Weekend Breaks
Oman & UAE

A guide to exceptional stays in the Gulf

Proudly supported by  **The Wave**
MUSCAT

i

Weekend Breaks in Oman and the UAE
ISBN 978-9948-03-337-0

Copyright © Explorer Group Ltd 2008
All rights reserved

All maps © Explorer Group Ltd 2008

Front cover photograph – Pete Maloney

Printed and bound by Emirates Printing Press, Dubai, UAE

Explorer Publishing & Distribution
PO Box 34275, Dubai , United Arab Emirates
Phone (+971 4) 340 8805   **Fax** (+971 4) 340 8806
info@explorerpublishing.com   www.explorerpublishing.com

While every effort and care has been made to ensure the accuracy of the information contained in this publication, the publisher cannot accept responsibility for any errors or omissions it may contain.

Welcome...

You know the drill – spend all week at work looking forward to those two precious days off, and then come Friday morning you're at a loss for things to do. Weekend Breaks in Oman and the UAE is here to help you plan the best weekends of your life; with 52 reviews of the best hotels (that's one for every weekend in the year), as well as pages of essential information on camping, shopping and going out in each area, you'll never need to endure a boring weekend again.

So whether you choose to luxuriate in the isolated desert surroundings of Al Maha (p.86), camp atop the peaks of the Hajar mountain range (p.45), enjoy a fun-filled family getaway at Shangri-La Barr Al Jissah Resort (p.28), or take in a bird's-eye view of Dubai from your own private balcony at Raffles Dubai (p.120), all the information you need is in these pages.

Your weekend starts here...

Many thanks to: Sharjah Commerce & Tourism Development Authority for images in the Northern Emirates and East Coast sections, Mohsen Al Dajani for the image on p.52, and the entire Explorer team for their contribution.

Contents

Introduction

Oman

UAE

Index

Getting Around

Most destinations in Oman and the UAE are within easy driving distance; however, regional airlines offer an extensive network of flights that will get you there much quicker.

Car Rental

Oman

Avis	24 607 235	www.avisuae.com
Budget Rent A Car	23 235 160	www.budget-uae.com
General Automotive Co LLC	24 492 143	www.zaleasing.com
Hertz Rent A Car	24 566 208	www.nttoman.com
Sixt	24 482 793	www.sixt-oman.com
Thrifty	24 489 248	www.thrifty.com
Value Plus Rent-A-Car	24 817 964	www.valueoman.com

UAE

Autolease Rent-a-Car	04 282 6565	www.autolease-uae.com
Avis	04 295 7121	www.avisuae.com
Budget Rent A Car	04 295 6667	www.budget-uae.com
Diamond Lease	04 343 4330	www.diamondlease.com
EuroStar Rent-a-Car	04 266 1117	www.eurostarrental.com
Hertz	04 282 4422	www.hertz-uae.com
National Car Rental	04 283 2020	www.national-me.com
Thrifty Car Rental	800 4694	www.thriftyuae.com
United Car Rentals	04 266 6286	www.unitedcarrentals.com

Regional Airlines

Oman

Emirates Airline	24 792 222	www.emirates.net.com
Etihad Airways	24 823 555	www.etihadairways.com
Gulf Air	24 703 222	www.gulfairco.com
Oman Air	24 707 222	www.oman-air.com
Qatar Airways	24 787 070	www.qatarairways.com
Saudi Arabian Airlines	24 789 485	www.saudiairlines.com

UAE

Air Arabia	04 508 8888	www.airarabia.com
Emirates Airline	04 214 4444	www.emirates.com
Etihad Airways	04 505 8000	www.etihadairways.com
Gulf Air	04 271 3222	www.gulfairco.com
Oman Air	04 351 8080	www.oman-air.com
Qatar Airways	04 229 2229	www.qatarairways.com
Saudi Arabian Airlines	04 229 6111	www.saudiairlines.com

Driving Distances

Use this handy reference table to plan your road trip. Don't forget to allow extra time for border crossings, which are usually busier over weekends and holidays.

	Abu Dhabi	Ajman	Al Ain	Al Buraymi	Al Hamra	Ar Rustaq	As Seeb	Bahla	Barka	Dhaid	Dibba	Dubai	Fujairah	Hatta	Ibra	Ibri	Jebel Ali	Kalba	Khasab	Khor Fakkan	Liwa	Masafi	Mirbat	Muscat	Nizwa	Ras Al Khaimah	Salalah	Sharjah	Sohar	Sur	Umm Al Quwain
Abu Dhabi		175	160	165	435	430	450	405	425	235	305	145	315	245	605	305	110	305	340	350	225	235	540	500	440	250	1225	165	275	740	190
Ajman	175		150	160	430	435	410	410	370	60	130	30	125	120	570	310	70	135	160	155	365	95	1375	460	445	70	1440	10	225	665	15
Al Ain	160	150		5	275	270	290	245	265	135	205	125	215	145	445	145	140	205	310	240	270	165	1135	340	280	220	1065	140	115	580	165
Al Buraymi	160	160	5		270	265	285	240	260	130	200	120	215	140	440	140	135	200	305	235	265	160	1140	335	275	215	1060	135	110	585	160
Al Hamra	435	430	275	270		265	155	135	190	400	470	390	415	410	235	120	415	405	610	440	545	450	980	220	45	495	910	415	315	345	440
Ar Rustaq	430	435	276	308	264		115	295	85	330	325	415	265	260	265	240	450	255	460	290	540	300	1180	160	260	375	1110	390	165	425	380
As Seeb	450	410	290	201	157	115		190	40	350	345	435	285	280	160	285	410	275	480	310	560	320	1070	50	155	395	1003	410	185	315	430
Bahla	405	410	245	250	20	295	188		280	380	450	370	395	390	225	100	385	385	595	420	515	430	965	210	35	475	895	390	295	335	420
Barka	425	370	265	270	235	85	40	280		320	315	395	255	315	190	230	445	245	450	280	545	290	1105	85	185	365	1035	375	155	350	365
Dhaid	235	60	135	130	470	330	350	380	320		70	75	65	100	505	280	125	70	170	90	425	30	505	395	415	80	1200	55	165	730	50
Dibba	305	130	205	200	470	325	345	450	315	70		145	60	170	505	365	195	70	170	35	495	40	1355	395	500	80	1285	125	175	660	115
Dubai	145	30	125	120	415	415	435	370	395	75	145		150	145	570	270	35	160	195	180	335	110	1260	480	405	105	1190	20	250	745	50
Fujairah	315	125	215	215	410	265	285	395	255	65	60	150		60	435	360	190	10	190	25	505	35	595	330	430	110	1280	120	100	595	110
Hatta	245	120	145	140	235	260	280	390	315	100	170	145	60		430	290	130	60	60	205	470	80	525	325	425	125	1210	130	95	660	120
Ibra	605	570	445	450	235	265	158	225	190	505	505	570	435	430		325	555	425	630	460	715	470	1030	180	190	545	960	585	335	160	620
Ibri	305	152	145	235	300	290	100	230	290	280	365	270	360	290	325		285	350	495	385	415	335	990	305	135	375	920	290	200	430	315
Jebel Ali	110	70	140	135	415	450	410	385	445	125	195	35	190	130	555	285		185	205	220	300	155	520	515	420	140	1205	55	225	790	85
Kalba	305	135	205	200	610	225	275	385	245	70	70	160	10	60	425	350	185		205	35	495	40	1340	320	420	115	1280	130	90	585	110
Khasab	340	160	310	305	610	460	480	595	450	170	170	195	190	60	630	495	205	205		145	525	145	1485	525	630	90	1445	175	305	790	145
Khor Fakkan	350	155	240	235	440	290	310	420	280	90	35	180	25	205	460	385	220	35	145		540	60	1375	355	455	115	1305	150	125	560	140
Liwa	225	365	270	265	545	540	560	515	545	425	495	335	505	470	715	415	300	495	525	540		425	1405	610	550	440	1335	355	385	850	380
Masafi	235	95	165	160	980	300	320	430	290	30	40	110	35	80	470	335	155	40	145	60	425		1300	365	465	75	1230	135	135	630	80
Mirbat	540	1375	1135	1140	980	1180	1070	965	1105	505	1355	1260	595	525	1030	990	520	1340	1485	1375	1405	1300		1090	930	1355	70	1250	1185	1140	1300
Muscat	500	460	340	335	220	160	50	210	85	395	395	480	330	325	180	305	515	320	525	355	610	365	1090		175	440	1025	500	230	205	205
Nizwa	440	445	280	275	45	260	155	35	185	415	500	405	430	425	190	135	420	420	630	455	550	465	930	175		500	865	425	330	300	450
Ras Al Khaimah	250	70	220	215	495	375	395	475	365	80	80	105	110	125	545	375	140	115	90	115	440	75	1355	440	500		1285	85	210	775	55
Salalah	1225	1440	1065	1060	910	1110	1003	895	1035	1200	1285	1190	1280	1210	960	920	1205	1280	1445	1305	1335	1230	70	1025	865	1285		1210	1120	1070	1235
Sharjah	165	10	140	135	415	390	410	390	375	55	125	20	120	130	585	290	55	130	175	150	355	135	1250	500	425	85	1210		345	315	515
Sohar	275	225	115	110	315	165	185	295	155	175	175	250	100	95	335	200	225	90	305	125	385	135	1185	230	330	210	1120	345		495	210
Sur	740	665	580	585	345	425	315	335	350	730	660	745	595	660	160	430	790	585	790	560	850	630	1140	205	300	775	1070	315	705		210
Umm Al Quwain	190	15	165	160	440	380	430	420	365	50	115	50	110	120	620	315	85	110	145	140	380	80	1300	205	450	55	1235	515	25	210	

Basic Arabic

Introduction

I am from …	anaa min ….
Britain	braitani
Europe	oropi
India	al hindi
America	ameriki

Route Related

Is this the road to …	hadaa al tariyq ila
Right	yamiyn
Left	yassar
Straight ahead	siydaa
North	shamaal
South	januwb
East	sharq
West	garb
Turning	mafraq
First	awwal
Second	thaaniy

Road

Road	tariyq
Street	shaaria'
Roundabout	duwwaar
Signals	ishaara

Accidents

Police	al shurtaa
Permit/licence	rukhsaa
Accident	Haadith
Papers	waraq
Insurance	ta'miyn

Questions

How many/much?	kam?
Where?	wayn?
When?	mata?
Which?	ayy?
How?	kayf?
What?	shuw?

Why?

Why?	laysh?
Who?	miyn?
In/at	fee
From	min
And	wa
There isn't	maa fee

Numbers

Zero	sifr
One	waahad
Two	ithnayn
Three	thalatha
Four	araba'a
Five	khamsa
Six	sitta
Seven	saba'a
Eight	thamaanya
Nine	tiss'a
Ten	ashara

Hotels By Category

There are enough hotel reviews in this book to be able to stay at a different one on each of the 52 weekends of the year. However, just in case you can't manage one hotel a week, these are Explorer's top picks in the following categories:

Oman

Stunning scenery, friendly locals and a relaxed pace combine to make Oman the perfect weekend getaway.

Oman

Oman
essentials

Nestled in the south-eastern quarter of the Arabian Peninsula, with a land area of 300,000 square kilometres, the Sultanate of Oman is phenomenally diverse. Spectacular geography marked by mountains and wadis, bustling city centres, serene beaches and a wealth of history and heritage make it a country with something for everyone.

The city centres are virtually devoid of skyscrapers, unlike many other cities in the region. Stout, pretty, whitewashed buildings sit alongside ornate mosques, low-rise hotels and luxury villas.

Oman is proud of its ancestry and traditions, and rightly so. The country has a long list of cultural attractions to be explored. From crumbling forts and ancient cities, to lively souks and fascinating museums, Oman has the history that many other GCC nations lack.

Outside of the cities, Oman's flora and fauna are equally appealing – more than 1,200 indigenous plant species, including its native frankincense tree (Boswalia sacra) thrive in the sultanate. Look out also for the wide variety of wildlife, including endangered species such as the Arabian oryx, Arabian leopard and tahr (a mountain goat now found only in Oman). Oman's waters are home to over 150 species of commercial fish and shellfish, and 21 species of whales and dolphins, including the humpback whale. There are four species of sea turtle that come ashore to lay their eggs.

Oman is unique in that every corner of the country has something special to offer. Adventure seekers will enjoy activities like desert driving, wadi bashing, diving and trekking amid the stunning natural beauty of Oman's scenery. Though much of the country is barren desert, a brief shower of rain quickly brings out the wild flowers. Coconut, banana and other tropical fruit trees thrive in the Salalah region in the south, whereas up north, dramatic fjords and natural lagoons offer a completely different perspective.

People & Traditions

As you explore the many sides of Oman, you'll find that the local people are warm and welcoming. Oman's historical position on an important trade route means that the Omani population has been exposed to many different cultures over the centuries, and locals are generally tolerant, welcoming and friendly. Because of the active efforts of the government to increase local participation in the workforce, a large percentage of jobs are held by Omanis, so you have more opportunities to interact with the locals than you might elsewhere in the region.

Muscat Festival

Food & Drink

Traditional local cuisine is fairly simple; typically rice is cooked with beef, mutton, chicken or fish, which has been marinated in a blend of herbs and spices. The country's restaurants serve up a range of excellent cuisine, particularly locally caught seafood. Both meat lovers and vegetarians will find plenty of choice on local menus. Although the nightlife is limited, with just a handful of nightclubs, Oman's many four and five-star hotels offer an excellent collection of fine dining restaurants and popular bars.

Ramadan

Ramadan is the holy month in which Muslims commemorate the revelation of the Holy Quran. For 30 days Muslims are required to fast during daylight hours, abstaining from eating, drinking and smoking from sunrise to sunset. The fast is broken with an Iftar, or feast. The start of Ramadan is determined by the sighting of the moon and usually happens 11 days earlier each year.

Non-Muslims are expected to respect this holy month and refrain from eating, drinking and smoking in public places, even in their cars, during the daytime. Most hotels will provide screened dining areas for those not fasting, but it's best to check when booking. Bars are closed during Ramadan, although some restaurants will still serve alcohol. Ramadan ends with a three-day celebration and holiday called Eid Al Fitr.

Language

Arabic is the official language in Oman, although English is widely spoken. In cities like Muscat and Salalah, most road signs and restaurant menus are in English and Arabic; in remoter areas, you may see less English. Learning a few words of Arabic will be useful, especially outside the cities. See p.ix for the Basic Arabic table.

Climate

Sunny blue skies and warm temperatures are normal throughout the year. The best time to visit is winter, which falls between October and April, when temperatures are milder. Summer temperatures can reach up to 48°C during the day, and average 32°C overnight. Humidity can rise to 90%, so it gets a bit sticky. The southern Dhofar region gets light monsoon rains between June and September.

Money

The monetary unit is the Oman rial (RO or OR), which is tied to the US dollar at a mid-rate of approximately $1:RO 0.385. The rial is divided up into 1,000 baisas and notes come in denominations of RO 50, RO 20, RO 10, RO 5, RO 1, 500 baisas, 250 baisas, 200 baisas and 100 baisas. Most hotels, shops and restaurants in Muscat will accept the UAE dirham, although outside of the city you will need local currency.

Tipping

Many hotels and restaurants automatically include a service charge of at least 5% (check the bottom of your bill). However, this is unlikely to end up with your waiter, so a tip of a few hundred baisas is always greatly appreciated. The same applies for petrol pump attendants, taxi drivers, hotel porters and anyone else providing a service.

Time

Local time is +4hrs UTC (Universal Coordinated Time, formerly GMT) with no summer saving time, so the clocks don't change. Some businesses still close for a long afternoon break (known as a 'split shift'), but most of the private sector works straight shifts from 09:00 to 17:00 or 18:00. Government offices are open from 07:30 to 14:30, Saturday to Wednesday.

Musandam

Oman

Border Blues

If you are heading for Oman from the UAE over a busy period (such as Eid, New Year or any long weekend), expect chaos at the border posts with too many visitors, not enough officials, and a general lack of efficiency. You now also have to pay to leave the UAE, which adds to the time you'll need at the border. Allow an extra hour or two, take a good magazine, and don't forget to pack your sense of humour – you'll need it.

Crime & Safety

While street crimes are uncommon in Oman and violent crimes are rare, it is wise to maintain a healthy degree of caution. Ladies are strongly advised to avoid taking the orange and white taxis if they are alone as there have been cases of harassment. Men stare but you can minimise the hassle by dressing modestly and staying away from lower-end hotels. Staring tends to be worst on the public beaches, but generally if you can ignore it you'll save yourself a lot of aggravation. If that doesn't help, call the police on 999.

Dos & Don'ts

Although Oman is a fairly liberal country, there are a few things to watch out for. When taking pictures, keep an eye out for signs banning photography – you'll see a few of these around, particularly near government buildings or military posts. Always ask permission before you take pictures of the locals, and if the answer is 'no', respect it. It is illegal to drink alcohol in public places, so limit drinking to licensed bars and restaurants. You are not allowed to bring alcohol into the country if crossing the border in your car, but if you are flying into Oman then you can bring alcohol in with you according to the current duty free limits. Comfortable, loose-fitting, conservative dress is ideal – ladies may feel more comfortable wearing something that covers the shoulders and is at least knee length. If you are visiting a mosque, then long sleeves and long trousers are a must.

Public Holidays

Public holidays in Oman often involve grand celebrations and can sometimes last a few days. Some dates are fixed while others are decided in line with the lunar calendar. Eid Al Fitr is a three-day holiday that celebrates the 'Feast of the Breaking of the Fast' at the end of Ramadan. Eid Al Adha, meaning 'Feast of the Sacrifice', is a four-day holiday marking the end of the annual pilgrimage to Mecca. It is celebrated 70 days after Eid Al Fitr. Lailat al Mi'raj celebrates the Prophet's ascension into heaven. Oman's national day is on 18 November, which is also the birthday of Sultan Qaboos. Renaissance Day, on 23 July, commemorates Sultan Qaboos' accession.

Annual Events

Khareef Festival

This festival is held in Salalah each year, from 15 July to the end of August, and celebrates the monsoon season. There are music and dance performances from different regions of Oman, and many stalls selling traditional Omani handicrafts.

Muscat Festival

The Muscat Festival is held over 22 days in January and February and showcases Oman's vibrant history and culture. Expect to see traditional dance displays, camel races, concerts, sports and educational events, and various activities for adults and children. It's a wonderful time to be in Muscat, although it is very busy, so book your hotel in advance. www.muscat-festival.com

Qurm Beach

Rally Oman

Oman's premier motorsport event is usually held over three days in early April. Family entertainment is also on offer including a freestyle motocross competition, music, and parachute displays. www.omanrally.com

Getting There

Those travelling to Oman from neighbouring UAE can drive via one of the official border crossings, or fly into international airports in Muscat or Salalah. Oman Air operates direct flights from various regional destinations (www.oman-air.com). From Muscat International Airport you can get domestic flights to Salalah and Khasab. You can also fly direct to Salalah from certain regional airports (such as Dubai).

Visas

There are four types of visa that are relevant to visitors – single entry, multiple entry, express, and common visa facility with Dubai. This last one is for visitors who have a valid visit visa for Dubai, meaning they can travel to Oman freely. For residents of the UAE, a single entry visa that is valid for one month costs RO 6, and a multiple entry visa, valid for one year for stays of up to three weeks each, costs RO 10. Visa application forms are available before passport control, or look out for the Travelex counter if you're flying into Muscat. Be sure to verify your visa expiration date before you leave the immigration counter; a hefty RO.10 penalty per day is enforced should you overstay your welcome. For further information, see www.rop.gov.om.

Getting Around

The Oman National Transport Company (ONTC) has a fleet of buses and coaches servicing various internal points within the country, as well as several routes to and from the UAE. Buses cover all areas of Muscat, and timetables, destinations and route numbers can be found at bus stops. Long distance routes depart from the

Nizwa Fort

central station in Ruwi, Muscat. See www.ontcoman.com for more information.
Many international car rental companies, as well as some local firms, have offices in Muscat and Salalah. Larger firms generally have more reliable vehicles and a greater capacity to help in an emergency. Make sure that you have comprehensive insurance that includes personal accident coverage. Most international and foreign licences are accepted. See p.vi for a list of car hire firms.
Driving is on the right hand side of the road and seatbelts are mandatory in front seats. The use of mobile phones while driving is banned. In the event of an accident, contact the police on 999. If you are driving to Oman from the UAE you will need Oman insurance, which you can either arrange through your existing provider, or through the insurance office near the border. You will be asked to show the papers at immigration.
Taxis are plentiful and nearly always driven by an Omani citizen. They are white with distinctive orange stripes, but not all are metered so arrange the price before you get in, and don't be bashful about negotiating. City Taxi (24 603 363) and Hello Taxi (24 607 011) are private taxi firms which may be safer and more reliable, especially when travelling at night.

Camel races, traditional concerts, dance displays and heritage activities make the Muscat Festival one of the region's most interesting celebrations of local culture.

Hiking

The mountains of Oman provide many wonderful opportunities for hiking. Rugged scenery, breathtaking views, dramatic canyons and gorges and rolling plains are just some of the things you can look forward to while hking in Oman. Various mountain trails have been carefully marked out for trekkers, ranging from short and easy walks to longer hikes over challenging terrain. Some trails take you through remote yet still-inhabited villages.

The main mountain range in Oman is Al Hajar, which runs from the Straits of Hormuz in the north, and spreads for 600 kilometres along the coastline. The range splits into the northern, eastern and western Hajars, and has many peaks towering 2,000 metres and upwards. Jebel Shams, in the western Hajars, is the highest peak at just over 3,000 metres. The spectacular 'Grand Canyon' of Oman is also in this area.

The Dhofar mountains in southern Oman reach a height of 2,000 metres. The range is topped by rolling plateaus and punctuated by deep wadis. From June to September, during the khareef season, the south-facing escarpments of this range are blanketed by rain clouds, and are therefore covered with dense woodlands.

The best time for hiking is during cooler months (October to April). Hiking in Dhofar during the khareef should be approached with caution; dense fog and damp conditions can make the going difficult.

Oman
Activities

In any country where you've got mountains, desert and beaches, you'll find a huge range of related activities and Oman is no different. Camping on the beach, dune driving through the Wahiba Sands and trekking along precarious mountain paths are all pursuits that you may want to experience while surrounded by Oman's magnificent scenery.

Off Roading

Picking your way over desert dunes or rocky wadis in a capable 4WD is one of the most popular activities to enjoy while in Oman. Venture off the beaten track and you'll be rewarded with jaw-dropping views, secret picnic spots and a better insight into the heritage and culture of the local people. The following routes are just some of the great trips you can take through the country:

Musandam: From the UAE you can drive up to Khasab via Ras Al Khaimah, right to the tip of the Arabian peninsula. The countryside ranges from mangroves, sabkha (salt flats), gravel plains and desert to stunning mountain scenery and the famous 'fjords of Arabia' where mountains plunge into the Straits of Hormuz. Alternatively, you can navigate your way along precarious paths through the mountains on the Musandam peninsula, driving from the fjords up to an altitude of almost 2,000 metres at the top of the pass. Once up, you can expect temperatures to be around 8°C cooler than they are at sea level, so you can still camp up here almost throughout the summer. See p.31 for more information.

Western Hajars: This magnificent mountain range is yours to explore, and easily accessible from several different starting

Hike along mountain pathways, drive through dramatic wadis, and explore the vivid colours of Oman's underwater world.

Clockwise from top left: Sea turtle, Falaj, Mountain range, Wadi driving

Oman

Coral reefs and shipwrecks attract a range of marine life, and you can expect to bump into turtles, cuttlefish, stingrays and moray eels as well as a rainbow selection of colourful fish.

points. Driving from Muscat, you can head through the scenic Samail Gap, a huge valley dividing the eastern and western Hajars. Alternatively, you can visit Wadi Damm, home to the ancient beehive tombs of Al Ayn and Bat. Jebel Shams is the highest point in Oman, so expect stupendous views – from here you are near the Abandoned Village Walk, undoubtedly one of the most rewarding hikes you can do. A trip to Sayq Plateau lets you explore more than 30 villages. Wadi as Sahtan provides a dramatic gateway to a host of roads leading to lovely villages, including several set right at the foot of the north face of Jabal Shams. Wadi Bani Awf is one of the most spectacular wadis in the country, where you'll find the village of Balad Sayt nestled at the base of Jabal Shams.

East Coast: Head for Sur – along the way you'll find some fascinating attractions such as Bib Maryam's tomb and a dhow building yard. Yiti and As Sifah beaches, while not a great distance from Muscat, feel a world away. Enjoy the picturesque pools and waterfalls amid date plantations in Wadi Ash Shab and Tiwi, or explore the famous turtle nesting beaches of Ras Al Jinz. Sand dunes and large open spaces make a great off-roader's playground in the Wahiba Sands, which are just over 200km from Muscat.

Dhofar: Whether you visit during the khareef season, when this part of the country catches the tip of the Indian monsoon season, or during winter, there is always a lot to do and see in Dhofar. Head for Wadi Darbat, where you'll find a wadi lake, a large sinkhole and some massive baobab trees. In good weather, you can't beat the campsites and viewpoints in this area. For more information, see p.56.

Diving

It's the sheer quantity as well as the spectacular quality of Oman's sea life that makes it a great diving destination. Waters are warm and there are areas suitable for all levels of divers; from the calm waters in some of Muscat's natural lagoons to the slightly more hairy conditions around Musandam's fjords. If you have previous diving experience, all you need to do is get a diving permit from the Royal Oman Police (www.rop.gov.om) before hitting the water. If you are new to diving, Oman has some wonderful places to learn. Fahal Island in Muscat has around 10 dive sites offering great diving in most weather conditions. In this area you can find isolated reefs, a swim-through cave and artificial reef balls. Non-divers can snorkel on the western side of the island.

Not far from Muscat is Bander Khayran, an area characterised by a small fjord system. Diving depth is up to 30 metres, and you can see a diverse range of beautiful corals and marine life. Al-Munassir Naval Shipwreck, near Bander Khayran, lies at a depth of about 30 metres. The rooms in the ship have been opened up to enable divers to get in and out easily.

The nine Daymaniyat Islands span around 20 kilometres from Seeb to Barka. The islands and their surrounding reefs are a national nature reserve, and access is controlled. Thanks to this there is an extensive coral reef and abundant sea life.

Dive Companies

Arabian Sea Safaris	24 693 223	www.arabianseasafaris.com
Blu Zone Diving	24 737 293	www.bluzonediving.com
Capital Area Yacht Club	24 737 712	na
Daymaniyat Divers	26 795 545	www.alsawadibeach.com
Global Scuba LLC	24 692 346	www.global-scuba.com
Gulf Leisure	99 819 006	www.gulfleisure.com
Hormuzline Tours Company	26 731 616	www.hormuzlinetours.com
Khasab Travel & Tours	26 730 464	www.khasabtours.com
Moon Light Diving Centre	99 317 700	www.moonlightdive.com
Musandam Extra Divers	26 730 501	www.extra-divers.li
Muscat Diving & Adventure Center	24 485 663	www.holiday-in-oman.com
Nomad Ocean Adventures	050 885 3238	www.discovernomad.com
Oman Dive Centre	24 824 240	www.omandivecenter.com

Night dives in Oman are popular, and you can rub shoulders with many nocturnal creatures that you wouldn't normally see. The phosphorescence in Oman's waters is visible after dark and this green-blue substance, released by plankton, makes for an amazing underwater display.

Muscat

Oman's capital is a striking city sandwiched between spectacular rocky mountains and beautiful beaches. With strong connections to its history and culture, and some of the friendliest locals in the region, you'll want to visit again and again.

Muscat, the capital of Oman, is one of the most attractive and charismatic cities in the Middle East, and once you've visited you'll understand why many residents count it as their favourite regional city. It is visually striking, perhaps because it looks so little like a normal city; rather than a bustling CBD characterised by countless skyscrapers, gridlocked traffic and dirty smog, Muscat has many separate areas nestling between the low craggy mountains and the Indian Ocean. There is no one area that defines Muscat on its own – each part has its own distinctive character and charm.

Great care has been taken to ensure that, while it is definitely a modern city, there is a cohesive and traditional Arabic element that remains. Visit the old town of Muscat or the Mutrah Souk for an idea of what life has been like for decades for the people that still live in the area. Muscat is clean and features a lot more greenery than you may be used to if you live in Dubai or Abu Dhabi. With beautiful beaches, bustling souks, a collection of great restaurants and cafes, and some fascinating museums, you'll need at least a few days to fully discover this friendly city. The main areas worth exploring are around the old town and the fishing port of Mutrah, although taking long walks

Clockwise from top left: View over Mutrah, Muscat mountains, Muscat gate

along the beach in Qurm or exploring the natural lagoons in Qantab are also activities worth doing.

The Old Town Of Muscat
The old town of Muscat is situated on the coast at the eastern end of the greater Muscat area between Mutrah and Sidab. It is quiet and atmospheric, based around a sheltered port that was historically important for trade. The area is home to some very interesting museums. Muscat Gate Museum is located in one of the fortified gates of the old city walls, and illustrates the history of Muscat and Oman from ancient times right up to the present day. The view from the roof over the old town is worth the visit alone. Bait Al Zubair is in a beautifully restored house and features major displays of men's traditional jewellery, including the khanjar, women's jewellery and attire, household items, and swords and firearms. The Omani French Museum celebrates the close ties between these two countries, and is on the site of the first French Embassy. Other highlights include the striking Alam Palace, home of Sultan Qaboos, and Jalali Fort and Mirani Fort overlooking the harbour.

Mutrah
Mutrah rests between the sea and a protective circle of hills, and has grown around its port, which today is far more vibrant than the port of the Muscat's old town. Mutrah Corniche is lined with pristine gardens, parks, waterfalls and statues. Further east you'll find Riyam Park, where a huge incense burner sits on a rocky outcrop, while nearby is an ancient watchtower overlooking Mutrah – the view at the top is lovely and well worth the steep climb. One of Muscat's most famous shopping experiences lies in this area: the Mutrah Souk. It is always buzzing with activity and is renowned as one of the best souks in the region.

Other Areas
Although primarily a residential area, Qurm has some great shopping, good quality restaurants and cafes, the city's largest park (Qurm National Park) and arguably the best beach in Muscat. It is also home to some of the top hotels, all of which have superb leisure facilities. The villages of Al Bustan and Sidab provide an interesting diversion from the main Muscat areas. Head south along Al Bustan Street out of Ruwi on the spectacular mountain road to get to the village of Al Bustan and the Al Bustan Palace Hotel, one of the most famous hotels in the region.

Further down the coast, the mountains increase in height and the landscape gets more rugged. However, this undulating rocky coastline hides a number of beautiful secluded coves. These bays, mostly reachable by roads winding over the mountains, are home to the beaches of Qantab and Jassah, the Oman Dive Center (www.omandivecenter.com) – one of the top dive centres in the world – and the new Shangri-La Barr Al Jissah Resort (p.28). Many of the bays in this area have stretches of sandy beach sheltered by the rocky cliffs, and crystal clear waters that are perfect for snorkelling, diving and fishing.

Outside Muscat
Not much further out of Muscat than the Shangri-La Barr Al Jissah Resort, Yiti Beach, while once a popular daytrip from Muscat, is now sadly becoming off limits due to the construction of a huge development called Salam Yiti. As Sifah beach, a little further down the coast, is very popular. The well-travelled path past the last of the houses in As Sifah leads to a beach which slopes gently towards the ocean at low tide. If you're keen to snorkel, head towards the headland at the northern edge of the beach. If you enjoy hiking, you can explore the headlands on foot (and maybe even find a secluded beach or two further along).

Feel The Burn
You can climb up to the base of the giant incense burner in Riyam Park. You might arrive a bit out of puff but you'll be rewarded with amazing views over the port to the north, and of Muscat old town to the south.

With beautiful beaches, bustling souks, a collection of great restaurants and cafes, and some fascinating museums, you'll need at least a few days to discover this friendly city.

Muscat

17

There are some excellent off-road routes you can do from Muscat within a day, or on an overnight camping trip. For more information on off-roading in Oman, get a copy of the *Oman Off-Road Explorer*.

Accommodation Options

Apart from the beautiful hotels listed in this section, there are other accommodation options in and around Muscat. The Oman Dive Center, just south of Muscat, is an amazing experience, whether you're a diver or not, offering a licensed restaurant and unique accommodation. You can book a barasti hut (they are actually made of stone, with barasti covering) for an average of RO.66 for two people (depending on season), including breakfast and dinner. They are air conditioned, en suite and feature shaded terraces with lovely sea views. The centre offers dive training and excursions, as well as boat tours. See www.omandivecenter.com or call 24 824 240 for more information.

Just north of Muscat on the road to Sohar and Dubai, the Al Sawadi Beach Resort is a quiet resort near the Daymaniyat Islands, a popular place for snorkelling and diving. Accommodation comes in the form of chalet-style rooms; alternatively you can camp on the private beach with access to the resort's facilities. These include a pool, a gym, tennis and squash courts, and mini golf. The hotel offers watersports such as windsurfing, waterskiing, jetskiing and kayaking, and the onsite dive centre offers PADI courses and regular trips to the islands. See www.alsawadibeach.com.

Camping

Of course, camping is a popular option for weekend breakers – apart from being cheap, it gives you the chance to explore new places where you can set up camp for a night or two. You'll find some great camping spots south of the Shangri-La Barr Al Jissah Resort and Yiti Beach – just try to set up somewhere where the construction won't bother you. For more remote camping, had south to As Sifa, where you will almost always be able to find a secluded spot.

If you're looking to escape the heat of summer, camping on the Salmah Plateau (around 150km from Muscat) is usually a much cooler area. The stargazing at night

Traditional dhow

is particularly good, as are the million-dollar views of the coastline.

Finally, camping on the beaches at Ras Al Jinz (350km from Muscat) comes with the added benefit of being able to watch nesting turtles clamber up the beach to lay their eggs, and then observe as the baby turtles hatch and make the journey back down to the sea. In the summer months you can see several hundred turtles nesting every night – you will still see them in winter, although in smaller numbers. Camping in this windy area is a challenge – pitching a tent in strong wind is not easy – but it is worth it if you can find a sheltered spot.

View over Muscat

Shopping

Muscat is home to a cosmopolitan range of shops, from boutiques and hypermarkets to handicraft stalls and international brands. But it is the lively and authentic souks (markets) that are the real attraction. The biggest and most famous souk in the city is Mutrah Souk, which is considered to be one of the most interesting in the region. It is a confusing labyrinth of alleyways, but getting lost inside the souk is the best part and could result in the most interesting purchases of the day. The amount of silver jewellery in the souk is staggering; many shops have multiple barrels brimming over with silver rings and if you have the time, you might unearth some unique pieces.

The Oman Heritage Gallery at the Jawaharat A'Shati complex sells genuine craft items such as carpets and pottery. The goods are more expensive than in other places, but there's not a piece of tat in sight. By providing an income for these skilled artists, you're also helping to keep traditional crafts alive (24 696 974). Because most goods are tax free, items like carpets, textiles and gold are often cheaper than they are in other countries. The key to shopping like a pro in Muscat is to bargain where possible, or wait for

the sales when prices can be cut by up to 70%. In souks and markets however, you are expected to haggle – if you drive a hard bargain and pay with cash, you'll find that you can knock a significant amount off the original price.

Shopping Malls

Al-Araimi Complex: Upmarket mall in Al Qurm with more than 70 shops. 24 566 180

Jawaharat A'Shati Complex: Located near the beach in Shati Al Qurm, this small centre is home to two Muscat must-dos: the Oman Heritage Gallery and D'Arcy's Kitchen, a cafe serving delicious home-style meals. 24 696 974, www.jascomplex.com

Markaz Al Bahja: This spacious mall houses Marks & Spencer and Danish furniture outlet ID Design, among others. Great for families, with plenty of entertainment and food options. 24 541 952, www.markazalbahja.com

Gone With The Wind
Escape the constant wind of the Ras Al Jinz area by forgoing camping and booking in at Al Naseem Tourist Camp (www.desert-discovery.com). It is just a few minutes from Ras Al Jinz, and has accommodation in the form of permanent cabins.

19

Muscat City Centre: Big and busy, although located a little distance from the centre of Muscat, MCC is a good place for fashion and lifestyle shopping as well as local specialities like halwa and dates. 24 558 888, www.citycentremuscat.com

Sabco Commercial Centre: Worth a visit for high-end jewellery, local perfume and the 'souk' that sells Omani silver, handicrafts and souvenirs. 24 566 701, www.sabcogroup.com

Kargeen Caffé: A mix of Arabic food and comfy majlis-style seating in verdant alfresco surroundings. Madinat Sultan Qaboos Centre, 24 692 269

Golden Oryx: Offering a mix of Chinese and Thai dishes, as well as a Mongolian barbecue, this popular outlet is consistently excellent. Try the snake coffee for a novel end to your meal. Ruwi, 24 702 266

Le Mermaid Café: Enjoy an Arabic meal, a shisha or one of the best fruit cocktails in the city; alternatively, grab a juice and wander down to the beach to watch the locals playing football. Near the Grand Hyatt, Shati Al Qurm, 24 602 327

Mumtaz Mahal: Costumed waiters, traditional live music and a delectable menu of classic Indian dishes make for an authentic experience. Al Qurm, 24 605 907

Whether you're after five-star finery or cheap chow, you'll find somewhere to suit your taste and budget.

Pavo Real: Sizzling Mexican food in a sizzling atmosphere, especially later in the evenings. Madinat Sultan Qaboos Centre, 24 602 603

Going Out

It may not be a party hotspot like Dubai, but there are some great eating and drinking venues in Muscat. A wide range of cuisines is available, with Arabic and Indian food being particularly good. Whether you're after five-star finery or cheap chow, you'll find somewhere to suit your taste and budget.

Although many of Muscat's most popular restaurants are found within hotels, there are also some excellent independent outlets. Unlike neighbouring UAE, where restaurants can only serve alcohol if attached to a hotel or a sports club, in Muscat independent outlets may acquire an alcohol licence.

There is plenty to choose from and you'll probably find some great places just by driving around; however, here are some outlets recommended by Explorer:

Bait Al Bahr: Fresh, succulent seafood and amazing ocean views. Shangri-La Barr Al Jissah Resort, 24 776 666

The Restaurant: Sophisticated surroundings and a contemporary fusion menu of Mediterranean, Arabic and Far Eastern cuisines. The Chedi, 24 524 400

Tomato: Leisurely, well-prepared meals enjoyed alfresco amid beautiful gardens – breakfast here is a real treat. Muscat InterContinental, 24 680 000

City Of Views
The most striking views of Muscat are from vantage points among the craggy mountains overlooking the surrounding coastline. In Mutrah, an easy and short hill walk from Riyam Park offers spectacular views over the port town in a bay surrounded by a protective circle of hills. Another is from the Crowne Plaza Hotel (p.22), located on a cliff in Qurm Heights, which commands one of the best views of any hotel, overlooking Qurm beach stretching into the distance.

Sultan Qaboos Grand Mosque

This spectacular mosque looks striking from the outside, and is no less magnificent inside. It is one of the largest in the Arab world and also one of the highest, with one of its minarets reaching almost 100m. The mosque is open to non-Muslim visitors between 08:00 and 11:00, Saturday to Wednesday. Children under 10 not allowed.

Beaches

Muscat has some beautiful beaches, from the secluded shores between the rocks in Qantab and Sidab to the seemingly endless Qurm Beach, which starts from the Crowne Plaza Muscat and stretches through Shati Al Qurm to Azaiba and beyond.

Mutrah Souk

A visit to Muscat would not be complete without a stroll through this atmospheric souk. Stock up on silver jewellery, traditional Omani hats and frankincense and discover for yourself why it rates as one of the best in the region.

Must-Do Experiences

Muscat

Muscat's unique history and location result in a special mix of city bustle and waterside calm.

Muscat Festival

Held over 22 days in January and February, the Muscat Festival is one of the best times to visit the city. It showcases the rich heritage and culture of Oman, attracting crowds of locals and tourists. Various events are held throughout Muscat, but the main venue is Qurm Park, where a mix of traditoinal crafts, music, dance and food entertain visitors in a vibrant atmosphere.

Muscat Old Town

Historically an important trading port, the old town of Muscat is quiet and atmospheric, and a great place to walk around. The striking Alam Palace, home of Sultan Qaboos, dominates the area. Flanking this, two Portuguese forts, Jalali and Mirani, overlook the harbour. Also within the old city walls lie a number of museums worth a visit: Bait Al Zubair and Muscat Gate House Museum – the latter mainly for the view over the town.

Oman Dive Centre

For a nominal fee you can get a day pass into the ODC, which is one of the most renowned dive centres in the region. Take a dive class or head out on an expedition, or just laze by the shaded pool and watch the boats coming and going. Snorkelling gear and paddleskis are available for hire. There is an excellent, fully licensed restaurant serving breakfast, lunch and dinner. www.omandivecenter.com

Muscat

Crowne Plaza Muscat

Location, location, location – it's the principle that works just as well for hotels as it does for real estate. And that's why the Crowne Plaza Muscat is a serious contender for your weekend break business – it has, quite possibly, one of the very best locations in Muscat. Apart from being relatively centrally placed, the main reason that this hotel scores highly is its position on the edge of a cliff overlooking the area of Al Qurm, a long stretch of beach and the Gulf of Oman. At any time of day, it's a very impressive backdrop.

The hotel management is obviously aware of the advantages a great view brings, and have done everything they can to capitalise on it. Most of the 200 rooms have big windows overlooking the sea, and some of the on-site restaurants feature terraces to ensure you're getting a view along with your meal.

You may think that being on top of a cliff makes it impossible to offer beach facilities, but the Crowne Plaza has built a staircase down to the beach below to cater for guests who prefer the sand and the sea to lying by the swimming pool. There are even sun loungers and umbrellas down there. At low tide, you'll be able to walk a little way along the cliff face, and if beach walking is your thing you're in luck – you can stroll for almost five kilometres

along this particular stretch of coast, although only at low tide (at high tide, an inlet from the sea will block your way).

If you do spend time on the beach here, be warned that it's a pretty steep climb back up to the hotel afterwards. If that sounds far too strenuous to manage on a relaxing weekend break, you can enjoy a much more sedate pace around the hotel's large free-form swimming pool. There are plenty of sun loungers, and the food and beverage service is available throughout the day. A separate kids' pool is nearby.

The hotel is home to a large, modern fitness club, which is popular with Muscat residents as well as hotel guests. The club includes a large gym, a sauna and steam room, squash courts and tennis courts – plus there is a resident tennis pro should you need a few pointers on your backhand. There is also a spa offering a range of treatments.

In terms of food and drink, the Crowne Plaza has four recommended outlets. Shiraz is the hotel's Persian restaurant and is well known for authentic cuisine and a vibrant ambience. Outdoor seating is available so that you can enjoy the view.

Come Prima, the Italian restaurant, offers a range of classics prepared by an Italian chef, and complemented with a selection of fine wines. All-day buffet dining is available in the Tropicana restaurant, which is on the same level as the pool. While many buffets are average, the one at Tropicana is excellent, and the Friday brunch is always fully booked. Finally, The Edge is aptly named given its teetering cliff-top spot – the views don't get any better than they do here. Serving a selection of light meals and drinks throughout the day, The Edge is always a good choice if you don't want to stray too far from the pool (or the view).

For those people visiting from neighbouring UAE, the good news is that it's often a couple of degrees cooler sitting on this cliff in Muscat than anywhere near home, so if you want to escape from the summer heat, it's ideal.

While the 200 rooms are perfectly comfortable and equipped with standard hotel amenities, they are relatively small in comparison to some other regional hotels.

However, with such an ample mix of facilities on offer outside of the rooms, it is unlikely that you will be spending much time there anyway. Given that it has such a desirable location, is central (the hotel offers a complimentary shuttle service anywhere within a five kilometre radius), and has four superb dining outlets, this is an excellent choice for a weekend break.

Contact
Phone: +968 24 660 660
Email: cpmuscat@cpmuscat.com
Web: www.crowneplaza.com

Location
From Sultan Qaboos Street, turn left at the Sayh Al Malih Roundabout. Stay on that road for about three kilometres up to Qurm Heights, follow the signs for the hotel.

Food & Drink
Shiraz – Persian • Tropicana – international • Come Prima – Italian • Duke's Bar – English pub

Features
Beach • Dolphin watching • Pool & children's pool • Gym • Squash courts • Sauna • Spa

Nearby
Qurm National Park • Qurm Heights Park • Qurm Beach • Mutrah Souk • Majan Beach • Jalali Fort • Sultan Qaboos Grand Mosque

The Chedi Muscat

There's little fuss or frippery; just confident cooking, fresh ingredients and a beautiful setting (with semi-private dining rooms inside). Even the four show kitchens seem to take a backseat as you enjoy excellent Arabic, Mediterranean and Asian dishes.

This is possible thanks to the hotel's clever design, which creates space and relaxation from the moment you enter the majestic lobby. The whitewashed main Serai Wing, the Deluxe Rooms in the Chedi Wing and the standalone one and two-storey suites are linked by paths through beautiful, village-green lawns, and water gardens, meaning you're never hurried or surrounded by other guests.

The only colours you'll see are black, white, dark brown and the alluring glow of orange lights. These are beautiful, understated buildings, backlit and complemented by lighting that has a magnetic effect on your senses. It slows you down, shuts your mind away, and brings out a huge, contented smile. The Chedi's styling is clean and contemporary, with subtle Omani flourishes. It's a template that has been copied but never bettered elsewhere. The difference is that when The Chedi chooses to impress, it does so with supreme originality and that trademark confidence – take the huge, black-tiled Chedi infinity pool (adults only), surrounded by

There is a confidence that comes with knowing you're one of the best, and The Chedi has it in reserve. This beautiful boutique hotel on the shores of the Gulf of Oman, regularly voted among the world's finest, is a monument to civilised relaxation and serenity.

Stressed-out executives and newlyweds fly here from Europe and don't leave its manicured grounds for two weeks. But spend just a few days among its elegant straight lines and infinity pools and you'll understand why. The success of The Chedi lies in its seemingly effortless style and simplicity. Take the eponymous The Restaurant for example.

queen-size loungers, or The Serai Pool, the smaller of the infinities, which seems to slip beautifully away to sea.

If you choose to lounge on the private beach rather than the endless carefully placed beds you'll be interrupted only by the placement of a cooling towel, regular refills of ice cool water with fresh mint, and the sound of the sea.

If you manage to summon the energy to actually do something, there are two floodlit tennis courts, an outstanding spa, as well as a petite gym with excellent equipment – step on the treadmill and you'll be staring straight out to sea.

The choice of rooms will depend on the depth of your pockets, but a Deluxe Room is large enough for you never to want to leave. The hotel's trademark symmetry is repeated with the rain shower on one side, toilet on the other and matching washbasins inbetween. The low-rise, king-size bed faces sliding cupboards, split by bench seating, which reveal TV and a Bose all-in-one (pre-programmed Chedi tracks, of course). Narrow, strip windows offer views of the water gardens or the Hajar Mountains. High ceilings provide an added sense of space. There's free Wi-Fi, or you can take your laptop to The Library, where there's a good range of local interest and coffee table tomes. However, the fantastic room service menu – the equal of what's on offer in the restaurants – could prove too tempting.

If you can stretch to a one or two-storey Chedi Club Suite, you'll enjoy a bedroom with king-size bed, separate living area, and an outdoor balcony (some with views across the Gulf). Two iPod minis with 1,500 pre-loaded tracks, a sunken bath and free mini bar are included for good measure.

The cheapest (relatively speaking) option is the Serai Room. This is only six square metres smaller than a Deluxe and comes with a queen-size bed. It will also save you money, so you can dine at the hotel's other restaurant, the Chedi Poolside Cabana, which serves fine Mediterranean and seafood next to the beach. There's also good international bar food and light meals available next to the Serai pool.

A babysitting service and cots are available, but you'll see very few children at The Chedi. There is little to keep them entertained and they're not nearly stressed enough to appreciate its charms.

The hotel offers a popular summer promotion when prices are extremely competitive, even if the temperatures outside are choking. But it's worth saving for when the weather matches the perfect surrounds. Everyone should escape to The Chedi at least once. It's a reminder that life can be simple and outrageously luxurious at the same time.

Muscat

Contact
Phone: +968 24 524 400
Email: chedimuscat@ghmhotels.com
Web: www.ghmhotels.com

Location
Once in Muscat, turn off Sultan Qaboos Street at Al Ghubbrah Roundabout on to Street 38. At the roundabout, turn left on to Street 46, and the hotel is on your right. The Chedi is clearly signposted from the Airport Roundabout.

Food & Drink
The Restaurant – international • The Arabian Courtyard – Arabic • The Beach – seafood • The Lobby Lounge – cocktails • Chedi Poolside Cabana – Mediterranean

Features
Private beach • Two swimming pools • Tennis courts • Library • Boutique • Fishing • Spa

Nearby
Mutrah Souk • Sultan Qaboos Grand Mosque • Qurm Beach

InterContinental Muscat

A world away from the polished, formal modernity that is the main characteristic of some five-star hotels, the InterContinental Muscat offers a break from the rush and push of 21st century life.

Your first glimpse of the hotel may not cause too much excitement – the seven-storey building looks more city centre carpark than five-star hotel, but things get markedly better once inside.

Upon entering, your eyes are automatically drawn upwards. The interior is set around a vast central atrium, with the dark wooden roof beams exposed way up above.

The second thing to strike you will be the hotel's reduced noise levels, as though someone has knocked the volume down a couple of clicks. Maybe it's the church-like roof looming above, or the pervasive laid-back Omani vibe, but the atmosphere seems to be one of hushed reverence. A small water feature trickles in the distance, the clink of a cup resonates through the Majlis Al Shams lobby cafe, and a soft piano lullaby filters through the air. This introduction sets the tone perfectly.

The hotel has 258 standard rooms and 11 suites, including the two-bedroom Royal Suite. Priority Club members get to stay on the dedicated 'club floors', and gain access to a private check-in, free internet, buffet breakfast

and complimentary pre-dinner drinks in the dedicated lounge.

All rooms are described as having either a sea or mountain view (although there's a fair bit of urban landscape to look across before you see the Hajar Mountains in the distance). Each one has a balcony, and non-smoking rooms are available.

The rooms, while clean, comfortable, well-equipped and a good size, are beginning to show their age, with dated decor and furnishings. But one of the small pleasures of staying here is to be found in standing outside your room and observing the goings on in the lobby below – you'll witness guests checking in and out, tourists milling around and people sitting enjoying a leisurely coffee.

One floor below the lobby is where you'll find two of the hotel's restaurants. Musandam Café & Terrace is the buffet venue, open for breakfast, lunch, dinner, and Friday brunch, while Señor Pico serves up hearty portions of fine Mexican fare. Staff here mix a mean margarita, and the guitar and harp duo alone are worth the visit.

A branch of Polynesian-themed chain Trader Vic's is housed in a separate building just a few steps from the front entrance. It's pricier than the other venues, but a good choice for killer cocktails, romantic meals on the pretty terrace, and the best crepe suzette you've ever had.

For cooler days and evenings, Tomato is a smart open-air restaurant beside the pool and gardens, offering a tasty selection of Italian and Mediterranean favourites. And last but not least, Al Ghazal Pub is something of an institution in Muscat; authentic pub grub and beer accompany sport on the TV, regular live music and a lively atmosphere.

Aside from eating and drinking, there's plenty to keep guests occupied. Set amid a 35 acre oasis, the hotel boasts attractive lawns lined with mature trees. For serious swimmers there's a 25 metre length pool (with a wooden trellis offering slats of shade), but the majority of guests head for the more family-friendly main pool area. Water sprays and islands to swim around mean that cooling off needn't be boring; the islands even have room for a few sunloungers, so get

there early to bag the best spot.

The comprehensive sporting facilities continue, with six floodlit tennis courts, a football pitch, volleyball court and two glass-backed, air-conditioned squash courts. Indoors, the hotel's health club boasts a large gym, Jacuzzis, saunas, steam rooms and plunge pools.

Crossing the lush green expanse of lawn and passing through the gateway brings you to the wide expanse of free public beach. The beach is not owned by the hotel and so is open to all, and in places is not particularly clean, but a stroll along the sand is certainly recommended. Time it right and you'll see fishermen lugging sacks, heaving with the day's catch, from their small boats into beaten-up old pick-ups before driving off to market. Their nets are often spread out for hundreds of metres, drying on the sand, while gulls wheel above – take your camera for an excellent photo opportunity. For your own fill of fun on the water, Bait Al Bahar, operating from the hotel grounds, has boats, kayaks and windsurfers for rent.

The InterContinental isn't the place for a weekend of glamour and glitz, but that's part of its charm – it fits in perfectly with the Muscat experience, offering a wonderful feeling of what Dubai must have been like 20 years ago.

Contact
Phone: +968 24 680 000
Email: muscat@icmuscat.com
Web: www.intercontinental.com

Location
From Sultan Qaboos Street, follow the signs for the InterContinental and turn off on to Al Ilam Street towards Shati Al Qurm (Hayy As Saroj). At Al Kharijiyah Roundabout turn left and follow the street up to the signal and turn right.

Food & Drink
Musandam Cafe & Terrace – international • Trader Vic's – French-Polynesian & cocktail bar • Señor Pico – Mexican • Majlis El Shams – snacks • Tomato – Italian • Al Ghazal – English pub

Features
Two swimming pools • Jacuzzi • Sauna • Gym • Tennis courts • Two squash courts • Newsstand • Beauty salon • Spa • Gift shop • Children's activities

Nearby
Qurm National Park • Mutrah Souk • Qurm Beach • Majan Beach • Jalali Fort • Sultan Qaboos Grand Mosque • Children's Museum

Even the beauty of the spectacular long and winding road that leads to the Shangri-La's Barr Al Jissah Resort & Spa, framed by the rugged splendour of the Gulf of Oman's mountainous coastline, doesn't prepare you for the magnificence of the 124 acre resort that lies ahead. Your breath will be taken as you turn the final corner into a secluded bay on your journey to Shangri-La and see the traditional architecture and elegant luxury of the resort's three hotels.

Each hotel is aesthetically in keeping with the others, but with its own unique selling point. Al

Waha (oasis) has a definite family flavour; it is home to the Little Turtles children's club and contains various swimming pools designed to keep toddlers and older kids happy. Al Bandar (town) is the resort's centre, location of the majority of the Shangri-La's restaurants and bars, as well as various open spaces where entertainers set stage for evening performances during the cooler months, and Iftar tents are erected during Ramadan. There is also a souk area, which houses an interesting gallery showcasing local art.

The third and most luxurious of the hotels is Al Husn (castle), where the privileged few can take advantage of a totally opulent

Muscat

Shangri-La's Barr Al Jissah Resort & Spa

personal service. As well as the private beach and infinity pool, daily afternoon tea and stunning suites, there are little extras (such as complimentary iPod rental) that make this the perfect choice for those seeking exclusivity. However, if Al Husn is a little out of your price range the two aforementioned hotels have more than enough luxury detailing and potential for self-indulgence to make you feel like royalty.

Al Bandar's 1,400 square metre pool has partly submerged sunbeds for the ultimate lounging experience, while the guestrooms, regardless of classification (of which are there many), are soaked in modern luxury, each with a minimum size of 45 square metres and either a balcony or terrace. While the hotel's design is in keeping with traditional Omani architecture the rooms have a more 21st century feel, with leather, mahogany, rich colours and subtly placed amenities that make the 'do not disturb' sign a necessity (especially in the suites with baths the size of small swimming pools).

Al Bandar and Al Waha are connected by a lazy river, which at 250 metres in length invokes relaxation in the most impatient of natures. In addition to the various options for a dip there are a number of activities on offer in and around the resort. A Heritage Village gives you an insight into the traditional way of Omani life, while various watersports, including kayaking and windsurfing, are available from the beach. The resort also has its own marina and dive centre, offering dolphin and whale watching trips, plus PADI courses. While aquatic creatures tend to be rather shy in the Gulf of Oman, a couple of hours on a boat cruising around this wonderfully intricate coastline is well worth it. Just remember to bring your wet weather gear as bounding out to sea is a splash-happy affair.

Once evening draws in there are plenty of dining and drinking options available. Choices range from the buffet restaurant, Al Tanoor, which offers all-day dining and a dessert table (fully equipped with chocolate fountain) to make a dieter cry, to the auspicious fine dining restaurant Sultanah, serving international cuisine in the unique setting of a docked ship. There are six signature restaurants in all,

seven casual dining settings, three lobby lounges, two bars and a nightclub, each offering the highest quality service and remarkable attention to detail.

It is this meticulousness that is so obviously a driving force behind the management of the resort, which makes the guest experience so special. Touches like the dedicated Turtle Ranger, who can be seen at all times of the day tending to the protected creatures that still call this bay home, or the heavenly private spa suites where treatments are physically and spiritually matched to each client.

As you enjoy an alfresco sundowner, aperitif or nightcap overlooking the tranquil sea, blessedly untouched by the current craze for manmade islands, you can enjoy the relaxation of the hotel's remote location. Despite the large number of guestrooms – 640 in total – the sprawling design of the hotel means that even during peak season you won't feel crowded, and with the protective shadow of the mountainous backdrop you can enjoy a sense of intimacy often lost in resorts of this size. The only downside is that a weekend stay here really isn't enough time to truly appreciate all the facilities, activities, culinary delights and decadent pampering on offer – you'll leave wishing you could stay longer.

Contact
Phone: +968 24 776 666
Email: slmu@shangri-la.com
Web: www.shangri-la.com

Location
On Sultan Qaboos Street, follow the directions for Ruwi on to Nahdah Street. At the Ruwi Roundabout, turn off the highway and right into Ruwi. By the Sheraton, turn right on to Bait Al Fahal Street. Keep on this street up and over the hill, then turn right on to Qantab Road to get to the resort.

Food & Drink
Al Tanoor – Arabic • Bait Al Bahr – seafood • Capri Court – Italian • Samba – Latin American • Shahrazad – Moroccan • Sultanah – international • Tapas & Sablah – tapas & mezze

Features
Spa • Kids' club • Teen's club • Heritage village • Private beach • Three pools • Lazy river • Dive centre • Dolphin watching Trips • Snorkelling • Gym • Four tennis courts

Nearby
Mutrah • Bait Al Zubair Museum • Alam Palace • Sultan Qaboos Grand Mosque

Musandam

Spectacular mountains, beautiful fjords and remote villages, the Norway of Arabia is a must-see on any visitor checklist.

Musandam is the isolated mountainous Omani territory to the north of the UAE. The peninsula is dominated by the Hajar mountains, which run through the UAE and Oman, but is characterised by scenery that is totally different from the rest of the Middle East. Its distinctive landscape has earned it the moniker of the 'Norway of Arabia', with jagged cliffs plunging directly into the sea and a coastline punctuated with beautiful fjords and lagoons.

Natural attractions abound underwater too. Just off the shore are coral beds with an amazing variety of sea life, including tropical fish, turtles, dolphins, sharks, and even whales. Some of the best dive sites in the Middle East are found here, and the area is becoming increasingly popular with divers as a result. The lagoons offer a little more protection from the elements, and are great spots for snorkelling.

The capital, Khasab, is a quaint fishing port largely unchanged by the modern world. Aside from its charm, the main attractions are Khasab Fort (mainly for its impressive setting dominating the coastline near the older part of town), and the port, from where you can book a boat trip into the fjords – a great way to sample the beauty of Musandam. Keep an eye out for the regular flow of high-powered speedboats smuggling cigarettes to Iran, just 45km away across the Strait of Hormuz.

Clockwise from top left: Clownfish, Diving in, Khasab mountain route

Dibba

At the southern end of Musandam, straddling the border with the UAE, Dibba is a small town made up of three fishing villages. Unusually, each part comes under a different jurisdiction: Dibba Bayah is in Oman, Dibba Al Hisn belongs to Sharjah, and Dibba Muhallab is part of Fujairah. The three villages share an attractive bay, fishing communities, and excellent diving locations – from here you can arrange dhow trips to take you to unspoilt dive sites along the remote eastern coast of the Musandam peninsula. The Hajar mountains provide a wonderful backdrop, rising in places to over 1,800 metres. There is a good public beach too, where seashell collectors may find a few treasures. Dibba is also a good starting point for some stunning off-road driving into the mountains.

The Omani part of Dibba is also home to Dibba Castle, a strongly fortified, double-walled castle built by the Al Shuhah tribe over 180 years ago. You can access the rooms, and provided you don't mind pigeons you can climb all the towers for some great views over the surrounding area and out to sea.

Accommodation Options

Most of Musandam is very remote and there are few towns or villages of any size, so apart from the capital Khasab, where there are a couple of other options, the only real alternative to staying at the hotels featured is to camp. In Khasab, the Khasab Hotel (+968 26 730 267, www.khasabhotel.net), is a small, friendly place located in the middle of town with a swimming pool and one international restaurant. Rooms are either in the older, one-storey wing around the pool, or in the new building. It's a bit more basic than the Golden Tulip, and this is reflected in the price. There are also some self-catering apartments, such as Esra Hotel Apartments, run by Khasab Tours (+968 26 730 464, www.khasabtours.com). Ideal for larger groups, the Extra Divers Villa (+968 26 730 501, www.musandam-diving.com) is situated just outside of Khasab. Rooms can be hired

individually, or you can book the whole villa, which has six double bedrooms, bathroom, and kitchen. Weekly barbecues are organised alongside other evening events.

For camping, the public beaches along the road north of the border offer some nice spots to pitch a tent, as does the promontory that juts out to the north of the bend in the road near Al Harf, before you reach Khasab. For more remote beaches, it is possible to hire a boat from the port to drop you off in your own private bay 15 to 30 minutes away from Khasab and pick you up the day after. You should negotiate the fee before setting off, and don't pay them until you're back in port. Obviously you'll also have to make sure you have everything you need with you, and there won't be any way back until your boat ride comes for you. Try to get a mobile phone number in case of emergencies.

If you want to venture inland, there are some great remote places on the main off-roading route – the Sayq Plateau (at 1,600 metres above sea level, it's a lot cooler than the coast) and the acacia forest near Sal Al A'la. The track leading to these locations is long and remote, so be prepared before setting off. In Dibba, the beach is a good place for camping, so you can roll out of your sleeping bag and into the sea for a morning swim. Further inland, you can head up the Wadi Bih route into the mountains for a complete change of scenery.

Activities

This is not a place to come if you want a weekend of shopping or eating out, so be prepared to make do with the comforts of the hotel and the fulfilling experience of being among some wonderful scenery. This does make it a good place to escape the daily grind, particularly with the wide range of outdoor activities.

Boat Trips

An essential activity on any trip to Musandam, a dhow cruise around the fjords is a truly memorable experience. You

Searching for dolphins

Known as the 'Norway of Arabia', Musandam is home to spectacular fjords which are best explored from the deck of a traditional dhow.

From left: Spectacular diving, Dolphin watching

can hire a dhow or a speedboat from the harbour at Khasab (remember to negotiate the rate before you leave, but expect to pay about Dhs.100 per hour for a speedboat and Dhs.250 per hour for dhows). Leisurely dhows are more stable and spacious – large enough for 20 to 25 people. Allow a minimum of three hours to explore the inlet closest to Khasab; tours usually include Telegraph Island and Hidden Cove. Alternatively, try the longer trip out to Kumzar – an ancient village set in an isolated inlet on the northernmost end of the peninsula.

On a full-day trip you'll see remote coastal villages, get a chance to swim and snorkel in the calm waters, and you are almost guaranteed to see dolphins. Khasab Travel & Tours (Dubai +971 4 266 9950, Khasab +968 26 730 464) operates a number of dhows, or you can just turn up at the harbour and bargain hard with the independent boat owners to arrange your own private cruise. You can also just hire a small boat to take you out and drop you off on your own private beach, only 10 to 20 minutes from Khasab, then pick you up at an agreed time. It's common to pay only when you have returned to port, otherwise you might get left there for longer than you planned.

Off Roading

To see the other side of Musandam, you can also drive up to the plateau beneath Jebel As Sayh (Jebel Harim), the highest peak in the area at 2,087 metres. This is an excellent area for camping, hiking, views across the mountain tops, and as a base for further exploration. Most of the year you can get to the top in a saloon car. If you have a 4WD, there are a number of tracks worth exploring that head over the mountains to more secluded places such as Khawr Najd, the only beach accessible by car in the fjords, or the acacia forest near Sal Al A'la. For more detailed routes see the *UAE Off-Road Explorer*.

Visas

Visas for Musandam are required for most people, and the majority of visitors will be able to obtain one on arrival, regardless of whether they are UAE residents or tourists. For residents of the UAE the cost is usually Dhs.20 to exit the UAE and Dhs.10 to enter Musandam, however as rules can change with little notice, it is wise to carry a bit of extra cash with you. For tourists, entry is usually free, but again you may be asked to pay on the day. For more visa information, see the Oman section.

There is also a border post entering the Omani part of Dibba; you won't need a visa, but you may be asked for ID. Check that everyone in your party has their passport before setting out.

Boat Trip

The best way to get up close to the stunning scenery and appreciate the scale of the fjords, a trip on a dhow will let you discover the inlets, islands and remote settlements. You'll be able to enjoy isolated beaches, and may even see dolphins swimming along next to you. You can arrange trips from either Khasab port or Dibba.

Hiking

This is a great area to get outside, stretch your legs and admire the scenery. There are hikes to suit all levels, including some challenging routes for the serious hiker, and the mountainous backdrop provides some fantastic views. If you like the idea of a hike without the hassle, try Khasab Travel & Tours (+968 26 730 464) in Khasab, or Absolute Adventure (+971 4 272 9594) in Dibba, who will organise the hike, so all you have to do is turn up.

Must-Do Experiences

Musandam

With distinctive scenery Musandam is a great place to get out and explore, whether on land or at sea.

Off-Road

Khasab is already off the beaten track in comparison with most places, but if you want to venture even further into remote terrain there is an excellent off-road route that takes you all the way from the fjords to the mountains where heights are approaching 2,000m. For a full guide to the routes see the *UAE Off-Road Explorer* or *Oman Off-Road Explorer*.

Diving & Snorkelling

There are endless possibilities for divers off the rugged coast of Musandam. There are more than 20 separate dive sites along the east coast for experienced divers, while some of the sheltered inlets and bays are ideal for snorkelling. You can book dive trips from your hotel, or through companies such as Al Boom Diving (+971 4 342 2993, www.alboomdiving.com) and Al Marsa Travel & Tourism (+968 26 836 995, www.musandamdiving.com).

Absolute Adventure

Absolute Adventure has its home base in Dibba, an old fishing port set in beautiful surroundings on the southern edge of Musandam. If you are travelling from the UAE, you don't need a visa to enter the area; instead you can simply drive across the border (with usually just a check of ID common – bring your passports to be on the safe side), making it an easy coastal escape offering different scenery from the flat lands along the shores of the Arabian Gulf.

Memorable views come courtesy of the crystal blue waters of the Gulf of Oman, juxtaposed against the rugged mountains. The quiet town of Dibba exudes a serenity that is a welcome break from the real world with its office deadlines, ringing mobiles and roads choked with traffic.

In the northern outskirts of the town you will find the Absolute Adventure camp, which is an oasis of landscaped gardens, barasti lookouts and a bonfire pit, which comes in handy for those rare chilly evenings during the winter. The traditional Arabic house has a communal lounge area, with majlis seating, and an adjoining dorm-style room with bunk beds that can sleep up to 14. All towels and sheets are provided.

In the evenings, gather round the sizzling barbecue and enjoy a feast of grilled meat, home-made soup, rice and vegetable dishes, followed by dessert. Just a note: if you are vegetarian, inform the camp in advance, so that staff can cater for you. Breakfast is a simple affair of toast and boiled eggs, with tea, coffee and juice.

And then the adventure starts. You can choose from a range of activities including mountain biking, sea kayaking, treks through secluded mountain villages, scuba diving, canyoning, exploring caves and secret staircases, hang gliding, mountain safaris and wadi bashing. Each activity is rated by how challenging it is, so you know what to expect. Everything is conducted in line with tight (and reassuring) international safety standards. Before you set off, the guides will run through a few procedures, and let you know of any difficulties you may encounter (such as

trekking over tricky terrain). You'll be given a Camelpak (a backpack that carries a few litres of water) and a packed lunch, consisting of sandwiches, fruit and a drink, as well as a few other snacks to keep you going. After a morning's activity, you can stop for lunch in a date plantation, on a rocky outcrop or on a deserted beach.

It may not be as luxurious as staying in a four or five-star hotel, but a weekend with Absolute Adventure will provide thrills and a sense of accomplishment that you won't get elsewhere.

Musandam

Contact
Phone: +971 4 345 9900
Email: info@adventure.ae
Web: www.adventure.ae

Location
From Dibba, take the main Khasab road, looking out for signs to the Golden Tulip. Take the new tarmac road leading to the Golden Tulip hotel. After about 200m you will see the Adventure Centre on your left.

Food & Drink
All meals provided

Features
Traditional Bedouin tents • Large courtyard • Corporate & school adventures • Outdoor courses • Sailing • Mountain biking • Kayaking • Fishing • Snorkelling • Rock climbing • Trekking • Dog sledding • Horse riding

Nearby
Dibba Beach • Mountains • Wadis • Dibba Castle • Bidiyah Mosque • Snoopy Island • Boat trips

Golden Tulip Resort Dibba

Although it's a perfect base for exploring the east coast of the UAE, this little gem is actually situated in Musandam, Oman. The Golden Tulip sits in the north of Dibba right on the beach, nestled in between the Hajar mountains and the Gulf of Oman. Don't let that put you off heading there on a last-minute weekend break though – although Dibba is actually split into three (Fujairah, Sharjah and Oman all have jurisdiction over a third of the town), at time of writing you don't need to worry about sorting out visas to cross the border to get to the hotel (although you might need to show ID for everyone in your party at the checkpoint – take passports to be on the safe side), and you will also need car insurance for Oman.

Heading north through Dibba, the town thins out, and the UAE flags change to Omani colours. At the end of the road, just before the mountains meet the coastline, sits the Golden Tulip, a world away from the hustle and bustle of the UAE's big cities. Barely visible from the road, the 52 room low-rise hotel is cosy, intimate and family friendly. Arabic lanterns decorate the steps up to the entrance, giving an inviting welcome. The hotel may not be flash by UAE standards, but its small scale makes for a genuinely caring, friendly atmosphere.

The building is designed so that all rooms feature a sea view. Rooms on the ground floor open on to a patio that gives easy access to the pool and beach, while rooms on the first floor have balconies, so you can sit and have your breakfast or an evening drink while looking out to sea. The rooms themselves are basic but comfortable and spacious, with large beds, table and chairs, an en suite bathroom, and large TV with cable channels. There are also three suites available.

In between the hotel and the beach are a swimming pool, whirlpool bath, lawn area and children's playground. The leisure facilities are fairly basic, but if all you want is to just lounge by the pool in the sun while the kids keep themselves busy, then this is a good spot. There's a basketball court on the beach too, although Hurricane Gonu did its best to drag half of that into the sea in 2007. Drinks and food are all served poolside, and there are regular buffets served alfresco too. Inside the hotel, kids – and adults – can let off steam by playing table tennis, table football or darts.

A slightly limited international menu is served at the Khasab restaurant, off the hotel lobby, while the Zebra Bar serves a range of alcoholic beverages. The food is adequate but not overly inspiring, so if you're after gourmet fare you may need to take a little drive back down the coast to some of the bigger Fujairah hotels. The real benefit of staying here, however, is the proximity to the attractions of the east coast and Musandam peninsula. There is a tour desk within the hotel from which you can book activities such as diving, snorkelling,

dhow cruises, hiking and kayaking. Some of the region's best dive sites are scattered around this area, and there is some great trekking to be done in the mountains. The friendly Al Marsa Tours company can arrange your preferred activity, or tailor a day's programme to suit your party. If you're only staying for one night though, it's probably worth calling ahead (+968 26 836 995) to make sure you can do your activity of choice. It's also only a 20 minute drive down the coast to snorkelling hotspot Snoopy Island, and there's some great off roading to be done right on the doorstep.

It may not be the flashiest hotel in Arabia, but if you're after a good value, quiet getaway, a base for an active weekend, or a glimpse of Musandam without the visa hassles, the Golden Tulip fits the bill.

The Dibba Dead
A vast cemetery on the outskirts of town is said to be the last resting place of over 10,000 rebels who died in a great battle fought in 633AD, when the Muslim armies of Caliph Abu Baker were sent to suppress a local rebellion and to reconquer the Arabian peninsula for Islam. To find it, head out of Dibba towards Wadi Bih.

Contact
Phone: +968 26 730 888
Email: info@goldentulipdibba.com
Web: www.goldentulip.com

Location
From Dibba Town Centre the hotel is signposted from Dolphin Roundabout.

Food & Drink
Khasab Restaurant– international
• Cappuccino Cafe – cafe • Zebra – bar
• Pool Bar – snacks

Features
Private beach • Gym • Jacuzzi
• Swimming pool • Play area
• Play room

Nearby
Dibba Beach • Mountains • Wadis
• Dibba Castle • Bidiyah Mosque
• Snoopy Island • Boat trips • Fishing
• Snorkelling

Golden Tulip Resort Khasab

The Golden Tulip Resort Khasab was built in 2003 to provide comfortable accommodation for the many visitors who travel to the Musandam area to enjoy the beautiful fjords, either from above the water in a dhow, or below the water on a dive trip. It is situated along the mountainous coastline, so in terms of scenery, you have got the best of both worlds. It is a perfect place to spend a night or two while you explore the region.

The hotel has 60 rooms and suites in total, all with either a sea or mountain view. All rooms have generous balconies, complete with patio furniture, so that when you've finished a day of diving or exploring the area by boat, you can relax on the balcony and watch the sun set over the sea. Rooms are modern and certainly large enough for comfort. The suites in particular are very spacious, with a master bedroom and a separate, very large lounge and living area opening up on to the balcony. If you are planning a trip in advance and make your reservations early enough, try requesting one of the ground floor rooms that open directly on to the pool area. While you may lose out on the view that you would have from a room on a higher floor, these ground floor rooms are excellent for guests with children, as they offer easy access to the outdoor playground and pool.

The hotel also features a collection of chalets, which are located to the left of the hotel as you enter the lobby. These are comfortable, and suitable for larger families, although not all of them have a sea view.

One of the main reasons for visiting Musandam is to take a boat trip through the fjords, and you can arrange a morning, afternoon or full-day trip through Khasab Travel and Tours, which has an office in the hotel lobby. Prices for the tours vary according to season, but are reasonable. The full-day tour departs at around 09:30 and sails for around two hours before stopping for snorkelling.

During this time, you have an excellent chance of seeing some of the dolphins that inhabit the waters in this region. The boat staff are generally very good at finding the dolphins, and once they've found them, they each have their own techniques for enticing the dolphins to swim alongside the boat (such as clapping, whistling or shouting).

Once you've had an hour of snorkelling, the boat sets sail again before anchoring for a barbecue lunch. After more snorkelling, you'll turn around and head for home, and if you are very lucky, you will see dolphins on the way back as well.

Back at the hotel, the pool area is a wonderful place to relax either before or after your excursion out on the open water. The pool is big enough for crowds and has a large shallow area that is suitable for kids, as well as a separate kids' pool, and thanks to shelters made from barasti there is plenty of shade should you need to wheel your sun lounger somewhere a bit cooler. Snacks and refreshments are available around the pool, and the waiters from the poolside cafe will be happy to bring a nice frosty drink right up to your lounger. What makes the pool area even lovelier is the setting – you are very close to the sea, and while there is no beach, the pool has lovely sea views. There is a small playground near the pool.

From the pool area you can also find the access point for the dive centre. The area is renowned for its excellent diving, thanks to warm waters and deep drop offs. Inexperienced divers may find easier diving in secluded bays formed by mountainous outcrops jutting out into the sea, which may feature weaker currents in an area otherwise known as being a fairly challenging dive destination. However, if you dive with an instructor and can get used to the currents, you'll be rewarded with a beautiful collection of varied marine life, and beds of coral that stretch out for miles in some places. The dive centre is operated by Extra Divers (+968 26 730 501, www.musandam-diving.com), and welcomes divers of all levels.

As for food and drink, the hotel has the Dibba Restaurant that serves buffet breakfast, lunch and dinner. There is also a small a la carte selection, although the buffet is of a fairly good quality and has a great range of dishes. The hotel has a bar and a cafe, but with such great poolside service you could almost do all your eating and drinking around the swimming pool.

Daytrips
Khasab Travel & Tours has an office located in the Golden Tulip Resort Khasab, where tours and dhow trips can be booked directly. If you want to be super organised, and arrange your trip before you arrive at the hotel, you can call them on +968 26 731 351, or at the Dubai office on +971 4 266 9950.

Musandam

Contact
Phone: +968 26 730 777
Email: info@goldentulipkhasab.com
Web: www.goldentulip.com

Location
From Ras Al Khaimah, follow signs for Khasab. Just before you enter Khasab, the hotel is on the left hand side of the main road, and is signposted.

Food & Drink
Dibba Restaurant – international • Cappuccino Cafe – cafe • Darts Bar – bar

Features
Dive centre • Children's playground • Swimming pool • Children's pool • Gym • Table tennis • Dhow cruises • Mountain safari • Dolphin watching • Snorkelling • BBQ nights • Tour desk in lobby

Nearby
Khasab Fort • Telegraph Island • 'Fjords of Arabia' • Acacia forest • Mountains

Nestled next to a remote fishing village in the spectacularly secluded Zighy Bay, this hideaway certainly lives up to the prime reputation of the Six Senses brand. Protected by the majestic mountains of Musandam, there is only one access road to Six Senses, which was carved out of the imposing rock for the exclusive use of the hotel. However, that doesn't mean there is only one way to reach this retreat. In fact there are three modes of arrival – by the rocky, windy road in one of the hotel's 4WD vehicles, by speedboat into the bay, or if either of those seemingly daredevil entrances is not adrenaline-pumping enough, you have the option of paragliding into the resort. Whether you arrive by sea or sky, or stick to the road, by the time you enter the impressive Omani doors you'll be walking on air. The resort has been designed with traditional architecture in mind and each guest room is an individual bungalow. The style is certainly rustic, and not the standard 'faux rustic' where a few touches are thrown in to try and mask modern luxury. Instead, stone, marble and wood are the main materials here and the furniture is all hand-crafted by local carpenters.

Six Senses Hideaway Zighy Bay

However, don't assume that lavish comfort is absent; quite the opposite. Once you enter your private residence the serenity that washes over you will defrazzle the most tightly wound of city dwellers. Modern amenities are subtly disguised by clever design and stunning craftsmanship, while nature is served with a side order of indulgence, in the form of a lavish four-poster ebony bed covered by wicker fans, an outside shower, and a lounge area adorned with the most sumptuous of pillows. Each of the bungalows has its own private pool, with a cushioned, bamboo-protected majlis that's perfect for sipping fruit cocktails. The poolside area is perfect for a romantic dinner, which can be cooked and served by your own chef and waiter.

The alternative options for dining are no less impressive. The main restaurant, Dining on the Sand, can cater to couples or groups. The cuisine is a fusion of Asian, Arabic and European, and the colour of the cushions change depending on the hour of the day – an interesting gimmick amid the muted rustic decor. If the paragliding didn't take your breath away then the mountain-top restaurant, Dining on the Edge, certainly will, with its a la carte dining and exquisite drinks menu, and a magnificent view of the bay below. Chill is an inviting bar with raised booths and a terrace overlooking the main pool, where the cocktails come creatively chilled. Wine bar Vinotheque houses an impressive cellar and a spiral staircase leading to an intimate rooftop – the perfect spot for a sundowner.

If total relaxation isn't what you have in mind, there are plenty of activities to keep you busy. The hotel can organise an afternoon of trekking along footpaths through the mighty Musandam mountains, or there's snorkelling and fishing in the remote bay. The resort, while not exactly sprawling, does have a spacious feel and you can potter around the main pool or head down to the beach on the set of bikes stored in front of each bungalow.

Six Senses resorts are renowned for their spa offerings, and Zighy Bay is no exception. The luxurious spa provides a range of treatments, focusing on a holistic approach to mind and body. If you aren't already on cloud nine after a weekend at this resort, the highly skilled spa therapists and exquisite, tranquil surroundings of the spa will get you there. The spa offers relaxing and beautifying treatments such as holistic massages, natural body scrubs and henna treatments. The traditional Arabian Hammam, while not for the bashful, is a unique treatment specific to the region. This slice of heaven on earth certainly doesn't come cheap, but it really is worth every penny. You may leave with a lighter wallet, but you'll take with you a sense of enlightenment that you'll want to hang on to for as long as possible after you return to the real world.

Contact
Phone: +968 26 735 555
Email: reservations-zighy@sixsenses.com
Website: www.sixsenses.com

Location
From Dibba, turn left at Dolphin Roundabout and follow the road through the UAE border post. Take a left at Mosque Roundabout and left again. Turn right at the dam, and the road will turn into a track, which you should follow for around five kilometres until you see the gates on your right.

Food & Drink
Dining on the Sand – Asian & Middle Eastern • The Deli – snacks • Dining on the Edge – tapas & bar • Chill – cocktail bar • Vinotheque – wine cellar

Features
Spa • Gym • Game fishing • Swimming pool • Artisan gallery • Tours • Private cooking classes • Snorkelling & excursions • Water activities • Paragliding • Mountain biking • Trekking

Nearby
Dibba Beach • Mountains • Wadis • Dibba Castle • Bidiyah Mosque • Snoopy Island • Boat trips • Fishing • Snorkelling

Western Hajar

This imposing range of mountains may look other-worldly and barren at times, yet it is home to fascinating wadis, fertile plateaus and jaw-dropping views. There is a variety of terrain to explore, from lush oases, pools, streams and waterfalls to remote villages nestling beneath towering cliff faces.

Further Reading
For first-hand advice on tackling this part of Oman, including details on specific routes to follow, see the *Oman Off-Road Explorer*. Apart from maps and waypoints for each route, and suggestions for things to see along the way, it also offers important safety information that is essential reading when exploring this challenging terrain.

The Hajar Mountains are often called the backbone of Arabia. These other-worldly, serrated lumps of rock spread across northern Oman to the eastern extremes of the UAE. The barrenness of this range can be both daunting and spectacularly beautiful.

The Western Hajar area is home to two of the biggest (literally) attractions in Oman; Jebel Shams and Wadi Nakhur. Jebel Shams, or 'mountain of the sun' in Arabic, is the highest point in Oman at 3,009 metres, and has several hikes, some of which are quite challenging but offer amazing views. Right next to this, and fondly known as Oman's Grand Canyon, the depths of Wadi an Nakhur offer opportunities for more exploring and breathtaking scenery.

Above: Balad Seet, Below: Hiking

Further east, 25 kilometres from Nizwa, is the Sayq Plateau, located on top of Jebel Akhdar (the green mountain). The plateau is home to over 30 villages set among a maze of roads and trails, and it feels like it's a world away from the rest of Oman. As well as being significantly cooler, with elevation varying mostly between 2,000m and 2,400m, the high level of rainfall (up to six times the amount that falls on the plains below) means there is a surprising amount of greenery on the terraces and plantations at the edge of the plateau. It also home to the Jabal Akhdar Hotel (p.52), the perfect base for your exploration of the mountains. Currently it is the only hotel located so high up, but it may soon be joined by others, as there are more projects planned for this area.

One of the best times to visit is around March and April, when the roses and fruit trees are in full bloom. There is a security checkpoint where the driver will be asked to produce their passport, driving licence and car insurance – and only 4WD vehicles will be allowed to pass, even though it is a tarmac road.

In between these two high points lie the historic hotspots of Nizwa and Bahla, with lots to see and do in and around the old towns. Exploring the nearby village of Misfat Al Abriyyin is also recommended, as it has one of the most beautiful and intricate falaj networks (traditional irrigation channels used in plantations and farms) to be found in the region. It is also unusual in that whereas most plantations are on flat ground, its falaj feed an impressive set of terraces on very steeply terraced hillsides.

The spectacular mountain scenery of Oman, with its miraculous staircases crisscrossing the mountains, is paradise for those who like exploring the country by foot. The climate in the higher areas is also usually significantly cooler at altitude, so when the summer temperatures get too hot to handle, many intrepid weekend breakers head for the hills. The caves in the area provide a mystical underground world containing glittering stalagmites and stalactites, white gypsum crystal and underground lakes. Unless you are an experienced caver, use an experienced guide when you explore the caves.

Close to Jebel Shams, Al Hoota Cave is well worth a visit. It is home to some amazing rock formations and an underground lake, which together with natural air, support a fascinating subterranean ecosystem. Other facilities include a great restaurant and a natural history museum. At various stations throughout the cave, you will find a knowledgeable Omani guide who can tell you about the history of the cave and its ecological significance. The cave is very humid inside, with temperatures of around 25°C throughout the year, so you can leave your woolly jumper in the car, along with your camera, as photography is not allowed inside the cave. All visitors need to book at least 24 hours in advance, as only a limited number of people are allowed into the cave at a time – ask your hotel for assistance, or call the cave office directly. Al Hoota Cave is well signposted from the Nizwa-Bahla Road, heading towards Al Hamra Village (+968 24 490 060, www.alhootacave.com).

Another attraction worth visiting is the ruins of the Al Sulaif Fortress Town, on the road from Nizwa to Buraimi. If you are driving from Muscat, these intriguing ruins are clearly visible on the left-hand side of the road just before you reach Ibri. Dating back to the 11th century, this surprisingly large deserted village is home to old mud houses and a fort, and offers many opportunities for exploring.

Western Hajar South

Nizwa

About 140 kilometres south-west of Muscat, Nizwa is a popular destination for tourists and residents of Oman. Nizwa was Oman's capital in the sixth and seventh centuries, and the centre of trade between the coast and the interior regions. It was historically a haven for poets, writers, intellectuals and religious leaders, and is still one of the largest and most important towns in the interior. Positioned next to two wadis, Nizwa is a fertile sea of green, with an oasis of date plantations stretching eight kilometres from the town. You

can also see ancient mud-brick villages among its date palms and the wadis.

The 17th century Nizwa Fort (www. omantourism.gov.om) is surprisingly large, and although not quite as visually impressive as the others, it is one of the most interesting forts to visit. You can wander through the maze of passageways and up to the battlements, where the views out over Nizwa in all directions show the sheer size of the oasis, with palm trees extending as far as the eye can see. High-tech displays and areas with extensive exhibits are recent additions, transforming it into a top-class attraction where you could easily spend a few hours.

Bahla

Just 40 kilometres west of Nizwa, Bahla is believed to be one of the oldest inhabited regions in Oman, and archaeologists have found artefacts here dating back to the third century BC. While it is not yet on the mainstream tourist map (although efforts are being made to attract more tourists to the area), anyone interested in archaeology and history will find it well worth a visit.

The town is enclosed by a protective, fortified wall that stretches for 12 kilometres. Although large sections of the wall are still standing, parts of it are in ruins and earmarked for eventual reconstruction. In the centre, Bahla Fort is the oldest in Oman, and definitely a must-see. Currently undergoing careful and extensive restoration sponsored by Unesco, the ruins rise 50 metres above the surrounding dwellings, and its now diminished windtowers were once said to be the tallest structures in Oman. The deserted mud-brick villages surrounding the fort are great to explore. The ruins of the mosque are particularly interesting.

Apart from the historical buildings and the traditional way of life, Bahla also has a rich and diverse ecology – a balanced mixture of fertile land, mountains, wadis and desert. This area is a good source of high-quality clay, which led to the town being known for its distinctive pottery. You shouldn't leave without buying some, or at least visiting the traditional pottery site near the souk or the smaller

Snake Canyon

Escape the heat by camping on the Sayq Plateau, where temperatures can be significantly cooler. The best time to visit is around March or April, when roses and fruit trees are in full bloom.

workshops where you can see potters working, and a wide variety of pots in various states. The town is characterised by its many winding roads, some so narrow that you have to pull over to let an oncoming car pass. Whether you explore the town on foot or by car, you will find an eclectic balance between the new, functioning town, the ancient, fascinating ruins, and the many date plantations that make perfect picnic spots.

Jabrin

Located about 12 kilometres south of Bahla is the fascinating three-storey Jabrin Fort, which is interesting for its wall and ceiling decorations and the water channels running through the kitchens. Kids especially will love finding secret passageways and staircases, and climbing up the towers, which offer views out over the surrounding barren countryside. For more information on this and other forts in Oman, visit the website of the Ministry of Heritage and Culture (www.mhc.gov.om).

Western Hajar North

Nakhal

Driving north-west from Muscat up the coast road will get you to Barka, where the 'Rustaq-Nakhal Loop' (Route 13) takes you south towards the mountains. One of the main towns in the area, Nakhal (75km from Muscat) is derived from the word 'Nakheel', which means date palm, and large date palm plantations are one of the area's main draws. There is an imposing restored fort set on a hill; if you stand at the top of the watchtowers you will have magnificent views of the surrounding countryside and town.

The area is also well known for the A'Thowarah hot springs, which can be found by following the main road past the fort. A twisty road leads you through the palm plantations and you catch glimpses of old ruins interspersed among the palms. The springs are a popular spot for picnics, and there are some covered picnic tables, but these often get busy with other picnickers. Head away from the crowds and you'll find plenty of shady places to stop. A concrete tube (with waterfall) provides a pleasant area to bathe in the springs, and there is also a small souk.

Rustaq

Another 45 kilometres along the main road takes you to Rustaq (or Ar Rustaq). In the middle ages, this town was the capital of Oman. Today, it is best known for its large and dramatic fort, which has been extended over the years. It was well placed to withstand long sieges because it has its own water supply. Near the fort you'll find a small souk, as well as some hot springs, which have now been enclosed into bath houses for men and women. Just 20 kilometres north of Rustaq is Al Hazm Castle, a fascinating castle with a colourful history and extensive tunnel and dungeon networks. It was once believed to be connected to the Rustaq fort by underground tunnel. The castle was closed in 2008 for renovation, but is scheduled to open again in 2009.

Accommodation Options

Apart from the stunningly located Jabal Akhdar Hotel (p.52), there are a few other hotel options in the area, mostly located in and around Nizwa. These hotels are close enough to the south of Nizwa to make them convenient starting points from which to explore the mountains in the Western Hajar South area and all its main attractions. This is also prime camping country – for more information on that, see p.50.

Al Diyar Hotel (+968 25 412 402, www.aldiyarhotel.com) offers an uncomplicated stay, with a swimming pool and gym. The Falaj Daris Hotel (+968 25 410 500, www.falajdarishotel.com) has landscaped gardens and a pool. The Nizwa Hotel (+968 25 431 616, www.nizwahotel.net) features amazing views of the Hajar Mountains and has 40 guest rooms, a swimming pool, an international restaurant and two bars. Also in the same area, the Safari Hotel (+968 25 432 150) is a small, friendly hotel that offers reasonable rates and has a restaurant serving a wide range of good value food.

For those who like to 'camp' with a few creature comforts, Jebel Shams Camping Centre (+968 24 635 222, www.rahaloman.

The Al Hoota Cave features a collection of amazing rock formations and an underground lake, which is home to a subterranean ecosystem and a rare species of blind fish. Knowledgeable guides are on hand at various points throughout the cave to provide information.

com), on top of Jebel Shams, has a great site with permanent tents and small chalets. This is a great base from which to make the most of the area's hiking routes; it is near Oman's 'grand canyon' and features amazing views.

Camping

The Western Hajars offer many places to set up camp in wadis or along hiking routes. Don't miss out on the magnificent views and photo opportunities to be had on Jebel Shams or the Sayq Plateau. You'll find that the higher areas are a lot cooler – temperatures average around 10 to 15 degrees cooler than down below, so it can therefore be more appealing than camping at lower altitudes. It is even possible to camp high up in the middle of summer.

On the Sayq Plateau, a popular place to camp is Diana's Viewpoint (named after Princess Diana, who visited in 1990). It is on the edge of a promontory with spectacular views, and there is plenty of space. As with camping anywhere in the wilderness, minimise your impact and leave no trace of your stay behind. On Jebel Shams there is a good campsite at the start of the W4 hike, at around 1,950 metres. Also in the area, the off-road route to Qiyut off the Nizwa-Bahla road gets you quickly up high to masses of camping spots and great views.

On the northern side of the mountains you can camp in Wadi Al Abyad next to the pools, perfect for a dip to cool off in warmer weather, or try one of the campsites set spectacularly beneath the awesome north face of Jebel Shams in the 'treasure chest' of Oman, Wadi As Sahtan, which has almost endless possibilities for exploring.

Hiking

Oman has plenty to offer hikers, and the best area of all is the Western Hajar Mountains. There are many excellent routes to be enjoyed, ranging from short easy walks to spectacular viewpoints, to longer, more arduous treks up high peaks. Jebel Shams has numerous impressive hikes. One of the shorter ones is the four-hour Balcony Walk along Jebel Shams Plateau, which has incredible canyon views. Be sure that on any hike, short or long, you consider the weather conditions. Always carry plenty of water and food, check your routes before setting out, notify someone as to your itinerary, and wear appropriate clothing. Be warned: no mountain rescue services exist, so anyone venturing out into mountains should be experienced, or be with someone who is.

Shopping

There is no better place to rub shoulders with the locals than at the souks in Bahla and Nizwa. In both places, in the alleyways leading away from the central livestock trading areas, you'll find many small shops that sell traditional crafts, Omani antiques, rugs, spices and nuts. You can watch the local silversmith at work, repairing khanjars and jewellery in the same way it has been done for generations. The souks also sell fruit and vegetables, all of which are locally produced, and the locally grown dates are delicious. In Bahla, a great souvenir is some of the distinctive and famous local pottery. If you can time your trip to Nizwa to catch the atmospheric Friday morning livestock market, you'll be rewarded with being able to observe a colourful local experience that hasn't changed in generations.

Nizwa Market

Wadi Al Abyad

Just over an hour west of Muscat, the pools of Wadi Al Abyad are a great place to visit throughout the year. From the end of the track, a short stroll will get you to increasingly larger pools where you can easily spend the whole day. Alternatively, you can take the easy two-hour hike through the wadi to the town of Al Abyad.

Forts

In the Western Hajar South, Nizwa Fort is one of the most interesting to visit, while Oman's oldest is in Bahla. Jabrin Fort, originally a 17th century palace, has been restored and visitors can see the living quarters of the Imam, his family and their servants, including the dining room, prison, school and majlis. In the north, Rustaq and Nakhal have forts which are worth a visit, as is Al Hazm Castle, north of Rustaq. It is a fascinating place, with a colourful history, and although currently closed for renovation, it will open again in 2009.

Oman's High Country

Jebel Shams, Jebel Akhdar and Wadi An Nakhur are definite must-sees. Jebel Shams, the 'Mountain of the Sun', has a rugged terrain that is actually a fairly easy trek with several good camping locations. Below the summit, Wadi An Nakhur has some of the most stupendous views in the country, offering ample photo opportunities as you drive through the 'Grand Canyon of Oman'. The Sayq Plateau on top of Jebel Akhdar has spectacular scenery and beautiful little mountain villages.

Wadi Mistall

Wadi Mistall's fruitful plantations are a balm for those tired of arid climes. The hanging gardens at the end of the wadi are lovely, as are the plantations growing alfalfa, limes, dates, apricots, figs, pomegranates and grapes at certain times of year. From here there are several sidetracks up to Sayq Plateau's villages and the Jabal Akhdar Hotel.

Must-Do Experiences

Western Hajar

The craggy terrain of the Western Hajar forms an adventure playground for outdoorsy weekend breakers.

Snake Canyon

Adventurers wishing to complete this spectacular, challenging hike should know that it involves some daring jumps into rock pools and a fair bit of swimming through ravines. It takes around three to four hours, and is something you'll remember forever. Keep a close eye on the weather, as rains from miles away could cause flash floods in a matter of minutes.

Misfat Al Abryyin

This ancient village, with terraced palm plantations built unusually on a steeply sloping hillside, is just a short distance from Al Hamra. Rich red soil, ancient houses and the ruins of a watchtower perched on the mountain add to the character of Misfat Al Abryyin. The falaj network is one of the most intricate in Oman and snakes its way around banana, lemon and date trees.

Al Hoota Cave

This long cave features a large subterranean chamber and an 800m underground lake which is home to a rare species of blind fish. The cave has been developed so that it can be enjoyed by those without proper caving experience and equipment, and it now includes a train and a sound and lighting system. www.alhootacave.com

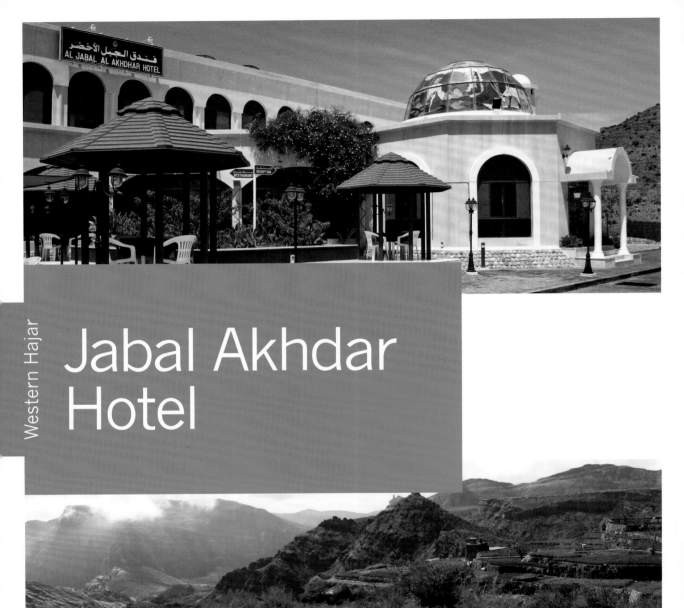

Jabal Akhdar Hotel

Tucked away a little further south of the better-known Jebel Shams, but in the same range of mountains, Oman has a hidden mountain playground for the adventurous to explore. Just 25 kilometres from the busy market town of Nizwa, you'll find Jebel Akhdar (the green mountain). And because it is less famous than Jebel Shams, it is even more peaceful.

This is partly because, until recently, tourists couldn't get up it. Like something from a Bond villain's most despicable schemes, a defence base sits on this isolated part of the planet. But in 2004, the Oman Ministry of Defence, in a show of un-villainous magnanimity, allowed everybody else to come and play. Provided you smile sweetly at the soldiers at the bottom of the hill and are driving a 4WD, that is. Manage this much, and your journey can begin.

If you make the ear-popping drive all the way up, you won't regret the trip. Particularly if you can time your ascent to coincide with sunset, when the sun falls slowly, painting the sky a mesmerising shade as you climb and climb and climb. Although not a drive for the faint hearted, the journey is very impressive. The scenery is just as stark as other parts of the Hajar range, and almost sinister in its beauty. While there may not be Bond villains, it looks alien enough that the appearance of a bug-eyed Martian might not be entirely surprising. When you do eventually reach the top, which is 2,400 metres above sea level, you'll find the sleepy Jabal Akhdar Hotel. Once the sun sets up here, it becomes cold and dark, but the hotel's friendly staff welcome guests with warm smiles.

While the hotel is not somewhere that could be described as luxurious – some of the finishes are a bit tatty, and the food is basic – it has everything that a mountain explorer might need. This is not a place to come for a raucous time. Instead, rise early for the hotel's basic breakfast and get out for the day – the staff are keen to offer advice on how to spend your time in the area.

Armed with some local knowledge and a good map, you can explore the mountain. There is only one road in and out, and beyond the hotel, you'll see the defence base, before coming to some beautiful little villages clinging to the side of the mountain as if they didn't care that the rest of the world existed. But get out and look around, and you'll find that visitors are still rare enough to cause curiosity and get welcoming greetings from the locals.

Oman's Ministry of Tourism is encouraging the development of facilities for outdoor activities such as hiking, and has created a network of signposted trails across the country including several on and around the Sayq Plateau. Details of all these hikes, including the superb route through the picturesque villages on the edge of the plateau – one of the best in the whole country – can be found in the *Oman Trekking Explorer*. And for more information on what there is to see on the plateau, the *Oman Off-Road Explorer* is an essential on any trip to this area. It also has detailed descriptions and maps of how to get there.

As Jebel Akhdar's popularity grows, so too do the many enquiries from tour operators in Europe. Jebel Shams has had the limelight for too long. Jebel Akhdar is just as beautiful, and perhaps even more so, because it has so few visitors.

Contact
Phone: +968 25 429 009
Email: jakhotel@omantel.net.om
Web: www.jabalakhdharhotel.com.om

Location
From Nizwa, follow signs for Jabal Al Akhdhar; the hotel is also signposted. Remember – only 4WDs are allowed up through the checkpoint.

Food & Drink
International restaurant, plus room service

Features
Mountain views • Complete tranquility

Nearby
Nizwa • Wadi Bani Habib • Hiking routes

Salalah

In the land of frankincense and summer rains, lush greenery and cool weather combine to make the ultimate short break from sticky desert climes elsewhere in the region.

Salalah is the capital of the southern province of Dhofar, and its most populated city. It is around a thousand kilometres from Muscat, near the border with Yemen, and the only area on the entire Arabian Peninsula to catch the tip of the Indian monsoon season. And therein lies the main attraction of Salalah: its climate. Throughout the year it is relatively greener than other areas, but from June to September you can enjoy the *khareef*, or monsoon season. A thick blanket of fog settles on the mountains and the natural environment flourishes, with flowing rivers and waterfalls punctuating the greenery. The mountains themselves are especially beautiful and definitely worth exploring; they seem to stretch as far as the eye can see, and a short hike will uncover intriguing caves and dramatic wadis hidden within.

The pace of life in Salalah is as calming as the surroundings. Friendly locals are usually only too happy to chat to you about the beauty of their town, and may even offer helpful suggestions for things to do and see before you leave.

Frankincense is another attraction of the area. Dhofar frankincense is regarded as the finest in the world, and once made this area immensely wealthy and important. In fact, it was historically the centre of the frankincense trade, and locally produced frankincense remains an important export for Dhofar.

You'll find an impressive grouping of trees in Wadi Qahshan, which runs through the mountainous backdrop of the Mughsayl-Sarfait Road linking Salalah with the Yemen border. This is where frankincense trees are farmed by local villagers. They cut into the trunks and allow the sap to seep out and harden into lumps that are then scraped off and traded in bulk. You can find Dhofar frankincense in souks throughout the country.

Above: Rolling greenery, Below: Tomb of Bin Ali

Salalah

Other Areas

Salalah is relatively small and, depending on the length of time you are there, you may wish to explore further afield. Wadi Darbat is within easy driving distance from Salalah, and features some great attractions. The Travertine Curtain, which looks like a huge pitted wall and is over 150m high, turns into a spectacular waterfall during the *khareef* as the entire contents of Wadi Darbat flow over this escarpment – it's Arabia's answer to Niagara Falls. There are several paths taking you towards the base of the cliff, with the going getting easier as you move past the trees towards the open grassland. Enjoy the spectacular views, and don't forget the camera. On a safety note, there are no guard rails, and the edge drops off steeply, so keep children well back.

Dhofar's prosperity was built on frankincense, the hardened resin of the boswellia tree. Burned for its aromatic, medicinal and insect-repelling qualities, the precious commodity was traded throughout Arabia, India and Europe, often pound for pound with gold. Dhofar frankincense was (and still is) considered the best in the world; as a result, the Dhofar region was historically the centre of the lucrative frankincense trade.

Wadi Darbat itself is misty, moody and muddy during the *khareef*, but in winter it is a verdant oasis. As you approach the wadi, just two kilometres from the Darbat turnoff, look out for the natural arch up to your right – this interesting feature can be reached with a short hike, and offers superb views over the surrounding valley, as well as a collection of small caves with stalagtites and stalagmites. As inviting as it may seem, the water in Wadi Darbat is not for swimming in, due to the risk of picking up a bilharzia infection.

Khor Ruwi, which is near the coastline in the Wadi Darbat area, used to be a bustling seaport, although it's hard to believe now. It is also home to an

The Travertine Curtain turns into a spectacular waterfall during the *khareef* as the entire contents of Wadi Darbat flow over the escarpment – it's Arabia's answer to the Niagara Falls.

Blowhole rest area

important archaeological site that was once the palace of the famed Queen of Sheba, and is where the waters of Wadi Darbat flow before finally reaching the ocean. The area is great for birdwatching, and flamingos are common from autumn to spring. From Khawr Ruwi you can hike up to the headlands above the eastern entrance to the lagoon – a large, flat plateau eventually leads to an abrupt edge with a 30m drop to the ocean.

Accommodation Options

Apart from the Hilton and the Crowne Plaza, which are detailed on the following pages, there are a few other options. Bear in mind that during *khareef* season hotel rooms get booked up months in advance and room rates skyrocket. If you can't get in the Hilton or Crowne Plaza, try the Dhofar Hotel (23 292 300) or the Hamilton Plaza Hotel (23 211 025), both of which are rated three star. Alternatively, stay in one of the three-bedroom villas or one-bedroom apartments in the Samharam Tourist Village (23 211 420).

Camping

While you won't find any organised campsites (that is, campsites with facilities) in Salalah, there are plenty of spots to pitch your tent. Just 20km past the turnoff to the Tawi Atayr sinkhole, you'll find several sidetracks to the edge of the escarpment overlooking the east coast and the sleepy town of Mirbat. In winter the views are consistently spectacular and this is a highly recommended camping spot. Although the water is not safe for swimming in Wadi Darbat, if you walk down the length of the wadi you will find many secluded campsites between the trees. In Khor Ruwi, you'll find some great campsites near the mouth of the lagoon, on the low, flat rocks just up from the beach. Just over 15km from the main road running along Jabal al Qamar, there's a stunning birds'-eye view of the secluded beaches on Oman's south coast. There are several spots perfect for camping just before and just after this viewpoint; however please remember not to disturb the locals, and if you camp here during the *khareef* be prepared for mud.

Shopping

With a reasonably small town centre, shopping in Salalah is all about the souks. Al Husn Souk is the place to head if you're after silver jewellery or traditional souvenirs. It's also an excellent place to pick up some fine Dhofar frankincense. At Al Hafah Souk, south of Salalah, you'll find plenty of perfume and locally prepared food. Al Sinaw Souk is where Bedouin tribes used to conduct their business, and is famous for authentic Bedouin jewellery. If you are camping and need to get supplies, you'll find a branch of Lulu's Hypermarket in Salalah, which offers a wide range of goods.

Going Out

The restaurants and bars within Salalah's hotels are your best bet for a night out. Both the Hilton and the Crowne Plaza have various outlets, which are popular with locals and tourists.

Frankincense Trail

Wadi Dawkah, with its resident frankincense trees, is a Unesco World Heritage Site. After a short drive along a graded road, you will reach an outcrop overlooking several trees. The main areas of trees have been fenced off for protection, but if you want to get closer there are a few trees just near the parking area.

Mountain Drive

Head off road and you'll be rewarded with spectacular views over Salalah and out to sea. A short drive takes you past attractions such as a small lake in a stunning wadi, a large sinkhole and even some massive baobab trees. In good weather, the viewpoints and campsites are unparalleled.

Salalah Museum

Get a feel for what life was really like for the small, yet growing, population of Salalah from as early as the 11th century. See ancient writings and manuscripts, traditional equipment, old pottery and the earliest forms of currency. Contact the museum on 23 294 549 for current opening hours.

Must-Do
Experiences

Salalah

Savour the natural wonders of blowholes and panoramic mountain vistas.

Blowholes

If you visit during *khareef*, drive along the coastline at Al Mughsayl to find one of the most spectacular natural sights in Oman – the Al Mughsayl blowholes. Thundering waves have eroded caverns underfoot and the only way out is up through small openings below the metal grates. Stand well back; the force generated is quite astonishing.

Nabi Ayoub's Tomb

Nabi Ayoub (also known as the prophet Job) was a respected religious figure who is said to have used this area to conduct his daily prayers. He dedicated his life to God and was put to rest in the same spot – facing Jerusalem – where he chose to worship. Located 40km from Salalah, this shrine is a popular tourist attraction.

Crowne Plaza Resort Salalah

When it's hot, humid and dusty throughout the region, Salalah is unbelievably green and cool thanks to the Indian monsoon season and the resulting *khareef*. No surprise then that crowds of hot, sweaty and flustered weekend breakers make the journey down to cooler climes for an escape, despite it being around a thousand kilometres from Muscat.

The Crowne Plaza Resort is one of only two five-star hotels in the area and prides itself on being able to cater to a range of guests, from teams of professionals on business trips to small families on holiday. The facilities are extensive – definitely in line with those you would expect from a resort rather than just a hotel. Set on 45 acres of land, one of the most impressive features of the resort is the nine-hole golf course and driving range.

Between greens and the range are the outdoor swimming pools. The swimming area has been designed to enable parents to relax while kids have fun in the pools – a water slide and special dedicated children's area will provide them with hours of entertainment. This, along with other special touches for kids (including a child-sized check-in desk at reception), make this an especially suitable resort for family holidays.

In the middle of the three pools you'll find the Splash Pool Bar, complete with underwater bar stools, snacks and a cocktail menu that is perfect for sunny afternoons. The outdoor Jacuzzi is yet another luxury feature of the swimming area, and is just a few strokes away from the pool bar. If you'd rather swim in the sea, the beach is a short walk away. It is equipped with sun loungers and umbrellas, and there is a lifeguard on duty throughout the day.

For dining, the Crowne Plaza has many options, including the Darbat restaurant just off the reception area, where breakfast is served overlooking the sea.

The Dolphin Beach Restaurant is definitely the resort's best offering; set right on the beach, this open-air restaurant comes alive in the evenings with a buffet-style menu that changes daily. Choose from a wide range of starters and mains, but leaving room to tuck into the heaving dessert table of course. During your meal a live band plays a popular yet relaxed repertoire of hits, adding to the ambience of the evening.

After dinner, there's more entertainment in the Al Luban nightclub, where you can catch the live band and dancers (who are particularly popular with the visiting business crowd). Comedy acts entertain the guests with a range of sketches, while on other nights you may find yourself watching belly dancers or even a show-band.

For those who wish to wind down and relax, there is a health club on site offering treatments such as manicures, pedicures, facials and haircuts. Massages are also available, from relaxing rubdowns to more intense therapeutic sessions. There is also a gym with a good selection of cardio equipment and free weights, two tennis courts (which are floodlit at night), and a squash court.

The rooms are comfortable, with the standard ones being just what you might expect from a hotel popular with business travellers: from the kettle and mini-bar to the high-speed internet access and satellite TV channels, they are equipped with all the usual conveniences. If you're prepared to splash a bit more cash, check into a junior or royal suite to experience more space, more luxury and more comfort. All rooms have views across the swimming pools and out towards the sea, so you'll experience that holiday feeling from the moment you check in.

The hotel offers a host of services and below lobby level you'll find a gift shop, car rental facilities, and a watersports and dive centre. With a shuttle service which runs from the airport to the hotel, guests who fly in will

find that they are looked after from the very moment they arrive in Salalah. No matter how you arrive though, the warm welcome you receive at reception lasts for the duration of your visit.

Salalah

Contact
Phone: +968 23 235 333
Email: cpsalalah@cpsalalah.com
Web: www.crowneplaza.com

Location
Once in Salalah, take Highway 47 heading west of the city and the hotel is on the left, past the Tourist Village.

Food & Drink
Al Luban – themed buffet • Darbat – international • Al Khareef – bar • Dolphin Beach Restaurant – international

Features
Four swimming pools • Dive centre • Salon • Golf course • Gym • Tennis court • Squash court • Gift shop

Nearby
Old souk • Gold souk • Lost City of Ubar • Al Mughsayl beach • Khor Ruri • Travertine Curtain • Blowholes • Wadi Darbat • Frankincense trees • Nabi Ayoub's Tomb

Hilton Salalah

The Hilton is the other of the two five-star hotels located in Salalah. Although it is a slightly longer drive out of town than the Crowne Plaza, it is worth making the trip for the peaceful, beautiful location on the shores of the Arabian Sea.

The entrance to the hotel is grand, and you'll receive a warm welcome from the courteous, professional staff upon your arrival. This is an excellent choice of hotel if you're looking for a romantic getaway or just a weekend of sheer escapism. The atmosphere is calm and even when the hotel is fully booked, you'll feel as though you are just one of a handful of valued guests.

Despite the tranquility, however, there is no need to leave the kids at home because the Hilton has a well-organised kids' club that will take care of the little ones while you relax. From treasure hunts and organised beach walks to nature studies and sports, a team of experts will ensure that kids are stimulated and entertained for the duration of their stay. The hotel offers a range of dining options, lounge areas and entertainment venues. The beachside restaurant Palm Grove is a key feature and a fantastic place to dine.

Based at the rear of the hotel amid beautiful surroundings, it serves delicious seafood and Mediterranean cuisine, which, when combined with a balmy summer evening, can make for the perfect dining experience. If you'd like to crank the romance factor up a notch, request one of the beach pavilions – these specially designed Arabian-style tents, complete with cushioned seating, are right on the beach and ideal for a special candlelit dinner.

After your meal, head to the shisha terrace for a relaxing end to the evening. Settle down on traditional Arabian seating and let the shisha expert recommend the perfect flavour for your pipe while you enjoy the poolside ambience. A selection of drinks is also available.

If you'd rather forego the shisha and wind down in a more traditional pub setting, you can enjoy a full range of beers, wines, spirits and cocktails in the Mayfair Pub, which is open from 12:00 to 15:00 and from 18:00 until late. Alternatively, head to the Sunset Lounge where you can play board games, browse through a collection of books, or watch TV on the 42 inch plasma screen in comfortable surroundings. If winding down is not on your agenda, Whispers Lounge, on the ground floor, is a popular nightspot featuring live music and dance shows, attracting hotel guests and local residents.

The Dolphin Health and Fitness Club is the on-site treatment and sports centre. Here guests can work out from 06:00 until 22:00 in the indoor gym which, although on the small side, has a good variety of machines and is fully staffed at all times.

Next door to the gym is the sauna area for post-workout muscle treatments. Saunas are available in the male and female changing rooms, and both are extremely private. A selection of massages is also available in the spa, but for a really decadent treat you can enjoy the Wave Relaxation treatment, where a qualified therapist gives you a massage in one of the beach pavilions. Other treatments available in the spa include body scrubs, manicures and pedicures.

The Hilton has two floodlit tennis courts and a fantastic swimming pool that incorporates a kids' area, an infinity pool and even a water slide. As you might expect from a resort hotel, there are numerous organised activities on offer throughout the week, from water aerobics to beach volleyball. Of course, since you're right on the coast your stay won't be complete without a dip in the ocean, and you can hire a body board from the hotel, or even have a few diving lessons through the Sub-Aqua dive centre. If you are a certified diver, the Hilton offers special dive packages that include accommodation and a number of organised dives – check the website for details.

All of the rooms at the hotel are spacious and comfortable with extensive amenities, breathtaking views and modern bathrooms. Internet connection, satellite TV, a well-stocked minibar and a fruit basket are all standard conveniences. Deluxe rooms and suites all have balconies with either mountain or sea views.

All in all, a stay at the Hilton is pleasant at any time of year, so there's no need to wait for the *khareef* to roll into town.

Contact
Phone: +968 23 211 234
Email: salalah@hilton.com
Web: www.salalah.hilton.com

Location
Once in Salalah, head towards the coast, east of the city. The hotel is located off Sultan Qaboos Street.

Food & Drink
Al Maha – international • Sheba's – Arabic • Palm Grove – Asian & seafood • Mayfair – pub • Sunset Lounge – snacks • Whispers – cocktails & snacks

Features
Beach view • Fitness room • Playground • Swimming pool • Scuba diving • Sightseeing tours • Windsurfing • Children's activities

Nearby
Old souk • Gold souk • Lost City of Ubar • Al Mughsayl beach • Khor Ruri • Travertine Curtain • Blowholes • Wadi Darbat • Frankincense trees • Nabi Ayoub's Tomb

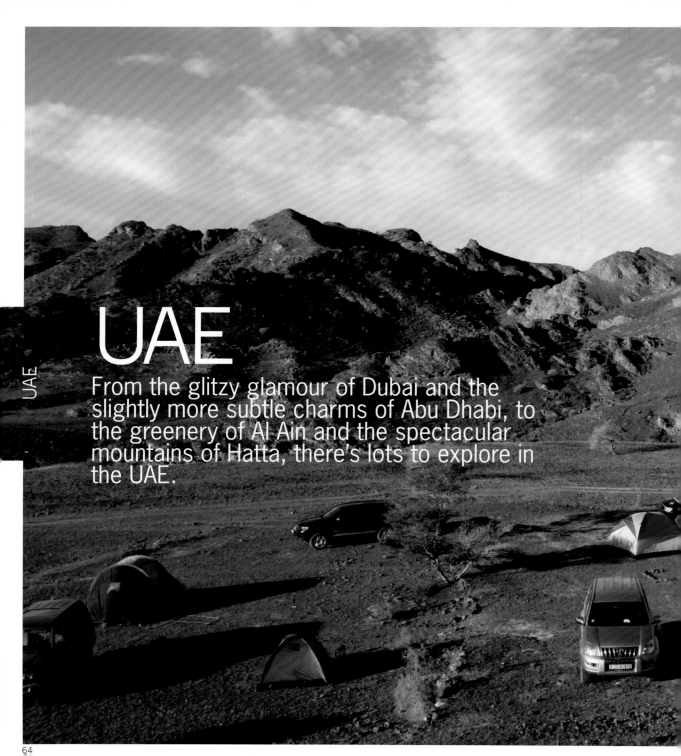

UAE

From the glitzy glamour of Dubai and the slightly more subtle charms of Abu Dhabi, to the greenery of Al Ain and the spectacular mountains of Hatta, there's lots to explore in the UAE.

UAE

Essentials p.68, Activities p.74, Dubai p.78, Abu Dhabi p.127, Northern Emirates p.155, East Coast p.179

UAE

The UAE is a remarkable country; it contains barren desert, craggy mountains, verdant patches of greenery, traditional rural villages and small trading towns, but it is also home to two of the most futuristic, modern cities of the 21st century.

It sits on the north-eastern part of the Arabian Peninsula, bordered by Saudi Arabia to the south and west and by Oman to the east and north, and is made up of seven emirates: Abu Dhabi, Dubai, Sharjah, Ajman, Umm Al Quwain, Ras Al Khaimah and Fujairah. Of these, Abu Dhabi is the largest, occupying over 85% of the land mass, and is home to the nation's capital city.

The island city of Abu Dhabi is a lush, modern metropolis, with tree-lined streets, futuristic skyscrapers, huge shopping malls and international luxury hotels. The city is surrounded by the sparkling waters of the Arabian Gulf, which offers a striking contrast to the large parks and green boulevards that spread across the island. From its origins as a centre for pearl diving and fishing, Abu Dhabi has developed at breakneck speed to become a truly 21st century destination. Elsewhere in the emirate, the important oasis town of Al Ain is a peaceful haven away from the big city.

Not to be outdone, the city of Dubai is the capital's bolder, brasher sibling. Here you'll find the world's tallest building, huge man-made residential islands, and a batch of new residential areas. Yet underneath the shiny surface there is more to Dubai than cranes and five-star cliche; you'll find Emiratis, fresh-faced expats, corporate climbers and sunburnt tourists, all enjoying and exploring the many sides to a surprisingly multi-layered city.

The other emirates all have their own characteristics and attractions too, detailed elsewhere in the book, while the dry landscape also has its charms. Off-road exploration of the desert and mountains makes for quite an adventure, and despite the scarcity of water and high temperatures, there are around a thousand plant species recorded in the country, as well as a range of fauna from the highly endangered Arabian leopard to a collection of gerbils and geckos. The animals you are most likely to see though, are camels and goats (often roaming dangerously close to the roadside). The birdlife is reasonably extensive but the most impressive array of natural life is to be found beneath the waves. A myriad of tropical fish, as well as dolphins, turtles, sharks, and the elusive dugong, are just some of the marine creatures you may spot along the UAE's east and west coasts.

People & Traditions

The UAE's culture is firmly rooted in the Islamic traditions of Arabia. Islam is more than just a religion; it is a way of life governing everyday decisions such as what

UAE
Essentials

Dubai Creek Golf & Yacht Club

to wear, eat and drink. People in the UAE are tolerant and welcoming; expats and visitors are free to practise their own religion, alcohol is served in licensed outlets (except in Sharjah) and the dress code is liberal. The family unit is important, and elders are respected for their experience and ability to give advice. Often, many generations will live together in the same house.

Rapid economic development has changed life in the UAE beyond recognition. However, the country's rulers are committed to safeguarding the nation's heritage, promoting cultural and sporting events that are representative of local traditions.

Food & Drink

You can eat your way around the world in the UAE, not just in the numerous five-star hotels, but also in independent street-side cafes where you can sample authentic cuisines from the Middle East and Asia at bargain prices.

Much of the Arabic food available in the UAE is based predominantly on Lebanese cuisine. Common dishes are shawarmas, falafel, hummus and tabbouleh. Emirati cuisine uses spices such as cinnamon, saffron and turmeric along with nuts, limes and dried fruit to add distinctive flavours. Culturally, eating in the UAE is a social affair, and the custom is for everybody to share a huge feast of various dishes, served in communal bowls.

Ramadan

Ramadan is the holy month in which Muslims commemorate the revelation of the Holy Quran. It is a time of fasting, and Muslims abstain from eating, drinking and smoking between dawn and dusk, before breaking their fast with Iftar in the evening. Non-muslims in the UAE are also expected to refrain from eating, drinking and smoking in public during daylight hours, as a sign of respect. Most hotels and many shopping centres now have at least one outlet that is open during the day for non-Muslims.

Language

Arabic is the official language of the UAE, although English, Hindi, Malayalam and Urdu are commonly spoken. Most road signs, shop signs and restaurant menus are in English and Arabic. The further out of town you go, the more you will find just Arabic, both spoken and on street and shop signs. Arabic isn't the easiest language to pick up, or to pronounce. But if you can throw in a couple of words here and there, you're likely to receive a smile – even if your pronunciation is terrible.

Climate

The UAE has a subtropical and arid climate. Sunny blue skies and high temperatures can be expected most of the year. Rainfall is infrequent and erratic, usually occurring on an average of only 25 days per year, mainly in winter (December to March). Temperatures in Dubai range from a low of around 10°C (50°F) in winter to a high of 48°C (118°F) in summer. The mean daily maximum is 24°C (75°F) in January, rising to 41°C (106°F) in August. Humidity is usually between 50% and 65%, and is slightly lower in the summer than the winter. The most pleasant time to visit is in the cooler winter months when temperatures are perfect for comfortable days on the beach and long, lingering evenings outside.

Money

Cash is still the preferred method of payment, although credit and debit cards are now widely accepted. Foreign currencies and travellers' cheques can be exchanged in licensed exchange offices, banks and hotels (a passport is required for exchanging travellers' cheques). If you're shopping in the souks and markets in the UAE, or in smaller shops, you're better off paying cash as it will help your bargaining power. The monetary unit is the dirham (Dhs.), which is divided into 100 fils. The currency is also referred to as AED (Arab Emirate dirham). Notes come in denominations of

Arabian lights

UAE

Salik Magic

Be aware that if you are driving into Dubai from out of town and intend to use the main Sheikh Zayed Road through the city, you'll need to sign up for Salik, an electronic tag that enables you to use the road toll system. These are available from any petrol station for a cost of Dhs.100 (including Dhs.50 of credit), and should be attached to the windscreen. There are four gates along the main stretch of Sheikh Zayed, and you'll be charged Dhs.4 for passing under a gate. If you pass the Barsha and Safa gates within one hour, you'll only be charged once. For more details visit www.salik.ae or call 800 72545.

Dhs.5 (brown), Dhs.10 (green), Dhs.20 (light blue), Dhs.50 (purple), Dhs.100 (pink), Dhs.200 (orange), Dhs.500 (blue) and Dhs.1,000 (browny-purple). The denominations are indicated on the notes in both Arabic and English. The dirham has been pegged to the US dollar since 1980, at a mid rate of $1 to Dhs.3.6725.

Tipping

Tipping practices are similar across hotels, restaurants and bars in the UAE. Tips are usually shared with the other staff. Many places now add a service charge on to the bill but no one really knows if this actually goes to the waiter, so many add a little extra. The usual amount to tip is 10%. Most restaurant bills in hotels should automatically come with 10% municipality tax and 10% service charge included, so check the bill carefully. In a taxi it is standard to round up the fare to the nearest Dhs.5 but this is not compulsory.

Time

The UAE is four hours ahead of UTC (Universal Coordinated Time – formerly known as GMT). There is no altering of clocks for daylight saving in the summer, so when Europe and North America lose an hour, the time in the UAE stays the same. Most offices and schools are closed on Fridays (the holy day) and Saturdays. This causes few problems for visitors but you might find shops don't open until later on Fridays.

Crime & Safety

While the crime rate is very low, a healthy degree of caution should still be exercised. Keep your valuables and travel documents locked in your hotel room or in the safe. When in crowds, be discreet with your money and wallet and don't carry large amounts of cash on you.

With a multitude of driving styles converging on the UAE's roads, navigating the streets either on foot or in a vehicle can be a challenge. When walking, you need to be conscious of the traffic as drivers often don't give pedestrians the space or consideration you might be used to. When crossing roads use designated pedestrian crossings wherever possible (jaywalking is illegal), and make sure all cars are going to stop before you cross.

Dos & Don'ts

The UAE is one of the most tolerant and liberal states in the region, but as a guest in a Muslim country you should act accordingly. Lewd and drunken behaviour is not only disrespectful but can lead to arrest and detention. Women should be aware that revealing clothing can attract unwanted attention, so very short skirts and strapless tops should be avoided. Public displays of affection are not allowed. With prices for cigarettes low, smoking is very common. However, new laws have banned smoking in malls and some restaurants so it's best to check the policy before lighting up. There's zero tolerance towards drink driving, even after just one drink. With thousands of low-fare taxis available there is no excuse or need. A prison sentence, and even possible deportation, awaits those who offend.

Public Holidays

The main Muslim festivals are Eid Al Fitr (the festival of the breaking of the fast, which marks the end of Ramadan) and Eid Al Adha (the festival of the sacrifice, which marks the end of the pilgrimage to Mecca). Mawlid Al Nabee is the holiday celebrating the Prophet Muhammad's birthday, and Lailat Al Mi'raj celebrates the Prophet's ascension into heaven.

As some holidays are based on the sighting of the moon and do not have fixed dates on the Hijri calendar, Islamic holidays are more often than not confirmed less than 24 hours in advance.

In general, public holidays have little bearing on daily life in Dubai, with shops opening perhaps a bit later. During the holy month of

Ramadan however, food and beverages cannot be consumed in public during the day and smoking is prohibited. Women should dress more conservatively. You'll find nightlife dies down for the month.

Annual Events

Abu Dhabi Classical Music Festival

The Abu Dhabi Classical Music Festival, organised by the Abu Dhabi Music & Arts Foundation (ADMAF), showcases the best in classical music each March, drawing on local talent as well as renowned musicians from overseas. www.adconcert.com

Abu Dhabi Golf Championship

The Championship puts Abu Dhabi into the international golfing spotlight as the first European PGA Tour ranking event of the calendar year. It has featured leading players such as Thomas Bjorn, Sergio Garcia, V J Singh, John Daly and Colin Montgomerie. www.abudhabigolfchampionship.com

Al Ain Aerobatic Show

This five-day annual air show, held at Al Ain Airport in January, attracts flying daredevils from around the world. Both military and civilian planes take part in the aerobatic displays. There is also a biennial airshow event in Dubai (the next will be November 2009). www.alainaerobaticshow.com

Dubai International Film Festival

This hotly anticipated event, held in December, marks a real achievement for the UAE film industry. Premieres are held at Madinat Jumeirah, while screenings take place across the city. The festival brings together a collection of regional, Hollywood and international arthouse films. www.diff.ae

Dubai International Jazz Festival

The Jazz Festival in February attracts a broad range of artists from all around the world to a chilled and pleasant setting in Dubai Media City. Courtney Pine, David Gray and Jamie Cullum have all featured,

and John Legend and James Blunt are scheduled to appear in 2009. www.dubaijazzfest.com

Dubai Rugby 7s

This three-day rugby event attracts more than 70,000 spectators every November, now at the new Sports City venue. Top international teams compete for the coveted 7s trophy while local teams try their luck. www.dubairugby7s.com.

Dubai Shopping Festival

A combination of a festival and a shopping extravaganza, Dubai Shopping Festival is hard to miss. There are bargains galore in January and February at the participating outlets, and spectacular fireworks each evening. It's a great (although rather congested) time to be in the city. www.mydsf.com

Dubai Tennis Championships

The $1,000,000 Dubai Tennis Championships is a great chance to see the top men's and women's seeds in an intimate setting. Firmly established on the ATP and WTP circuit, the tournament attracts the world's best each spring. The women's tournament takes place in the first week, the men's during the second. www.dubaitennischampionships.com

Dubai World Cup

The Dubai World Cup is the richest horse race in the world. Held at the end of March at Nad Al Sheba, the prize for the Group One Dubai World Cup race alone was a staggering $6,000,000. With a buzzing, vibrant atmosphere, it's also one of the year's big social occasions, and the culmination of the racing season. www.dubaiworldcup.com

Formula 1

Abu Dhabi has secured the right to host a Formula 1 Grand Prix. The announcement followed the success of the first Formula 1 Festival that brought the top drivers (including world champion Fernando Alonso) and their cars to the streets of Abu Dhabi in

Whether it's Tiger Woods teeing off in the Desert Classic, Kylie Minogue singing at a grand private party, or George Clooney opening the film festival, the UAE has become a must-visit destination for the international jetset.

February 2007. A track is under construction at Yas Island, close to the capital, and the inaugural grand prix is set to take place in November 2009. www.abudhabigp.com

Powerboat Racing

The UAE is well established on the world championship powerboat racing circuit, with Formula One (onshore) in Abu Dhabi and Class One (offshore) in Dubai and Fujairah. Abu Dhabi International Marine Sports Club has a racing calendar running from October to May and hosts the final round of the Formula One series at the end of the season. www.adimsc.ae

Red Bull Air Race

The Red Bull Air Race World Series comes to Abu Dhabi every April, the first of eight rounds in eight different cities around the world. Dubbed 'Formula 1 racing in the sky', the sport is the ultimate test of a pilot's skill and precision. www.redbullairrace.com

UAE Desert Challenge

This is the highest profile motorsport event in the country and is often the culmination of the World Championship in cross-country rallying, held in October or November. It attracts some of the world's top rally drivers and bike riders who compete in car, truck and motocross categories. The course runs from Jebel Ali Racecourse into the Empty Quarter. www.uaedesertchallenge.com

Getting There

If you're flying to the UAE, there are two main choices of arrival location: Dubai International Airport and Abu Dhabi International Airport, as well as smaller regional airports at Sharjah, Ras Al Khaimah, Fujairah and Al Ain that connect to other parts of the Middle East and Asia. Dubai International Airport (DXB) is an important global hub; it handled more than 34 million passengers in 2007, and a third terminal was added in October 2008 solely for use by Emirates. Over 120 airlines use the airport, flying to over 200 destinations. Abu Dhabi International Airport is Etihad's home base. Both airports are a short taxi journey from the respective city centres. Connecting Dubai and Abu Dhabi is the E11 highway, approximately a 90 minute car journey on a clear road, centre to centre, while the E311 Emirates Road is a good road connecting to all the northern emirates, right up to Ras Al Khaimah. The E44 and E66 roads connect the UAE to Oman, meaning driving from Muscat is easily achievable in around five hours (visa and border restrictions apply, and your vehicle needs to be insured for both countries).

Visas

Requirements for entering the UAE vary depending on your country of origin. Regulations should be checked before departure. GCC nationals (Bahrain, Kuwait, Qatar, Oman and Saudi Arabia) do not need a visa to enter the UAE. Citizens from many other countries get an automatic visa upon arrival at the airport – check with your embassy for details. New visa laws, valid from 2008 onwards, dictate that some nationalities may only stay in the UAE for a maximum of 30 days. For more information, log on to www.government.ae.

Construction in Dubai Marina

Desert driving in Liwa

Getting Around

Public transport is not the strong point in the UAE's major cities, although the Dubai Metro transit system could change all that when it opens in late 2009. It aims to be the largest driverless metro system in the world, and will be focused on two lines. The Red Line starts at Dubai airport and travels alongside Sheikh Zayed Road to the new developments in the south of the city and Jebel Ali, while the Green Line will service the city centre and the Purple Line runs along the Al Khail Road.

There are public bus routes, which are cheap but can be crowded, or even full, at peak times. Contact the Dubai Road and Transport Authority (800 9090, www.rta.ae) or Abu Dhabi Transport (02 443 1500) for route plans and timetables.

Taxis are the most common way of getting around (other than private vehicles). In Dubai there are seven companies operating more than 6,000 metered taxis with a fixed fare structure. The pickup fare ranges from Dhs.3 to Dhs.7 (although from the airport you will pay Dhs.20 or more) depending on the time of day and taxi company. It is also possible to hire a taxi for 12 or 24 hour periods. Taxis can be flagged down by the side of the road or you can make a booking through Dubai Transport by calling 04 208

0808. In Abu Dhabi, you can book Al Ghazal or NTC taxis by phone (02 444 7787 or 02 622 3300).

If you want to drive, international car rental companies, as well as a few local firms, can be found in the UAE. Prices range from Dhs.80 a day for smaller cars to Dhs.1,000 for limousines. Comprehensive insurance is essential; make sure that it includes personal accident coverage.

To rent a car, you need your passport, a valid international driving licence, your credit card and two photographs.

Parking is free and plentiful at most malls and is cheap on the street, although spaces can be hard to find. Rush hour traffic can be horrendous. Be bold, use your indicators, expect the unexpected but anticipate the worst and you'll be fine.

Opportunities for boat travel in the emirates are limited unless you take a dhow, although crossing Dubai Creek by abra is a common method of transport. Abra stations have been upgraded recently, and fares cost just Dhs.1. Another recent addition to the creek is a fleet of air-conditioned water buses. These operate on four different routes crossing the creek, with fares set at Dhs.4 per trip. A 'tourist' route also operates, with a 45 minute creek tour costing around Dhs.25 per person.

After what seems like years of construction, the Dubai Metro is finally starting to come together, and large stretches of uninterrupted track can now be seen in certain parts of Dubai. The official opening date is 09.09.09.

UAE

73

Golf

The number of international-standard courses in the UAE grows each year, with recent additions including The Montgomerie in Emirates Hills and the Four Seasons Golf Club within Dubai Festival City. The world's first course designed by Tiger Woods will be created in Dubailand and is set to open in late 2009; Ernie Els's eponymous course will be in the same development. Other top courses include the Dubai Creek Golf & Yacht Club and the Emirates Golf Club, where the Dubai Desert Classic is played every year. The Abu Dhabi Golf Club by Sheraton and the Al Ghazal Golf Club are ideal for golfers taking a weekend break in the capital.

The Dubai Desert Classic, which takes place at the end of January or beginning of February every year, is one of the highlights of the UAE sporting calendar and attracts some of the sport's best names (www.dubaidesertclassic.com).

Non-professionals can play golf throughout the year – truly dedicated golfers will even sweat through a midday tee-off in the height of summer. Dubai Golf operates a central reservation system for those wishing to book a round on any of the major courses in Dubai. For further information visit www.dubaigolf.com or email booking@dubaigolf.com.

UAE Activities

There's a lot more to the UAE than shopping and sunbathing. Weekend breakers can look forward to recreational sports, luxurious pursuits, and even skiing on the region's first indoor ski slope.

Diving

The waters around the UAE are rich in a variety of marine and coral life as well as several submerged wrecks (some deliberately sunk to form offshore reefs). The great thing about the location is that it is possible to dive all year round in the warm seas. In addition to exotic fish, such as clownfish and seahorses, you can see barracuda, spotted eagle rays, moray eels, small sharks, stingrays, sea turtles, to name just a few.

There are plenty of dive companies in the UAE offering all levels of courses, from introductory dives to instructor level and technical diving from international training organisations, such as CMAS, PADI and NAUI. Many good dive sites are easily accessible from Abu Dhabi and Dubai, including wreck or deep-water dives and reef dives. If you want to explore further in the UAE, the east coast is especially popular and is home to some stunning marine life. Most dive companies also organise trips to the spectacular area north of the UAE known as Musandam. Alternatively, from Dibba on the east coast, boats take divers as far up the coast as they desire. Most companies also offer snorkelling options too. For further information on diving in the UAE and Musandam, refer to the *UAE Underwater Explorer*, available at bookshops.

Skiing

You wouldn't normally associate desert with snow, but, amazingly, Dubai has its very own ski slope. Ski Dubai, the Middle East's first indoor ski slope, in Mall of the Emirates, has five runs in total (including a black run), chair lifts and annoyingly cool instructors. You will have to have some skiing or snowboarding ability before you're allowed on the slopes; a full range of lessons is available for those who have never skied before or who need a refresher course. Even if you don't ski, just looking at the slope is a spectacle not to be missed, and for the kids, it has the world's largest indoor snow park. The best views are from the restaurants and bars overlooking Ski Dubai, especially Après. A two-hour slope pass including equipment hire costs Dhs.220 – bring your own gloves and hat (04 409 4000, www.skidxb.com).

Golf Courses

Abu Dhabi	Abu Dhabi Golf Club	02 558 8990	www.adgolfsheraton.com
	Al Ghazal Golf Club	02 575 8040	www.alghazalgolf.ae
Al Ain	Al Ain Golf Club	03 768 6808	na
	Palm Sports Resort	03 768 4888	www.palmsportsresort.com
	Hilton Al Ain Golf Club	03 768 6666	www.al-ain.hilton.com
Dubai	Arabian Ranches Golf Club	04 366 3000	www.arabianranchesgolfdubai.com
	Dubai Creek Golf & Yacht Club	04 295 6000	www.dubaigolf.com
	Els Club Dubai	04 425 1000	www.elsclubdubai.com
	Emirates Golf Club	04 380 2222	www.dubaigolf.com
	Four Seasons Golf Club	04 601 0101	www.fourseasons.com/dubaigolf
	Jebel Ali Golf Resort & Spa	04 883 6000	www.jebelali-international.com
	The Montgomerie Dubai	04 390 5600	www.themontgomerie.com
	UAE Golf Association	04 368 4988	www.ugagolf.com
Ras Al Khaimah	Al Hamra Golf Club	07 244 7474	www.alhamragolf.com
	Tower Links Golf Club	07 227 8555	www.towerlinks.com
Sharjah	Sharjah Golf & Shooting Club	06 548 7777	www.golfandshootingshj.com
	Sharjah Wanderers Golf Club	06 558 6239	www.sharjahgolf.com

Dive Companies

Abu Dhabi	Abu Dhabi Sub Aqua Club	02 673 1111	www.the-club.com
	Al Jazira Dive Centre	02 562 9100	www.goldentulipaljazira.com
	Arabian Divers and Sportfishing Charters	02 665 8742	www.fishabudhabi.com
	Blue Dolphin Company LLC	02 666 6888	www.interconti.com
Dibba	Scuba 2000	09 238 8477	www.scuba-2000.com
	Nomad Ocean Adventures	050 88 53238	www.discovernomad.com
Dubai	Emirates Diving Association	04 393 9390	www.emiratesdiving.com
	The Pavilion Dive Centre	04 406 8827	www.thepaviliondivecentre.com
	Scubatec	04 334 8988	www.scubatec.net
	Sharjah Wanderers Dive Club	06 566 2105	www.sharjahwanderers.com
Fujairah	Sandy Beach Diving Centre	09 244 5555	www.sandybm.com
	Scuba International	09 222 0060	na
Khor Fakkan	7 Seas Divers	09 238 7400	www.7seasdivers.com
	Divers Down	09 237 0299	www.diversdown.ae

BurJuman shopping mall

Sailing

With calm waters and year-round sunshine, the UAE offers ideal conditions for those wishing to sample life on the ocean waves. A number of companies provide boat charters, offering everything from sundowner cruises of a couple of hours and overnight trips with snorkelling stopovers, to scuba diving excursions to remote destinations such as Musandam. Large sailing yachts, speedboats and other motorboats can be hired for private charter and corporate events; other companies offer outings on dhows and also cater to weddings and birthday parties. Fishing trips and watersports packages are also available. If you're on the east coast and fancy a traditional boating experience, large independent groups can charter a dhow from the fishermen at Dibba. If you haggle you can usually knock the price down substantially. Respected UAE charter companies include ART Marine (www. artmarine.net), Bristol Middle East Yacht Solution (www.bristol-middleeast.com), Leisure Marine (www.leisuremarinecharters.com), Marine Concept (www.marine-charter-concept.com) and Ocean Active (www.oceanactive.com).

Off Roading

The UAE is full of wadi beds, mountains and dunes, all waiting to be discovered, either in your own 4WD or with a specialist tour company. The *UAE Off-Road Explorer* lists a great range of routes, and gives advice on how to stay safe, where to camp and things to do along the way. Some of the regional highlights are listed below.

Northern Emirates: For a full day out, with some of the best driving in the emirates, combine the mountains around Wadi Bih, near Ras Al Khaimah, with one of the interesting wadi routes on the east coast.

Spas

Abu Dhabi	Eden Spa & Health Club	Le Meridien Abu Dhabi	02 644 6666	www.abudhabi.lemeridien.com
	Hiltonia Health Club & Spa	Opposite Hilton Hotel, Corniche Rd West	02 681 1900	www.hilton.com
Dubai	Akaru Spa	Aviation Club, Garhoud	04 282 8578	www.akaruspa.com
	Amara Spa	Park Hyatt Dubai	04 602 1660	www.dubai.park.hyatt.com
	Elixir Spa & Health Club	Habtoor Grand Resort & Spa	04 399 5000	www.habtoorhotels.com
	Givenchy Spa	One&Only Royal Mirage	04 315 2140	www.oneandonlyresort.com
	Lime Spa	Desert Palm Hotel	04 323 8888	www.desertpalm.ae
	Rafflesamrita	Raffles Dubai	04 314 9869	www.raffles.com
	Satori Spa	Bab Al Shams	04 809 6232	www.jumeirahbabalshams.com
	SensAsia Urban Spa	The Village Mall, Jumeirah	04 349 8850	www.sensasiaspas.com
	Senso Wellness Centre	Radisson SAS	04 366 9111	www.dubai.radissonsas.com
	Solesenses Spa	Le Méridien Mina Seyahi Beach Resort & Marina	04 318 1904	www.lemeridien.com
	Talise Spa	Madinat Jumeirah	04 366 6818	www.jumeirah.com/talise
	The Grand Spa	Grand Hyatt Dubai	04 317 2333	www.dubai.grand.hyatt.com
	The Spa	Jebel Ali Golf Resort & Spa	04 883 6000	www.jebelali-international.com
	The Spa	The Palace, The Old Town	04 428 7888	www.theaddress.com
	The Spa at Shangri-La	Shangri-La Hotel	04 405 2441	www.shangri-la.com
Fujairah	Spa Al Aquah	Le-Meridien Al Aqah Beach Resort	09 244 9000	www.lemeridien-alaqah.com
	Zen Spa	Fujairah Rotana Resort & Spa	09 244 9888	www.rotana.com
	Zen Spa	Hotel JAL Fujairah Resort & Spa	09 244 9700	www.jalhotels.com
Ras Al Khaimah	Spa	Hilton Ras Al Khaimah Resort & Spa	07 228 8888	www.hiltonworldresorts.com
	Spa	Khatt Springs Hotel & SPA	07 244 8777	www.khatthotel.com
Sharjah	Bay Club	Radisson SAS Resort	06 565 7777	www.sharjah.radissonsas.com
Umm Al Quwain	Imar Spa	Umm Al Quwain	06 766 4440	www.imarspa.com

East Coast: From Dubai, the east coast can be reached in about two hours. The mountains and beaches are fantastic spots for camping, barbecues and weekend breaks, as well as various other activities. There are some great wadi and mountain routes here, and the area is also renowned for its diving and snorkelling opportunities, particularly around Snoopy Island.

Hatta: The Hatta region is home to the popular 'Big Red' sand dune, a huge draw and a must-do challenge for off roaders and quad bikers, as well as the Hatta Pools, a great swimming spot in the Hajar Mountains.

Al Ain: Near the attractive oasis town of Al Ain, worthy of a visit in its own right, are natural attractions such as the imposing Jebel Hafeet and Hanging Gardens, a great trekking spot.

Liwa: A trip to Liwa is one you'll never forget – it's one of today's few chances to experience unspoiled dunes. The drive from Abu Dhabi or Dubai is long, more suitable for a two or three day camping trip, but the journey is worth it. Prepare for the most adventurous off-road driving the UAE has to offer, and some of its most incredible scenery.

Shopping

Dubai and Abu Dhabi are either a shopaholic's dream or nightmare – depending on who's paying the bill. The rapid development that both cities continue to experience is inextricably linked to shopping, and with each new development seems to come a new mall. The Dubai Shopping Festival (p.71), a month dedicated to consumerism, has taken place annually for more than 10 years.

Shopping revolves around the malls, both big and small – Mall of the Emirates in Dubai and Marina Mall in Abu Dhabi are the current cream of the crop – but it is also well worth checking out the independent shops and traditional souks. Dubai Mall, the largest mall in the Middle East, opened to much fanfare in November 2008. It is home

to a gigantic aquarium, an Olympic-size ice rink and some super shops. Practicality plays a large part in mall culture, and during the hotter months they are oases of cool in the sweltering city – somewhere to walk, shop, eat and be entertained – where you can escape the soaring heat for a few hours. The popularity of the malls is evident by the crowds that they pull, particularly at the weekends. It takes a brave and dedicated shopper to tackle them on a Friday evening. While average prices for most items are comparable to elsewhere in the world, there are not many places that can beat the UAE's range and frequency of sales.

Spa

The UAE's focus on luxury tourism is fortuitous for people who love to be pampered. Nearly every five-star hotel has at least one spa, many of which are renovated every few years to keep up with the latest developments and design trends. Several venues utilise brand name treatment products, while others focus on unique treatments, such as Moroccan baths. Treatments for men and male-only spas are increasing in popularity. Keep in mind that the range of spas is huge, and many of the lesser known options are just as good and often cheaper.

From luxurious spa treatments to rugged off roading over dunes or through wadis, the UAE offers a wide range of must-do pursuits.

Al Asalla Spa, Dubai Ladies' Club

Dubai

For 21st century high living mixed with traditional Arabian heritage, the buzzing, growing metropolis of Dubai offers the ultimate east-meets-west experience.

Dubai

Dubai, The City of Gold, is an ever-changing, thriving urban landscape. Having transformed itself from a stark desert outpost just a few decades ago to the self-styled city of luxury and opportunity you see today, Dubai offers a modern take on old traditions and customs. East meets west in a burgeoning melting pot, drawing tourists, developers and residents from all over the world, eager to live it up in sleek skyscrapers and shiny new developments. A coastal town, Dubai's premium seaside location, with golden shores, is a great draw for lazy beach days, while its glittering malls offer almost every kind of shop imaginable, plus a host of entertainment options.

This is the place to come to indulge. Treat your tastebuds to dinner at one of the city's outstanding restaurants – Michelin stars, celebrity chefs and cuisines from around the world top the bill at many hotels. Surrender yourself to a weekend of relaxation by visiting some of Dubai's heavenly spas. Take advantage of the first-class sporting facilities, including playing some of the world's best golf courses or watching prestigious tennis, horse racing and golfing events. Or escape the city altogether at one of the emirate's desert retreats. The choice is yours.

But there is more to this city than just being a sun and shopping holiday hotspot. In the land of 'anything is possible' you can take yourself skiing on snow-covered slopes, have drinks and dine at over 40 storeys above street level, take to the desert sands on a dune

Clockwise from top left: Bastakiya, Creek skyline, Golfing, Jumeira Beach Park

Dubai

80

safari, or have a go at one of the plethora of watersports available. There are also some more traditional spots to explore, such as the impressive architecture of the Bastakiya area of Persian housing, the comings and goings of the wooden passenger and cargo boats on the creek, or the detailed, fascinating history of the region on display at Dubai Museum.

By contrast, drive out of the city to experience a taste of the beguiling desert landscape that surrounds the metropolis. Relax among the dunes at peaceful retreats such as Al Maha (p.86) and Bab Al Shams (p.92), or visit the small mountain town of Hatta and learn about a different way of Emirati life.

Even if Dubai is the place you call home, there are plenty of opportunities to take advantage of all it has to offer, and get away from it all without leaving the city or Emirate. As befits an area where, for generations, pearl fishing was the main industry, in today's Dubai the world is most certainly your oyster.

Hatta

One of the most popular spots in the UAE for off-roaders, the mountain town of Hatta offers pleasing respite from the city, only 100km from Dubai. With natural rock pools that are easily accessible, an interesting heritage village that provides an insight into traditional living, and the excellent Hatta Fort Hotel, the area is a great spot for a break.

The drive from Dubai to Hatta, along the E44, provides some welcome diversions and opportunities for off-roading, including the famed dune Big Red where you can take your own 4WD over the sand, rent quad bikes or dune buggies and even try sand skiing.

There are great possibilities for exploration, especially when you combine visiting the pools with a trip to the neighbouring villages and a spot of adventurous driving, hiking or mountain biking.

For a more sedate activity, visit the Hatta Heritage Village (04 852 1374), where you can explore the narrow alleyways and barasti houses or shop for traditional handicrafts. Hatta is also home to the oldest fort in the Dubai emirate, built in 1790.

Accommodation Options

Hotel apartments lead the way in budget, self-catering accommodation, and with Dubai being a busy hub for business travellers, there are plenty of them around. The Golden Sands area in Bur Dubai is named after the cluster of apartment buildings offering both long and short-term accommodation (www. goldensandsdubai.com). Hotels such as the Dusit Dubai (www.dusit.com), the Grand Hyatt (http://dubai.grand.hyatt.com) and the Fairmont (www.fairmont.com) all offer luxury, fully serviced hotel apartments, but they'll cost you a pretty penny.

Cheaper apartments include Al Mas Hotel Apartments in Bur Dubai (04 355 7899, www. almashotelapartments.com), Embassy Suites in Deira (04 269 8070), or the Winchester Hotel Apartments in Bur Dubai (04 355 0111, www.winchester.com).

The cheapest accommodation in town is at the Dubai Youth Hostel, located near Al Mulla Plaza. It's not luxurious, but it is clean and safe, and certainly cheap (04 298 8161).

Camping

There are no official campsites in Dubai, but there are plenty of places to camp informally. You won't find facilities such as power points and showers, but you will find the ultimate in peace and quiet, and, depending on where you camp, super views. Near Dubai, the desert dunes on the way to Hatta are a good option, as are the mountains a little further on. Jebel Ali beach, which used to be one of the most popular camping spots, is now completely closed off because of construction on the Jebel Ali Palm. You can still camp on the beach at Saih Ash Shaib, which is a bit further down the coast past Jebel Ali, heading towards Abu Dhabi.

Shopping

Shopping experiences don't get much better than a visit to Dubai. The city has it all, from the high street to the high life, and luxury goods in particular abound.

In this part of the world, the mall is most

Heading For Hatta
The road to Hatta from Dubai, the E44, passes through an Omani enclave. There's no border as such, but technically your vehicle should have insurance that covers Oman. Many off-road routes around Hatta are also inside the Oman border, so it's definitely worth being covered.

Dubai has one of the highest concentrations of luxury hotels per capita in the world. However, there are many other options – and the only limit is deciding how much cash you're willing to part with.

definitely king. But a shopping mall is not just a place to shop; far from it. Mega malls like Mall of the Emirates, Festival Centre and the latest debutant, Dubai Mall, are showpieces, and offer everything from restaurants to cinemas and theatres, and, at Mall of the Emirates, even a fully functional snow-covered ski slope. But don't forget about the shops. From H&M and Topshop to Chanel, Fendi and Dior, Dubai aims to please the most ardent spender.

There's plenty of variety on offer too. Saks Fifth Avenue in the Burjuman Centre (04 351 5551, www.burjuman.com) is home to beautiful shoes in the form of the great Manolo Blahnik and delicate intimates in cult lingerie store Agent Provocateur, among other delights. Meanwhile, quirky independent boutiques such as S*uce in the Village Mall (04 344 7270, www.thevillagedubai.com) and concept store Five Green (04 336 4100, www.www.fivegreen.com) offer an enticing selection of clothing, accessories and lifestyle goods. The best time to shop here is during the Dubai Shopping Festival (DSF). Held from December to February each year, it's the perfect opportunity to snap up some great deals, with massive discounts in many stores, raffles and promotions. It's a wonderful, if busy, time to visit the city, with fireworks displays and coloured lights adorning streets and shop windows adding to the festive flavour. See www.mydsf.com for more information. Dubai's success as a shopping paradise is not

solely down to events such as the DSF, or to universal chain stores. For those looking for the old world charm of the souks, the covered markets either side of the creek are a great experience. These are grouped into different types of product, with the textile souk on the Bur Dubai side of the water, and the gold, spice and electronics souks on the Deira side of the Creek. They are the place to go for a spot of friendly haggling and a traditional Middle Eastern style shopping experience. For a modern-day take on the souk experience, Souk Madinat Jumeirah (04 366 8888, www.jumeirah.com) is an air-conditioned covered maze of alleyways bearing street stalls, stores and pretty waterfront cafes and restaurants. The shops here are fairly upmarket, and the prices are fixed. Khan Murjan at Wafi (www.wafi.com) offers a similar experience but with a more Arabic-style selection of outlets, and Souk Al Bahar in the Old Town area offers more of the same in the shadow of new icon the Burj Dubai. If you're staying near Dubai Marina, the outdoor Marina Market is held every weekend from October to May, between 11:00 and 19:00, and sells great gifts, fashion, home accessories, art and toys; it's a very relaxing way to spend a few hours.

Going Out

Dubai does going out better than anywhere else in the region – there's never a dull

Malls Of Dubai

The Boulevard	Emirates Towers	www.jumeirahemiratestowers.com	04 319 8999
BurJuman	Bur Dubai	www.burjuman.com	04 352 0222
Deira City Centre	Deira	www.deiracitycentre.com	04 295 1010
Dubai Festival Centre	Garhoud	www.dubaifestivalcity.com	04 213 6213
Dubai Outlet Mall	Al Ain Road	www.dubaioutletmall.com	04 367 9600
Dubai Mall	Downtown Burj Dubai	www.thedubaimall.com	04 362 7500
Ibn Battuta Mall	Nr Dubai Marina	www.ibnbattutamall.com	04 362 1900
Lamcy Plaza	Oud Metha	www.lamcyplaza.com	04 335 9999
Mall of the Emirates	Umm Suqeim	www.malloftheemirates.com	04 409 9000
Mercato	Jumeira	www.mercatoshoppingmall.com	04 344 4161
Souk Al Bahar	Downtown Burj Dubai	www.theoldtownisland.com	na
Souk Madinat Jumeirah	Umm Suqeim	www.madinatjumeirah.com/shopping	04 366 8888
Times Square Center	Al Quoz	www.timessquarecenter.ae	04 341 8020
Village Mall	Jumeira	www.thevillagedubai.com	04 349 4444
Wafi Mall	Umm Hurair	www.waficity.com	04 324 4555

moment when the sun goes down, with endless bars, pubs and clubs to entertain every taste. From chic wine bars to novelty theme pubs, sports bars, intimate dance spaces and superclubs, the options are many. Dubai has a liberal attitude to alcohol compared with some of the neighbouring emirates and every hotel has at least one type of bar or restaurant serving drinks and cocktails. Most places also serve up shisha, coffees and teas, and a range of mocktails and juices.

The sheer variety of cuisines available in Dubai is enough to make even the most jaded foodie's mouth water. Not only can you find a selection of five-star cuisine, but there are also many independent restaurants where you can sample authentic dishes from India, Pakistan, the Philippines, Sri Lanka, Thailand and the Middle East for rock bottom prices. Dubai's nightlife is electric, with Thursday night being the liveliest on most weekends. For a self-contained night out, head to Souk Madinat, which is home to a vast collection of restaurants, cafes and bars. Below is a list of Explorer's favourite nightspots, whether you're eating, drinking or dancing:

360° – This circular rooftop bar boasts striking views of the Arabian Gulf and the Burj Al Arab; from 16:00 grab yourself a beanbag and a cocktail and experience the ultimate weekend feeling. Jumeirah Beach Hotel, 04 348 0000

Al Mallah – Stand-out Lebanese street cafe on Satwa's busiest strip; munch on a succulent five-dirham shawarma and watch the boy racers cruise up and down in their sports cars. Al Mallah has the best falafel in town, if not the world. Al Diyafah Street, 04 398 4723

Asha's – This celebrity restaurant is decked out in Indian summer reds, yellows and oranges; the menu features Indian classics as well as some of Asha Bhosle's signature dishes and some interesting fusion choices. Wafi Pyramids, 04 324 4100

Barasti – A laidback bar that is a must-do, no matter how long you're in Dubai. A meaty menu, jugs of Pimms and panoramic views, not to mention a friendly crowd and the fact that you can wear flipflops, make this a weekend winner. Le Meridien Mina Seyahi, 04 399 3333

Bateaux Dubai – Fine dining aboard a glass-topped boat; this is no ordinary dinner cruise. Bateaux is a top pick for a romantic dinner or a weekend treat, and sails daily from near the British Embassy. Bur Dubai, 04 399 4994

Boardwalk – The ultimate alfresco venue for light meals and casual cocktails. Grab a table on the wooden deck and enjoy the passing creek traffic (mainly abras and seagulls) while you savour the holiday feeling. Dubai Creek Golf & Yacht Club, 04 295 6000

Chi @ The Lodge – Dubai's favourite superclub features different theme nights throughout the week; the most popular regular event is undoubtedly Cheese Night with legendary roller-skating DJ Tim Cheddar. Check the website for upcoming events (www.lodgedubai.com). Al Nasr Leisureland, 04 337 9470

Ginseng – An understandably popular Asian bar where the designer cocktails flow and the

Downtown Burj Dubai

crowds gather. Enjoy a selection of eastern finger foods while you peruse the lengthy drinks menu. Wafi Pyramids, 04 324 8200

Irish Village – Not your bog-standard olde Irish pub, 'the village' is always busy with Dubai expats who appreciate the beauty of drinking cold beer in the warm sun. Big-screen sports and live music, as well as one of the city's best New Year's Eve parties, please the crowds. Garhoud, 04 282 4750

Lime Tree Café – Lunch with the ladies of leisure at this suburban haven of coffee and home-made food. Lime Tree features a hearty menu of quiches, salads, paninis and couscous – and don't you dare leave without ordering the carrot cake, which is legendary. Beach Road, 04 349 8498

Lobby Lounge – Take time out for a traditional English afternoon tea at the Ritz-Carlton's Lobby Lounge; a teetering tower of delectable pastries and sandwiches is there to be devoured while your tea is brewing in its silver pot. Ritz-Carlton, 03 399 4000

Spectrum on One – Dine your way around the world in this restaurant, which features cuisines from Europe, Asia and the Middle East. All food is prepared in gleaming open kitchens and complemented by a large, well-stocked wine cellar. Fairmont Dubai, 04 311 8000

Spice Island – 'All you can eat and drink' nights are an essential part of Dubai dining, and this lively venue does it well. Choose from a selection of house beverages and a jaw-dropping buffet of international specialities, all for one surprisingly reasonable, all-inclusive price. Renaissance Hotel, 04 262 5555

Teatro – Offering a true fusion of cultures and tastes, Teatro is undoubtedly one of Dubai's best restaurants. The menu is a mix of Japanese, Chinese, Indian and European, and the food is guaranteed to please; it is complemented by a moody, modern decor and beautiful views of Sheikh Zayed Road. Towers Rotana, 04 343 8000

Yalumba – Weekend brunch at Yalumba is the stuff of legend; for one all-inclusive price you can indulge in the five-star cuisine until you're full to bursting, washing it down with endless refills of posh hampagne. By 15:00, everyone is dancing round the tables. It's a must-do, but you have to book early. Le Meridien Dubai, 04 282 4040

Left: Jumeira Mosque, Right: Khan Murjan at Wafi

Water Parks

Pack your trunks and a towel and head to one of Dubai's exhilarating water parks. Wild Wadi (04 348 4444, www.wildwadi.com) is a favourite among thrill seekers, with networks of rides, a wave pool and the white-knuckle Jumeirah Scarer. New on the scene is the Aquaventure water park (www.atlantisthepalm. com) at Atlantis on the Palm Jumeirah, which includes a ride that takes you through shark-infested waters (behind glass, thankfully).

Souks

Still an essential part of life for many people, Dubai's souks should be visited at least once. Check out the colourful textile souk in Bur Dubai, the Fish Market in Deira or Karama, and Deira's Spice Souk for the aromas and Gold Souk to discover why Dubai is called the City of Gold.

Bastakiya

Stroll through historical streets lined with the traditional windtowers, courtyards, museums and galleries that characterise this heritage-rich part of the city. Learn ancient facts at Dubai Museum (04 353 1862, www.dubaitourism.ae), stop for coffee at the Basta Art Café (04 353 5071) or enjoy a meal in the atmospheric Bastakiah Nights (04 353 7772).

Abra Ride

Take in the panoramic views along both sides of Dubai Creek on a boat ride from Bur Dubai to Deira by traditional wooden abra. You can take the normal crossing along with other commuters for just Dhs.1, or hire your own abra for a longer tour for under Dhs.50 per boat. Head to the official RTA stations on either side of the creek to book your passage.

Must-Do Experiences

Dubai

Don't leave Dubai without ticking these essential activities off your to-do list.

Ski Dubai

In a city where anything is possible, it should come as no surprise to find an enormous ski slope towering above a shopping mall. There are a number of runs, all with real snow, and lessons are available for non-skiers and boarders. Alternatively, you can just go to the Snow Park for a spot of tobogganing and a snowball fight (04 409 4000, www.skidxb.com).

Jumeirah Mosque

Discover more about local culture, Islam and what goes on inside a mosque through the informative organised tours held here four days a week. You don't need to book, but tours start at 10:00 sharp. You'll need to adhere to the conservative dress code (04 353 6666, www.cultures.ae).

Desert Safari

A trip to the desert is an absolute must. Surfing over the dunes in a 4WD at seemingly impossible angles is great fun and part of the essential desert experience. Add to this a camel ride, climbing a sand dune, sandboarding, star gazing, eating your fill at the barbecue and learning how to belly dance. Most tour operators offer various excursions at competitive rates, bookable through hotels.

Al Maha Desert Resort & Spa

Desert breaks don't get more luxurious than this. From the moment you turn off the E66 road, 45 minutes from Dubai, and leave your car at the entrance to the conservation area within which the resort is situated, you enter a whole new world of high-class serenity. It's not only your car you leave behind at the gates either – every ounce of stress, worry and city strife disappears in an instant at Al Maha. Set in 225 square kilometres of desert, the Al Maha Desert Resort & Spa, a member of The Leading Small Hotels of the World, is the definitive place to get away from it all. Here, you get a personalised service like no other. A dedicated field guide greets you on arrival,

transferring you from your car into an off-road vehicle and driving you across the dune tracks to the resort at the heart of the reserve. The resort itself, congruously set on the slopes of a rising dune in the form of a Bedouin camp, blends into the desert as if it had been there as long as the sands. Wild Arabian oryx (maha) wander the resort, putting you as close to nature in the UAE as you can get. Each guest room is a standalone property, designed to resemble a traditional Bedouin tent, and each is the epitome of luxury. Surrounded by colourful private gardens, and accessed by chauffeur-driven golf buggy, every one of the 42 suites features a private wooden-decked terrace and infinity plunge pool, from which you can marvel at both your own personal man-made surroundings as well as the wider environment. Inside, the circular suites are full of gloriously decadent touches. The main living area features a king-sized bed, two chaise longues, writing desk, huge TV with DVD player, a radio and CD player, and regal drapes, all given an authentic Arabian feel with an array of fascinating regional artefacts and decorations, and the canvas, tent-like roof. The bathroom is equally luxurious, and bigger than some hotel rooms; it has a king-sized bath, walk-in shower, and his-and-hers sinks. Toiletries come in the form of top-end brand Bulgari.

The living area is surrounded by panoramic windows that look out over the desertscape, and doors that open on to the patio area. Table and chairs for private dining plus two comfortable loungers furnish the deck, which is the perfect place to make use of a couple of the suite's accessories – a pair of powerful binoculars to spot roaming wildlife, and an artist's easel and pastels, for when inspiration takes hold. Should you fancy a spot of night swimming, there are pool lights to help you see where you are going, and the water temperature is adjustable (just call the reception to request a change).

If you don't opt for private dining on your patio (an experience you should definitely try), you can head to Al Diwaan restaurant for breakfast, lunch or dinner. As you'd expect, the quality of food here is excellent. The lunchtime Middle Eastern and Mediterranean buffet offers a vast selection – the only challenge is not to over indulge too early in the day. Indian, Sri Lankan and Japanese dishes are also served, and there is a great wine list.

If your own personal pool isn't enough, wander over (or take a buggy) to the Timeless spa. A large outdoor pool, indoor whirlpool bath, sauna, steam room and ice pool are open to all guests, and you can also book yourself in for a treatment. Choose from a wide selection, ranging from couples' Swedish massage to an Algae Detox Bath.

If all that relaxing sounds too much, there are several activities on offer. One of the most popular is a sunset camel ride and champagne toast on the dunes – a great way to mark your first evening there, and give you a true feel of the landscape. If you're an early riser, the sunrise falconry display lets you experience a traditional Arab sport. Other options include horse riding, dune safaris, nature walks and archery. Just tell your field guide what you're interested in, and they will arrange it.

Spend one night at Al Maha and you'll feel like you've been on relaxation duty for a week, and spend several nights there and you'll feel like you've left the real world behind for good. It's that special.

Dubai

Contact
Phone: +971 4 832 9900
Email: almaha@emirates.com
Web: www.al-maha.com

Location
Take the E66 Al Ain road from Dubai, and look for the small, signposted slip road after the Lahbab turn off. Follow the signposts up the track to the resort gates. Park here and a ranger will collect you and drive you into the resort.

Food & Drink
• Al Diwaan – Middle Eastern
• Al Maha's Bar

Features
Private plunge pools • Leisure pool
• Library • Majlis • Spa • Falconry
• Camel treks • Horse riding • Archery
• Dune safari • Mountain safari • Hatta excursions • Al Ain excursions

Nearby
Desert • Hajar Mountains • Dubai Outlet Mall (www.dubaioutletmall.com)

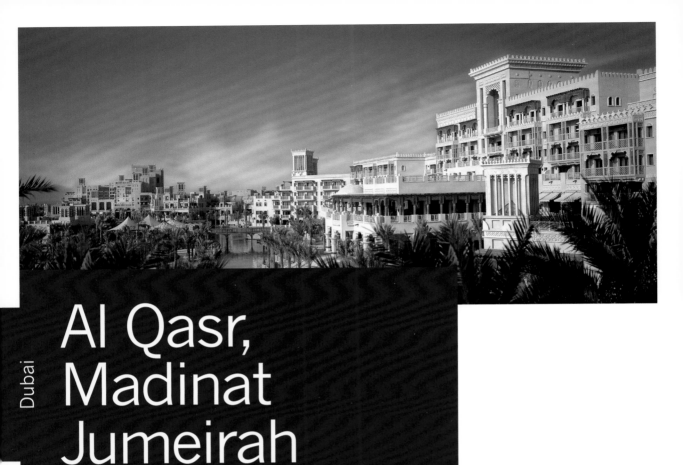

Al Qasr, Madinat Jumeirah

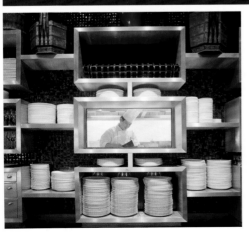

Madinat Jumeirah is an impressive collection of shopping, accommodation and nightlife, and Al Qasr is 'the palace' of the complex. It oozes grandeur from the moment you enter the extravagant entrance, lined with gold statues of prancing Arabian horses. This regal mansion hotel is designed to reflect an authentic experience of staying in a sheikh's summer dwelling, and while it certainly achieves that aim, it also has a contemporary feel that mirrors the traditional/modern duplicity of Dubai.

Al Qasr sits on an impressive kilometre-long stretch of private beachfront, and has the iconic Burj Al Arab and Jumeirah Beach Hotel as neighbours. Surrounded by water, this five-star deluxe hotel forms an island overlooking traditional windtowers, azure swimming pools, winding waterways and the dazzling white sand of the beach.

There are 292 rooms and suites in 10 different sizes, from the Arabian Deluxe room measuring 55 square metres, right up to the Royal Suite, which measures a whopping 550 square metres. Each room is carefully planned down to the last detail, from the Arabian hanging lamps to the elaborate carpets. Antique-style furniture throughout the hotel adds to the charm and character of the hotel. The high-quality linens and fabrics complement the Middle Eastern theme perfectly, and most importantly, they score top

marks for comfort. Views from the rooms look out across the resort and out to sea – your vista includes unrivalled views of the Burj and Palm Jumeirah.

If you are after additional privacy and a bouquet of extra services, reserve a Club Executive or Premium Leisure Club room, both of which offer exclusive bathroom amenities and unlimited access to the private lounges. The Ocean Suites offer a host of special features such as large private balconies, ideal for an intimate dinner overlooking the Arabian Gulf. There are two Presidential Suites at Al Qasr, each with two large bedrooms, a separate lounge area, a discreet individual lift, a large terrace and a walk-in rain shower. Finally, the Royal Suite is certainly fit for kings, with a majlis, a large private terrace, three bedrooms with private dressing areas, en-suite bathrooms, a huge lounge and separate dining area, and three lifts, offering ultimate privacy. It goes without saying that spending the night here comes at a royal price. All rooms have the usual amenities such as satellite TV and radio, room service, an in-room safe, and a minibar. Bathrooms feature neutral tones, huge mirrors and a good use of available space, and are ideal for long soaks in the oversized bath. Baby cots and rooms for disabled access are available upon request. Despite the luxury, kids are welcome here, and the hotel incorporates a kids' club and an adventure playground.

The leisure facilities at the hotel are plentiful, especially when you include those at neighbouring hotel Mina A' Salam and at Madinat. Al Qasr's swimming pool is one of the largest in the Middle East, and is even more impressive due to its aesthetic shape and lush surroundings. Talise Spa is one of the city's finest and offers a wide range of indulgent therapies and holistic healing treatments. Foodies are inundated with dining options here. Authentic Spanish flair can be found in the delicious dishes of Al Hambra's menu, and most meat lovers' search for the perfect steak ends in MJ's. Enjoy all-day dining in

Arboretum or in Khaymat Al Bahar, or some of the best Thai food in town at PaiThai. Other restaurants that are worth a special mention are seafood restaurant Pierchic; undoubtedly one of the most romantic settings around, being set at the end of a long pier where you can dine in virtual isolation aside awe-inspiring views of the Burj Al Arab, and Magnolia, which bucks the meat and seafood trend to offer delectable vegetarian dining.

Souk Madinat is an impressive recreation of a traditional Arabian market, and is a great place to spend some time (and money) in the varied collection of shops. It is also home to an impressive selection of food and beverage outlets, and is an essential nightlife destination for Dubai residents. Waterfront restaurants, cosy cafes and lively bars jostle for attention in this spectacular venue, which is often referred to as a 'city within a city'.

Dubai

Contact
Phone: +971 4 366 8888
Email: mjreservations@jumeirah.com
Web: www.madinatjumeirah.com

Location
Al Sufouh Rd (Beach Road), 200m south of Burj Al Arab (part of the Madinat Jumeirah complex).

Food & Drink
Al Hambra – Spanish • MJ'S – steakhouse • Arboretum – international • Khaymat Al Bahar – Arabic • Magnolia – vegetarian • Pai Thai – Thai • Pier Chic – seafood

Features
Private beach • Large pool areas • Kids' club • Health club • Tennis courts • Souk Madinat Jumeirah • Talise Spa • Madinat Theatre

Nearby
Ski Dubai (www.skidxb.com) • Mall of the Emirates (www.malloftheemirates. com) • Wild Wadi Water Park (www. wildwadi.com) • Miraj Islamic Art Centre • Gold & Diamond Park (www. goldanddiamondpark.com) • Emirates Golf Club (www.dubaigolf.com) • The Montgomerie (www.themontgomerie. com)

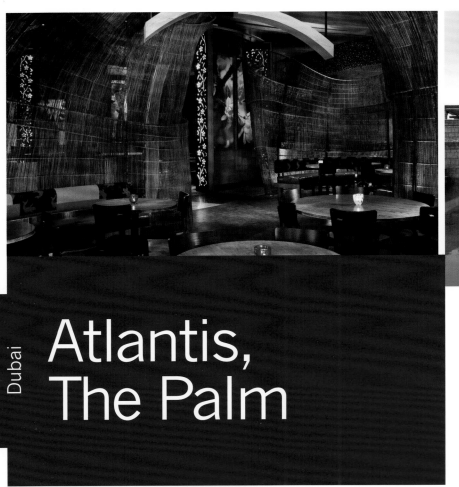

Atlantis, The Palm

Dubai

Not since the iconic Burj Al Arab opened its doors in 1999 has a hotel created so much buzz or so quickly become a Dubai must-do. However predictable it may be, it is near impossible to present any information on Atlantis without giving a rundown of some of the incredible, almost unbelievable, facts and figures. The hotel is set on 46 hectares of land on the crescent of the Palm Jumeirah – this includes 1.4km of beachfront. It is home to over 65,000 sea creatures, most of which swim happily in the Ambassador Lagoon, which holds a whopping 11 million litres of sea water. Over two thousand tons of marble and stone were used in the construction of the resort, there are a hundred thousand lights throughout Atlantis, and over 60,000 trees and shrubs. 3,000 staff are on hand to help you throughout your stay – this includes 500 chefs and 100 marine specialists.

Those are impressive numbers, but seeing them on paper simply cannot prepare you for the sheer scale of Atlantis once you arrive. The lobby is dominated by a huge and intricate glass sculpture; a work of art by renowned artist Dale Chihuly. It is made up of 3,000 hand-blown pieces of glass that were individually assembled to create a striking centrepiece. The lobby is also home to eight murals hand painted by Spanish artist Albino

Gonzales; these tell the story of the ancient mythological city of Atlantis.

After check-in, you can head straight up to your room in the Royal Towers. Of course, if you've got $25,000 in your pocket, you could check in for a night in the Bridge Suite, which spans the east and west towers and measures 924 square metres. It has three bedrooms, an 18 seat dining room table, a large living room and jaw-dropping views over the Palm, the Dubai skyline and out to sea. However, at the price it's likely to be out of reach for most weekend breakers, but fortunately the other rooms and suites in Atlantis, while no match in terms of size or luxury, all offer very high standards. The Deluxe Room, even though it is just the 'basic' room, is large and comfortable with amazing views. Apart from luxurious beds, beautiful interior design and a range of useful amenities, the rooms have lovely bathrooms that feature a separate rain shower and windows that open up into the lounge, enabling you to watch TV or enjoy the view while you languish in the bath. The Executive Suite features a similar bedroom, but also has a lounge, a guest bathroom, and a large oval bath with almost panoramic views. Rooms looking into the Ambassador Lagoon, the 11 million litre marine habitat, are just dreamy, and you'll feel like you're living in the world's most luxurious submarine. The variety of marine life is fascinating, as is the experience of waking up to see stingrays flapping gently past your bathroom window, or an inquisitive parrot fish grinning at you from the other side of the glass.

As nice as the rooms are, they are not where you are likely to be spending most of your stay at Atlantis – not when there are so many captivating features in the rest of the resort. Tummy-flipping thrills and waterside relaxation can be summed up in one word: Aquaventure. This humungous water park outshines all expectations, with 18 million litres of water and its great big Mesopotomanian-style Ziggurat temple. Ziggurat features seven daring rides, including the death-defying (but perfectly safe) Leap of Faith, down which you slide almost completely vertically before being

catapulted through a shark tank. The Lost Chambers, another aqua-themed feature of the hotel, is basically an aquarium; however it has been designed to look like the lost city of Atlantis, complete with relics and ruins and some of the strangest fish you've ever seen (and a scary tank of piranhas, who look quite friendly for flesh-eaters).

In total there are 17 food and beverage outlets in the resort, including (and this is definitely one of the unique selling points) four restaurants developed by celebrity chefs. So whether you're enjoying Japanese delicacies and the finest sushi in Nobu, authentic Italian fare in Ronda Locatelli, relaxed French cuisine in The Brasserie by Michael Rostang, or the freshest seafood In Santi Santamaria's Ossiano, you'll be experiencing Michelin-starred fine dining inspired by some of the world's greatest chefs. A beautiful spa, with 27 treatment rooms, and a variety of clubs to keep kids and teens supervised in age-appropriate environments, are additional features of Atlantis, which really is the resort that has everything. As a weekend break destination, this is probably as exciting as it gets; the only downside is that one weekend is probably not enough to get through it all.

Contact
Phone: +971 4 426 1000
Email: reservations@atlantisthepalm.com
Web: www.atlantisthepalm.com

Location
The far end of the crescent of Palm Jumeirah, which is accessed from either Al Sufouh Road or Sheikh Zayed Road.

Food & Drink
Nobu – Japanese • Ossiano – seafood • Ronda Locatelli – Italian • Rostang – French • Levantine – Arabic • Nasimi – Asian & European • Seafire – steakhouse • Kaleidoscope – international • Saffron – Asian • Nasimi – international

• Barazura – cocktail bar • Sanctuary – nightclub

Features
Aquaventure waterpark • Lost Chambers • Ambassador Lagoon • Spa • Beach • Pools

Nearby
Ski Dubai (www.skidxb.com) • Mall of the Emirates (www.malloftheemirates.com) • Dubai Marina • Emirates Golf Club (www.dubaigolf.com) • The Montgomerie (www.themontgomerie.com)

Bab Al Shams Desert Resort & Spa

Like a desert mirage come to life, Bab Al Shams is an absolute Bedouin fantasy escape set miles away from the hectic streets of Dubai. As you drive into the resort, bamboo torches guide you to the low-rise building that blends into the imposing dunes which surround it. Your welcome at reception, marked with the traditional ritual of dates and kahwa, is one of the many personal touches that infuse Bab Al Shams with Arabian hospitality and warmth. Once you've checked in, you will be guided to your room and given a brief explanation of how all the room features work.

The rooms, although luxurious, have been designed to evoke a feeling of Bedouin living; walls seem to be made of clay, furnishings are all crafted from dark wood, drapes are made of hessian. The bathroom is similarly designed, and features clay pots, rustic tones and a large bath that looks like it could have been carved from the earth.

The resort has made every effort to ensure your stay is as traditional as possible, right down to guest activities. At around 16:30 each afternoon, you can head up to the dunes for a ride on one of the hotel's 'ships of the desert'.

After your ride, you are allowed to take pictures and pet the camels. Afterwards, a falconry display begins nearby – you can even hold the falcon yourself for the ultimate photo opportunity.

If clambering up dunes and riding camels isn't your idea of relaxation, you can chill out in one of the outdoor holistic swimming pools. The infinity pool's horizon drops off into the sand dunes. Swim up to the in-pool bar for a cocktail or an icy cold beer and enjoy the splendour of the sunset over the dunes – you really do feel as though you are in an isolated world of tranquility here.

As the evening sets in, head to the Al Sarab Rooftop Lounge, where, under dimmed lighting projected from pretty Arabic lanterns, you can settle into cosy seating and enjoy shisha and a selection of drinks. For dinner, you could choose to eat in the hotel's Al Forsan restaurant, which serves an international buffet for breakfast, lunch and dinner. But the absolute highlight is Al Hadheerah. Set 300 metres away from the resort (a shuttle service is provided), Al Hadheerah is like a scene from Arabian Nights come to life. You enter by walking along a path of Arabic singers, and from then on the venue is nothing short of spectacular. As you are seated your waiter will bring you a plate of appetisers, and after that you can select your own feast from the vast buffet featuring the best of Middle Eastern and international cuisine. The dunes surrounding the restaurant are floodlit, providing an attractive desert backdrop, as well as a stage for the dazzling horse and camel displays that take place throughout the evening. The show doesn't stop on the dunes, however; as you enjoy your meal you can enjoy belly dancing and traditional music. A roving photographer is on hand to capture the fun, and you'll have the opportunity to buy the images at the end of the evening.

Spend the next day winding down in the luxurious surroundings of the Bab Al Shams Satori Spa, which offers a range of signature treatments. The Aromatic Massage, lasting for 55 minutes, is aimed to rebalance and rejuvenate using gentle music and expert

hands. Afterwards you can relax with a complimentary ginger tea.

A weekend at Bab Al Shams is an ideal way to feel as though you are getting away from it all, even though it's just a short drive from the city of Dubai (a free shuttle service makes it all the more accessible). The winding down process that transforms you from a stressed urban citizen to super-relaxed desert dweller begins the minute you drive through the front gates.

Dubai

Contact

Phone: +971 4 809 6100
Email: reservations@jumeirah.com
Web: www.jumeirahbabalshams.com

Location

The resort lies 40km inland from the Arabian Ranches roundabout – follow the signs right up to the private road leading to the resort.

Food & Drink

Al Hadheerah – Arabic • Al Forsan – international • Masala – Indian • Pizzeria Le Dune – Italian

Features

Pool • Arabian horse riding • Camel rides • 4WD desert exploration • Falconry • Spa • Bicycle rental • Outdoor archery • Lawn games • Gym

Nearby

Endurance City (www.dubaiendurancecity.com) • Arabian Ranches • Jumana Secret of the Desert at Al Sahra Desert Resort (www.alsahra.com)

This is quintessential Dubai: overblown, lavish and a lot of fun. The 19 exclusive Beit Al Bahar villas are found at the far corner of Jumeirah Beach Hotel, the city's second most famous five-star. It's a place you don't associate with peace and seclusion – its colour-clash lobby, complete with water feature, grand piano and chintz, signals its intent. But once you mention Beit Al Bahar to the concierge, everything changes. You are picked up by buggy and whisked from the main hotel, past pools, water features, bars and restaurants, where the pace noticeably slows. The villas each have a separate entrance, ornate wooden gate, and postcard-perfect views of the Burj Al Arab. Beit Al Bahar translates as 'house by the sea', and you'll notice your name already adorns the entrance next to the word 'Beit'. It's a winning touch, and one of the many designed to drive home the select club feel.

You are personally greeted inside your villa by two staff: one with hot towels, the other clutching a mocktail. They step aside to reveal a treasure chest overflowing with

Dubai

Beit Al Bahar
Jumeirah
Beach Hotel

fresh fruit. You haven't got enough hands to eat, mop your brow and down the orange cocktail, so you smile and take a plum. There is a living room with huge TV screen, imposing Bose sound system, two sofas scattered with gold lamé cushions, a laptop with free Wi-Fi, and doors leading to an ample terrace with dining table and chairs. The minibar has a great selection of teas; there's an excellent coffee machine – and presuming you can afford to stay here, you can sample the Johnnie Walker Black Label, huge cigars or a bag of jelly beans. Everything in the bedroom and bathroom is oversized and excessive. The bed is ridiculously big – large enough to house a healthy-sized family of four. The pillows could easily double as mattresses. The decor throughout isn't sure what it wants to be: there's Arabian glitz, a dressed-down Bedouin vibe, Roman touches, and stained-glassed windows to round out the look. The bathroom is brilliantly over the top; the only thing that is missing is gold swan taps. You can stand, or dance, in the sunken bath. There are more Bulgari products than you can possibly use in a month, and three types of sea salts. The only criticism is that the Jumeirah-branded ducks provided don't float. Next to the wash basins are sweatbands and a jogging map. At turndown, robes lie in waiting; towels are folded in the shape of ducks, bottled water is placed by your bedside and chill-out music plays on the stereo. Next to the fluffy slippers and room menu is a list of next day's activities at the hotel (all of which will be ignored in favour of three hours in the sunken bath). If this wasn't enough, Beit Al Bahar guests have access to the hotel's executive pool and lounge area (the pool has a fine bar and underwater sound system). A private sheltered pagoda will be reserved for you in the manicured grounds. Beyond is the beach, a beautiful, tranquil stretch of sand in the shadow of the Burj Al Arab that is rarely crowded (the proles from the main hotel aren't allowed on this bit). From here you can walk under the road that leads to the billowing sail of the Burj, and all the way up to Souk

Madinat Jumeirah. All the while tourists and daytrippers look back at you looking back at them. You know they're thinking 'how much is that a night'? And 'how can they afford it'? Breakfast can be taken on your terrace or as room service at Villa Beach restaurant, a clean, charming and stylish restaurant – less ostentatious than some of the hotel's other options. At night, it serves excellent Mediterranean cuisine with a flourish (the scallops are particularly recommended). Guests also have access to their own private pool among the Beit villas, where there are complimentary pre-dinner canapes and cocktails at Café Wadi.

Beit Al Bahar will appeal to a certain type of weekend breaker: those on a glitzy honeymoon, oligarchs, and the rest of us who can't resist an expensive glimpse of another world.

Dubai

Contact
Phone +971 4 406 8399
Email: beitalbahar@jumeirah.com
Web: www.jumeirahbeachhotel.com

Location
Just north of Burj Al Arab on Beach Road.

Food & Drink
Marina – seafood • Villa Beach – Mediterrannean • Beachcombers – South-east Asian • Latitude – international • Waterfront – healthy eating

Features
• Yacht chartering • Sea fishing
• Swimming pools • Gym • Squash
• Spa • Watersports • Children's club
• Diving • Golf • Access to Wild Wadi
• Private beach • Tennis courts

Nearby
Wild Wadi (www.wildwadi.com) • Emirates Golf Club (www.dubaigolf.com) • Ski Dubai (www.skidxb.com) • Mall of the Emirates (www.malloftheemirates.com) • Souk Madinat Jumeirah (www.madinatjumeirah.com) • The Palm Jumeirah (www.thepalm.ae)

Desert Palm

No matter how hard you work, it's unlikely that you'll ever actually be wealthy enough to live on your very own polo estate, surrounded by expansive green fields, beautiful horses and tasteful water features. However, it is possible to escape for a weekend and fantasise that this is the kind of life you lead – Desert Palm is set on a private polo estate just a very short drive out of Dubai, and offers a unique experience that you won't find anywhere else in the emirate.

As you enter the gates of the estate and approach the hotel, you'll notice that there are quite a few villas along the way. Desert Palm is home to around 90 residential villas, lived

in by a lucky few who get to experience this country-style living every day. The lobby of the hotel has been decorated to reflect the owner's good taste – neutral tones, dark wood features and splashes of colour create a peaceful, welcoming space that is luxurious yet subtle. There are only 24 rooms at Desert Palm, so it really does feel as though you are staying in a private lodge. The Palm Suites, which are in the hotel's main building, feature amazing views – floor-to-ceiling windows make the most of the spectacular view over the polo fields and all the way across town to the imposing skyline along Sheikh Zayed Road. The neutral, earthy tones that you saw in the lobby have been extended to the suites, which are large by most standards. Little luxuries make these rooms really stand out: a Bose surround-sound system, complete with pre-loaded iPod, Josephine Home linen on the gigantic, window-facing bed, original artwork courtesy of a prominent local photographer, a well-stocked minibar and a state-of-the-art coffee machine are just some of the amenities you can expect. Other accommodation options come in the form of one and two bedroom pool villas, which are set apart from the main building. These offer the ultimate in privacy for stressed-out city dwellers who want to get away from it all. Each villa has its own pool, sheltered from view by lush foliage, and you can spend the weekend lounging in the water, cuddled up in the poolside cocoon bed, or even enjoying a slap-up barbecue. The two bedroom villas have larger gardens, a study, and are particularly suited to families. The hotel's main pool is large and surrounded by comfy sun loungers, cocoon beds and even floating beanbags. Desert Palm is fast becoming renowned for its excellent onsite spa, Lime. Lime has six treatment rooms, including one double room for friends or couples to share – it comes complete with its own relaxation area and views over the polo fields. The Sublime relaxation area, available to all spa guests, truly is sublime – stretch out on the heated mosaic relaxation beds, curl up with a magazine on one of the comfy chairs, or request a colour therapy shower. There is also a boutique selling products used in the spa treatments, should you wish to recreate the glow at home.

Despite being a small hotel, Desert Palm is home to some excellent food and beverage options. Rare offers wood-fired steak and game in masculine, dignified surroundings. Surprisingly for a steakhouse, there is a good vegetarian selection too. In cooler months you can dine alfresco on the large terrace. Red bar opens at lunchtime and stays open through the afternoon and late into the evening – the adjacent wine cellar stocks over 300 labels, many of which are exclusive to Desert Palm or hard to find in Dubai. You can enjoy drinks and shisha, as well as a selection of bar food, on the terrace overlooking the polo fields – during winter there is polo every day.

But the showstopper is undoubtedly Epicure – a gourmet, deli-style market that offers a selection of home-made and luxury foods to the estate's residents. Open every day from 07:00, you'll see villa residents popping in and out to buy loaves of freshly baked bread, organic berries and gourmet pantry items. Epicure offers an all-day dining menu featuring the freshest ingredients, and the surroundings are just superb. Grab a seat at the long, bar-style table or on one of the comfy couches, and linger over your meal while you enjoy the

views of the swimming pool and the polo. It's a newcomer on Dubai's hotel scene, but it won't be long until Desert Palm is a household name on the lips of discerning residents who are looking for something unique; something different from the 'bigger, better' theme of most other hotels. Head out there while it's still one of Dubai's best-kept secrets.

Contact
Phone: +971 4 323 8888
Email: reservations@desertpalm.ae
Web: www.desertpalm.ae

Location
Drive past Dragon Mart on the Dubai-Hatta Road (E44). The entrance to Desert Palm is around two kilometres past Dragon Mart, and is clearly signposted.

Food & Drink
Rare – steak and game • Epicure – cafe • Red – wine bar

Features
Four polo grounds • Afternoon tea on the polo pavilions • Spa • Swimming pool • Two squash courts • Horse riding

Nearby
Ras Al Khor Wildlife Sanctuary (www.wildlife.ae) • Global Village (www.globalvillage.ae) • Dubai Festival City (www.dubaifestivalcity.com) • Dragon Mart (www.chinaexmart.com)

The Harbour Hotel & Residence

For a family break in the heart of New Dubai, you can't go far wrong with a stay at The Harbour – Emirates' city hotel right in the heart of Dubai Marina. Standing proud at the gateway to the buzzing Marina, this apartment-style hotel attracts everyone from weekend visitors looking to experience the best of 21st century Dubai's man-made attractions to long-stay business travellers who feel right at home here.

The hotel occupies a 52 storey skyscraper, one of the iconic structures of the area's mesmerising high-rise skyline. Vehicle access to the tower is, at present, fairly tricky, with diversions and construction still in full flow in this patch of the city. However, once checked in and escorted upwards to your room, you'll find no such spatial limitations. Suites are available in studio, one, two or three bedrooms (plus six extravagant penthouses, each occupying half a floor, if you've got the cash to splash).

Whatever size you opt for, the apartment comes equipped with a modern kitchen, meaning you have the option of some home cooking or 'dining out' at one of the hotel's restaurants. All rooms (apart from the studios) have a separate dining/living area, giving each a home-from-home feel rather than the standard hotel box shape. Interiors are tastefully furnished, mod cons such as 42 inch LCD TVs, DVD players and iPod docking

stations provide in-room entertainment, while the bathrooms contain a little splash of luxury too, featuring a range of L'Occitane products. Floor 41 up to the penthouse suites contain three-bedroom apartments only, while if it's a complete view you want (as opposed to building sites), make sure to request a sea-facing room. Although the large apartments may not be the first choice for an intimate weekend, the two and three bedroom suites are perfect for self-contained family outings, with sleeping options split between king-sized and twin rooms, and plenty of space for children to run around in.

There are other places for kids to let off steam, as well as for adults to soak it up. A terraced area, five floors up, houses a sea-facing leisure pool and sun deck, while across the road on the shore guests can access the beach facilities of Le Meridien Mina Seyahi. Inside, on the same floor as the pool, is the Emirates brand's top-of-the-range Timeless Spa. With treatment rooms for men and women, plus Jacuzzis, saunas and steam rooms, this is relaxation heaven. Calming vibes radiate around the spa area, and different types of massage are available, from aromatherapy-based treatments to Ayurvedic sessions.

The hotel's dining options are excellent too, ranging from deli-style food on the ground floor to gastro lounge with a stunning view on the top floor. If you're planning on self catering, Counter Culture is just the ticket. It's a licensed deli-cum-bakery-cum-barista coffee shop, and it's open 24 hours. If you want to get hold of the ingredients to cook up your own treat back in your apartment, you can get the ingredients you need here, at a reasonable price. From milk and bread to fish, pies and cakes, if they've got it you can buy it – and, for longer-stay guests, food can also be ordered in for you. Alternatively, opt for home cooking without the effort – simply present a recipe for your desired dish to the chef and, if he's got the ingredients, he'll rustle up the dish for you there and then.

For high-quality fare with a lovely Marina view, head to az.u.r on the fifth floor. With an emphasis on using the finer ingredients, be it carefully sourced organic produce from overseas, or the freshest local products available, the restaurant serves up a Mediterranean-based menu that focuses on blends of tastes and flavours (there are even 20 different types of water on offer, for H2O afficianados). During the cooler months, there's a terrace for alfresco dining.

For refreshments that will make you feel on top of the world (and fairly high above The Palm too), take the elevator up to The Observatory restaurant on the 52nd floor. With breathtaking 360° panoramic views of New Dubai and a stunning view of the Palm Jumeirah, this is, for now at least, Dubai's highest mainland restaurant. Enjoy dishes from an excellent gastro lounge menu, carefully and creatively put together using innovative cooking techniques, and then take in a close-up view through one of several telescopes lined up by the window. The vista at night is particularly memorable.

With the attractions of Dubai Marina and its numerous restaurants and parades of shops a stone's throw away, there are plenty of other eating, drinking and entertainment options on hand too, meaning everything you need for an indulgent weekend with the family is on The Harbour's doorstep.

Dubai

Contact
Phone: +971 4 319 4000
Email: ekresorts@emirates.com
Web: www.emirateshotelsresorts.com

Location
Al Sufouh Road (Beach Road) at the entrance to Dubai Marina, opposite Le Meridien Mina Seyahi.

Food & Drink
The Observatory – contemporary
• az.u.r – Mediterranean • Counter Culture – 24 hour deli

Features
Spa • Gym • Swimming pools

Nearby
Dubai Marina • Mall of the Emirates (www.malloftheemirates.com) • Emirates and Montgomerie golf courses (www.dubaigolf.com/egc) • The Palm Jumeirah (www.thepalm.ae) • Ski Dubai (www.skidxb.com)

Hatta Fort Hotel

The dramatic Hajar mountain range makes you feel like you are a world away from the artificial peaks of the city. And the Hatta Fort Hotel enjoys the perfect location from which to make the most of the Hajars – the low-rise hotel is actually a string of individual chalets stretched across a gap in the mountains. Each of the 53 rooms has, as you would expect in a mountain retreat, beautiful views of the surrounding range. From the outside, the rooms look unassuming enough, although once inside, each room has been beautifully decorated to further push home the idea that you are staying in a retreat, rather than in just a room. The walls have been crafted from stone, and high ceilings, complete with fans,

and dark, Arabian-style furnishings create an atmosphere that is instantly welcoming. The size of the rooms is a huge plus point too – each one is home to a luxurious king-size bed, a small dining table with two chairs, lounge seating, a minibar and TV, as well as a private patio or balcony that invites lingering sundowners spent gazing over the mountains with a good glass of wine in hand. Even the bathrooms are beautiful, fitted with a large bathtub and a walk-in shower. Rooms can sleep two adults and two children under 12 – special children's beds can be arranged at time of booking.

No matter how much you'll want to stay in the luxury of your room, the hotel has an impressive collection of facilities and activities that you shouldn't miss out on. It has two

lovely swimming pools, both of which can be used by hotel guests. The first pool is within the main part of the hotel, and is a tranquil area with shaded sections, plenty of sun loungers, and a bar service. The second pool is set about a hundred metres away from the main hotel complex, and is much bigger than the first, and usually a bit busier. This pool is open to day guests, who can pay an entry fee and use the facilities. It is also much more suitable for hotel guests with younger children, as there is a special children's pool and a playground nearby. This pool has been designed to appear as if it has been carved into the mountainous rocks, with two separate levels and an attractive rock feature complete with waterfall. Alongside the pool is a cafe and bar, so throughout the day you can select from the ample menu of light meals or cool yourself down with something frosty from the drinks menu. Both pools have amazing mountain views, so whether you're a hotel guest or a day guest, you will feel like you are a world away from the city.

Lounging by the pool, no matter how pleasant, is not the only activity on offer. At Hatta Fort Hotel Robin Hood wannabes can take an archery lesson with a qualified instructor – all equipment is provided.

The grounds of the hotel are expansive and contain a miniature golf course and a running track, so you can definitely incorporate plenty of relaxing activity into your weekend break. Then of course there are the activities outside the grounds – the hotel can arrange mountain and wadi safari tours for you, or if you've arrived with your own car you could go off and explore the surrounding countryside on your own. There are parts of the mountains that are accessible without an off-road vehicle – the famous Hatta pools, for example, are easy to get to in a saloon car (although you will have to park a short distance from the pools and walk the rest of the way). These natural rock pools are not signposted, yet just by word of mouth over decades they have become a significant tourist destination (sadly, this means that on some weekends they are so crowded and full of litter that it no longer feels

like a remote 'natural' attraction). But they are definitely worth a visit, especially since they are located just a short drive from the hotel. The UAE-Oman border is also just a quick drive from the hotel, making it a great stopover on your way to or from Muscat. When it comes to eating and drinking at the hotel, its remote location may seem like a distinct disadvantage: there are no nearby restaurants or bars to speak of, meaning that you are limited to the hospitality outlets within the grounds (of which there are only three, not including the pool bars). Fortunately, all offer excellent standards. Jeema is the main restaurant, and is located upstairs from the main hotel lobby. With a range of international options, the menu offers everything from seafood and steak to vegetarian and healthy options. The wine list is also superb and often the restaurant has food and beverage promotions, making it fairly reasonable for what you get. On certain nights of the week there is live entertainment. Café Gazebo is perched above the hotel's swimming pool, and offers light meals and buffet breakfasts in airy surroundings. Roumoul Cocktail Bar, just near Jeema, is a small but attractive bar that is perfect for pre-dinner drinks or that last nightcap.

Contact
Phone: +971 4 852 3211
Email: hfh@jaihotles.com
Web: www.jebelali-international.com

Directions
Follow the Dubai-Hatta Rd (E44), until you reach the Fort Roundabout in Hatta. Turn left here into the hotel, which is clearly signposted.

Food & Drink
Jeema – international • Café Gazebo – all-day dining • Roumool – cocktail bar

Features
Two temperature-controlled swimming pools • Golf driving range • 4WD driving tours • Gym • Table tennis • Billiards • Archery • Children's Club

Nearby
Hajar Mountains • Hatta Heritage Village • Hatta pools • Hatta Dam

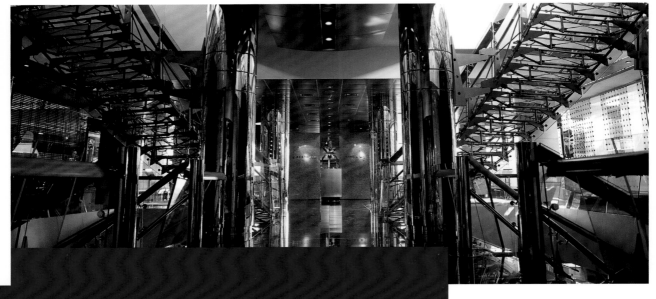

Hilton Dubai Creek

The contemporary, minimalist hospitality of the Hilton Dubai Creek forms a calm contrast to the frenzy of busy Deira, where it is located. Because of where it sits, on the bustling road that runs past the Dubai Creek and through Deira's prime commercial district, this hotel is understandably popular with business travellers. However, for weekend breakers there is a unique reason to pick this particular establishment out of the bounty of excellent hotels in Dubai: it is home to Michelin-starred Gordon Ramsay's first international restaurant, Verre. Since it opened in 2001, Verre has consistently impressed Dubai's diners with its fine food and five-star service, and has become the ultimate special occasion restaurant in the city. It's pricey, it's always fully booked, and it deserves respect – so choosing to extend your special night out with a stay in the Hilton, rather than heading back out to jostle with the Deira traffic, seems like a no-brainer.

The hotel's 154 rooms are stylish and unfussy, and most have great creek views. Splash out on a Queen Executive room for an added dose of luxury: these spacious rooms have floor-to-ceiling windows and sophisticated bathrooms with huge marble baths. Since this is predominantly a business hotel, you'll find that all rooms, while comfortable and modern, are functional and you won't find many of the superfluous trimmings that you might find

in a resort hotel. However, they are bright and beautifully decorated, and have handy amenities such as high-speed internet access, armchairs, a work desk and satellite TV.

The rooftop pool, on the 15th floor, has fantastic city views and on a clear day you should be able to see the Dubai Creek taper off towards the horizon. As you laze the day away on one of the wooden sun loungers, high above the hectic hustle and bustle below, you can enjoy a cocktail or a snack from the pool bar. The pool area is relatively modest in size, and can fill up fairly quickly at peak times, but if it gets too busy for your liking you can take advantage of the free, twice-daily shuttle service to the Hilton Dubai Jumeirah. Here you can soak up the sun around the (much bigger) pool area, or relax on the hotel's private beach.

The Hilton's proximity to the old side of town makes it an ideal location from which to explore Dubai's disappearing heritage and traditions. The city's famous souks are a short stroll away, so you can haggle for jewellery in the gold souk, enjoy the colours of the textile souk or take in the powerful aromas of the spice souk. Whether you're buying or just browsing, these souks are a great reminder that, before the glitzy malls and gleaming office towers, Dubai was a decidedly different place than it is today. For just Dhs.1 you can book your passage across the creek on an abra. These traditional water taxis may look rickety as they splutter along the width of the creek, but they are another way to immerse yourself in the history of Dubai, and you'll most likely be sharing your journey with an assortment of labourers, businessmen and tourists. Abra operators are usually willing, for a price, to take you on a half-hour ride up and down the creek if you'd prefer to take the scenic route. If you alight on the opposite side of the creek to the hotel, you'll be very near the historic Bastakiya district, home to a selection of art galleries, museums and cafes.

Back at the hotel, build the anticipation for dinner at Verre with a few well-mixed drinks at the Issimo Martini Bar – take your pick from the extensive cocktail menu and then relax in the futuristic surroundings while ambient jazz music plays in the background. However, your evening begins at dinner – Ramsay's Verre has scooped just about every restaurant award on offer, and is a perfect way to enjoy fine dining in stylish but surprisingly understated surroundings. It doesn't come cheap though: expect to pay around Dhs.400 per person for a starter and main course; that's without selecting a bottle from the large yet pricey wine list. But, on special occasions, who cares about the money? It's unlikely you'll be eating here on a weekly basis, so make the most of it. If your budget doesn't cover Michelin-starred cuisine, the Hilton is also home to the Glasshouse Mediterranean Brasserie, which offers down-to-earth, familiar dishes at more moderate prices. Glasshouse is under the same management as Verre, however, so you can be assured of superb quality. It also has a popular Friday brunch.

All in all, the Hilton Dubai Creek is an ideal weekend break for anyone who wants to soak up some local culture by day, and enjoy Dubai's finest cuisine by night.

Contact
Phone: +971 4 227 1111
Email: info.creek@hilton.com
Web: www.hilton.com

Location
Baniyas Road, on the Deira side of Dubai Creek just north of Maktoum Bridge.

Food & Drink
Glasshouse Brasserie – international • Verre by Gordon Ramsay – European Issimo – cocktail bar

Features
Creek views • Rooftop pool • Fitness room • Golf • Yachting • Dhow cruise

Nearby
Deira City Centre (www.deiracitycentre. com) • Creek Park (www.dm.gov.ae) • Gold Souk • Spice Souk • Abra Station • Dubai Museum (www.dubaitourism.ae) • Dubai Creek Golf & Yacht Club (www. dubaigolf.com) • Al Ghurair City (www. alghuraircity.com) • Al Ahmadiya School and Heritage House

The Hyatt Regency, on Deira corniche, was one of the first major hotels to be built in Dubai. Once a quiet part of town, with the sea right on its doorstep, this area is now teeming with hotels, shops, restaurants and apartments. Even the seascape is changing, with the Palm Deira development pushing Dubai's landmass further into the Gulf. The first stages of construction of this mammoth project are taking place almost on the Hyatt's doorstep, and where the views out to sea were once tranquil the waters are now a hive of activity, with ships and cranes busy creating this new part of the city. Luckily for the Regency and its guests, the angle of the hotel means that each of the hotel's 414 rooms boasts a great sea view, mainly unspoiled by the work.

Inside the recently refurbished hotel, the large lobby is a bustling centre for businessmen, holidaymakers, diners and wandering shoppers from the Hyatt's own precinct. The reception is more than just a formal place to check in, it's part of the hotel experience: this brightly lit area is designed to be the heart of the hotel.

Standard rooms come equipped with the usual amenities such as air conditioning, satellite TV and minibar, and all are finished with a sophisticated, contemporary touch. Or, if the occasion – and budget – permits, executive rooms can be booked as part of a Regency Club package (which includes use of The Regency Club on the 18th floor). All guests can access the hotel's fitness centre, Club Olympus, which includes a spa with an alluring range of treatments – try the personalised 60 minute Panpuri Journey massage for an absolute treat. The large outdoor temperature-controlled pool, surrounded by wooden sun

Dubai

Hyatt Regency Dubai

loungers, offers an inviting way to relax, with only minimal effort needed to order a cocktail from the well-stocked bar. There are also squash and tennis courts for those who want a more active break, as well as a Golf Park (pitch-and-putt and crazy golf) and ice rink (the latter is popular with families).

The hotel's corniche location means the attractions of downtown Deira are not far away – it's a short cab ride or winter walk to the gold, spice and electronic souks, and the lively fish market near the creek. Abras will take you across the bustling waterway if you want to explore further. However, if you're looking for a complete break from the outside world, the Regency is fully self-contained, featuring a shopping precinct, seven restaurants and bars, hair salon, cinema and babysitting service – you need never leave the hotel.

There is a diverse range of eateries to choose from. Italian restaurant Focaccia opens daily for lunch and dinner, and provides modern fare in a replication of a rustic Mediterranean house. Miyako offers the ultimate Japanese experience, with a variety of Japanese cooking methods including teppanyaki, teriyaki and sushi. If you are unable to finish your tipple at the end of the night Miyako provides a nice touch – staff will store your unfinished bottle for next time, something you'll be glad of the following evening (and morning).

At Shahrzad Iranian restaurant you can watch the chefs bake traditional bread in a tanour oven, or sit on the balconies overlooking the hotel lobby. This restaurant is dripping with tradition and offers tantalising lunch and evening fare. If you're undecided over what cuisine to plump for, The Kitchen offers a sophisticated mix of Asian, Middle Eastern and western food in a bustling area in the middle of the hotel lobby.

The dining high point – literally – is Al Dawaar revolving restaurant. Catch the exclusive lift from the lobby up to the 25th floor and take a 105 minute spin around Dubai while enjoying a buffet of Japanese, European and Middle Eastern dishes (the dessert table is also a scandalously good indulgence). Sip on your complimentary glass of fizz, soak up the

atmosphere, and watch the city sights glide by. This restaurant serves famously good buffet lunches by day (Dhs.155) and at night offers a great way to end your weekend with a romantic candlelit dinner (Dhs.185).

Your evening entertainment needn't stop at eating; the Hyatt also features several fun night spots. Visit The Bar for pricey but well-made cocktails in a quiet, stylish location with great views across to the Gulf. For those made of stronger stuff – or who have been on the stronger stuff – push aside your inhibitions and join the local crooners belting out typical hits in the hotel's karaoke bar, Hibiki Music Lounge, while the hotel's two clubs Frosty and The Premiere offer hedonistic partying to satisfy the most energetic holidaymakers.

Dubai

Contact
Phone: +971 4 209 1234
Email: dubai.regency@hyatt.com
Web: www.dubai.regency.hyatt.com

Location
Corniche Road, Deira, on the coast side of the road that flows out of the Shindagha Tunnel.

Food & Drink
Al Dawaar – international • Focaccia – Italian • Miyako – Japanese • Shahrzad – Iranian • The Kitchen – international

Features
Swimming pool • Swimming lessons • Tennis court & tennis coaching • Spa • Beauty salon • Fitness centre • Squash courts • Table tennis • Jogging track • Hyatt Golf Park • Ice rink • Galleria Shopping Mall • Emirates Bank • Pharmacy

Nearby
Dubai Creek • Gold Souk • Spice Souk • Fish market • Dubai Museum (www.dubaitourism.ae) • Al Ghurair City (www.alghuraircity.com) • Al Mamzar Beach Park (www.dm.gov.ae) • Al Ahmadiya School and Heritage House • Heritage and Diving Village

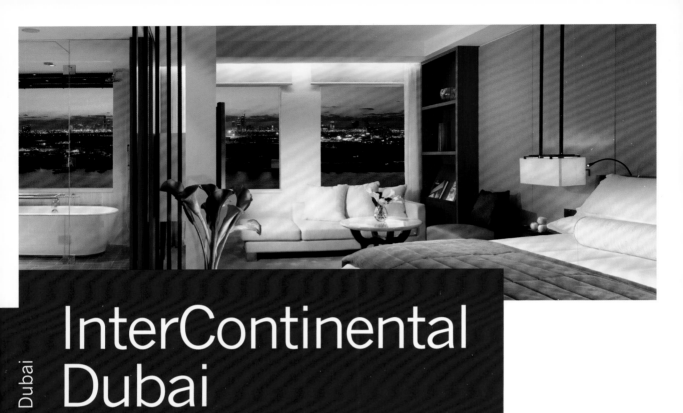

InterContinental Dubai Festival City

The InterContinental occupies a remarkable new waterfront location, with sweeping views over Dubai Creek. Poised to cater for the international jet set, this new establishment ticks all the right boxes – it's near the airport, has immediate access to the mammoth shopping haven that is Festival City, and offers a brand new view of Dubai.

The hotel looks set to dominate this area of the city not only architecturally but gastronomically too, with a varied collection of innovative restaurants and bars.

Inside, the set-up is ultra modern and conceptually interesting: from the quirky swing hanging from the ceiling (hard to resist the urge to jump upon) to the well-upholstered, comfortable bedrooms, this is a stylish hotel. Rooms are designed along classic, unembellished lines to enhance the feeling of spaciousness, with an emphasis on quality materials and simplicity. Flatscreen televisions offering a wide range of channels are installed for a touch of high-tech, while a sound system will relax you with soothing tunes as you take a dip in the luxurious bath to ease your traveller's aches and pains. Coffee and tea-making facilities are available and the beds are well proportioned. Rooms come with views including Festival Marina, Dubai Creek and the city's skyscraper-filled skyline.

The hotel is connected by walkway to the Festival Marina, which is a wonderful place for an evening stroll, and affords great sunset views over the water looking towards the city skyline. The opportunities for spending, browsing and eating in the Festival City mall are immense too – there are over 500 retail outlets and 90 restaurants and cafes to choose from.

If you'd prefer not to leave the comfort of the hotel, the dining opportunities within the InterContinental are first class. The arrival of the experiential guru Pierre Gagnaire, a Michelin-decorated master chef whose new Reflets restaurant is set to rival both Gordon Ramsay and Gary Rhodes's Dubai offerings, has given the establishment a thrilling global culinary reputation.

It's the Anise restaurant, however, that is its piece de resistance, with some sensational interior designing by the famously esoteric Japanese company Super Potato. Huge swathes of wood, steel and extraordinary lighting make this the inner citadel of the InterContinental palace. Dining here immediately upon checking in at the hotel sets a stylish tone for the rest of your stay. Immaculate serving staff offer five-star attention, greeting you warmly and guiding you effortlessly around the remarkably diverse Italian, Indian, Japanese, Chinese, and Arabian food stations, where chefs cook authentic food to your exact specifications and with a genuine passion for their enterprise. Fabulous desserts include petite French mesdames and ornate fruit tarts, while a mouthwatering, continental European or sizzling traditional English-style breakfast is available.

Elsewhere, elegant Parisian Bistro Madeleine allows you to sip hot chocolate and freshly baked croissants as sailors ready their yachts in the marina. The smell of the baking may incline you to while away your morning here, before you endeavour to burn off those calories in the gym or in the extensive spa and relaxation facilities (a swimming pool and spa pools, whirlpool, and an array of massage suites are on offer).

For some liquid refreshment, recline with a coffee or a refreshing long island iced tea in the Vista lounge bar, with its terrace, classically designed cocktail bar and trendy ambience. And if Vista doesn't chill you out then head up to the 26th floor to experience the Eclipse bar, where (as well as being that much closer to the moon) flickering neon and skyscrapers provide the backdrop. The InterContinental is part of a larger, ambitious complex with an attached Crowne Plaza, which houses the excellent Belgian Beer Cafe – a continental European-style drinking haven, complete with a great selection of real draught beer and subdued lighting.

The creek and attractions of Sheikh Zayed Road and Downtown Dubai are all nearby – ask the hotel concierge service what excursions or outings are available. But if it's shops, entertainment and creekside refreshment you're after, you really won't need to head beyond the confines of Festival City.

Dubai

Contact
Phone: +971 4 701 1111
Email: intercontinental@ichdfc.ae
Web: www.ichotelsgroup.com

Location
Festival City, on the Deira side of the creek and accessible from either Garhoud Bridge or Business Bay Bridge.

Food & Drink
Anise – international • Bistro Madeleine – French • Al Sultan Brahim Beirut – Lebanese • Reflets par Pierre Gagnaire – French

Features
Temperature-controlled swimming pool • Gym • Spa • Golf • Daycare & children's activities • Beauty salon

Nearby
Dubai Festival Centre (www.dubaifestivalcity.com) • Wafi Mall (www.wafi.com) • Belgian Beer Cafe (www.ichotelsgroup.com) • Four Seasons Golf Club (www.fourseasons.com/dubaigolf)

Jebel Ali Golf Resort & Spa

Jebel Ali Hotel opened way back in the 1970s, so it is a rare taste of 'old school' Dubai. The 128 acres of grounds are filled with a mix of mature trees and natural vegetation – home to chirruping birds and insects as well as the resort's famous peacocks. The gardens are populated by many varieties of palms and cacti, as well as an organic garden where fresh produce used in some of the resort's restaurants grows. Through the trees, the glimpses of the golfing greens are a pleasant surprise.

The main hotel, Jebel Ali Hotel, looks slightly dated from the outside, but the interior is tasteful, and it looks out over the gardens, the resort's marina and one of the longest stretches of private beach in Dubai. Rooms are on five floors, and are compact but smart and well appointed.

Outside, the resort has plenty of space. Vast lawns are scattered with sun loungers among tall shady palm trees, and sheltered by the Palm Jebel Ali, the bright, clear turquoise waters lap calmly on the white sandy beach. Surprisingly, the views over the grounds to the sea and the Palm have few cranes or signs of construction disrupting the scenery. Winding paths lead from the hotel over little wooden bridges crossing trickling streams, past fish-filled pools, waterfalls, and hidden grassy areas equipped with sun loungers, to the second property in the resort, The Palm Tree Court & Spa.

Slightly bizarrely, the reception here has a bit of a ski-lodge feeling, with natural stone walls and a tall, sloping, timber-framed roof. From here, you will be ferried by electric cart to your accommodation in two exclusive three-storey wings. Rooms in the front set have private terraces or balconies looking directly out towards the sea, and for those on the ground floor, private access out to the gardens and beach. The second wing is set further back, nestling on the small hillside among tall trees and thick tropical greenery, with paths weaving through the gardens to the Palm Tree Court.

Rooms are more spacious and luxurious than the main hotel, with more privacy afforded by direct private entrances.

The resort has all the usual leisure facilities such as tennis courts, a health club, a variety of watersports, and a luxurious spa offering more than 40 treatments, but few other hotels can boast their own marina (offering seaplane tours and a range of boat and fishing trips), a golf course and stables. In addition, there is a karting track next door, and the Jebel Ali Shooting Club is nearby. Kids can indulge their exuberance in the Peaco Club, which has its own pet corner. Babysitting services are available.

One of the main attractions is the hotel's own golf course. The nine-hole, par 36 course is good for a quick round, but it can also be played as an 18 hole course. Equipment is available for hire, and you can get in a good set of practice shots at the putting green before you tee off. If your game is too bad to be helped by putting practice, call in the professionals – there is an on-site golf academy offering coaching.

The resort has four temperature-controlled pools; a deep one at the hotel, another at Palm Tree Court, a small kids' pool and a salt-water pool, if you need help keeping afloat after indulging too much at the buffet. The two main pools have swim-up bars.

There's a great choice of food and beverage outlets. For the best views and atmosphere, a beach bar offers dining right next to the beach in a tasteful wooden shelter with a thatched roof, and a shisha terrace for puffing away under the starry skies after your meal. The buffet restaurants are decent, with staff who are helpful and flexible, but the flagship venues (which attract many diners from outside the hotel) are definitely worth visiting for a touch more sophistication and some top-quality food. On the ground floor, Signatures serves French cuisine from its open kitchen inside or alfresco looking out over the gardens. Upstairs, the terrace at White Orchid offers great views over the tops of the palm trees while you enjoy fine Thai,

Chinese and Japanese food. An Arabic BBQ is held on one evening a week, with a belly dancer to entertain.

With the rapid expansion of Dubai, Jebel Ali Resort is just far enough out of the city to escape the hustle and bustle, but still easy to get to. It has such a different feel to the rest of the UAE's resorts, and is definitely worth a visit when city life is getting too much. Fully equipped, luxurious surroundings and a peaceful atmosphere – it all adds up to a perfect place for a weekend break, or even longer.

Dubai

Contact
Phone: +971 4 883 6000
Email: jagrs@jaihotels.com
Web: www.jebelali-international.com

Directions
Nr Palm Jebel Ali, adjacent to Jebel Ali Free Zone. Take Sheikh Zayed Road (E11) until Interchange 10 (Exit 13) and follow the signs for Jebel Ali Golf Resort & Spa.

Food & Drink
White Orchid – Asian • La Fontana – Mediterranean • La Traviata – Italian • Ibn Majed – international • Shooters – American • Sports Café – Fusion • Signatures – French

Features
Spa • Golf course • Golf academy • Pools & beach • Watersports • Shooting club • Horse riding • Gym • Squash • Floodlit tennis courts • Croquet • Volleyball • Deep sea fishing • Snooker & billiards • Umbro Football Training Academy • Seaplane flights

Nearby
Ibn Battuta Mall (www.ibnbattutamall.com) • The Palm Jebel Ali (www.thepalm.ae)

Jumeirah Emirates Towers

The iconic Emirates Towers building along Sheikh Zayed Road is undoubtedly one of the enduring images of modern-day Dubai. This hotel has scooped numerous international awards, primarily in the business travel category. But it should not be overlooked as a luxury weekend break destination; from the grand lobby right up to Vu's Bar on the 51st floor, the hotel oozes elegance at every turn. Given that its clientele are mainly businessmen, the decor is understandably masculine. Most of the rooms are accented with dark colours and male grooming products. However, acknowledging that even the toughest businessmen have a soft side, bathrooms come with a rubber duck and an arrangement of candles next to the bathtub. In an effort not to exclude high-flying female business travellers, Emirates Towers has created a ladies' floor in conjunction with Chopard, where no men are allowed, and all staff members are female.

The rooms, even the 'standard' deluxe rooms, are sized generously and have all the usual conveniences, including a particularly attractive in-room bar. All rooms have sweeping views over the city of Dubai; fascinating, especially at night.

Emirates Towers has some of the city's top dining establishments. Top of the list, and of the building, are Vu's and Vu's Bar. The bar takes the top spot in terms of height; 51 floors up in a glass elevator is always going to be an interesting start to the evening. Try to get a table near the windows and you'll have almost panoramic views while you sip on a range of expertly mixed cocktails. However, Vu's restaurant, just one floor down, is undoubtedly the top spot in terms of food and service. The air of quiet elegance is apparent from the time you exit the elevator, carried through with the help of comfortable armchair seating, low lighting, muted background noise, and some of the most professional restaurant staff in Dubai. Spectacular views are once again the star of the show, and there aren't many places where you can dine at this altitude. The carefully planned menu is perfectly complemented by the impressive

wine list, although both will set you back a pretty penny.

For something a little less posh, other outlets in the hotel are worth mentioning. Al Nafoorah serves delicious Lebanese food from lunch until late. The Rib Room is a renowned steak and seafood restaurant, and Mosaico is open all day, serving an excellent Mediterranean buffet as well as a la carte options. In the adjoining Boulevard there are many more dining options, including Noodle House, tokyo@thetowers and Scarlett's. Enjoy a massive selection of wines in The Agency, or grab the mike at karaoke bar Harry Ghatto's. Soothe your hangover the next morning with a shot of pure oxygen at the H2O Male Spa, which also houses a flotation tank. It offers a comprehensive range of relaxation treatments for the stressed businessman. Ladies can enjoy a selection of spa treatments in the Health Club.

The swimming pool curves around the hotel, ending in a new pool bar offering a full service. Lying on a sun lounger, with the towering buildings of Sheikh Zayed Road over your head, you'll feel almost like you're playing truant for a day while everyone else is at work. And that's the beauty of this hotel – the atmosphere is so charged with the day-to-day business of hand-shaking and deal-making that it makes a 'for pleasure only' weekend break all the more relaxing.

Contact
Phone: +971 4 330 0000
Email: eth@emirates-towers-hotel.com
Web: www.jumeirah.com

Location
Sheikh Zayed Road, Trade Centre 2, near Dubai World Trade Centre.

Food & Drink
• Al Nafoorah – Lebanese • Corner 3 – contemporary • ET Sushi – Japanese • Mosaico – Mediterranean • The Noodle House – South-east Asian • The Rib Room – seafood & steakouse

• Scarlett's – Tex Mex & American
• Tokyo@The Towers – Japanese
• Vu's – contemporary

Features
Helicopter airport transfers • Charter tours • Modern shisha lounge • 25 metre pool • Health club • H2O The Male Spa • Signature shops

Nearby
Trade Centre • Jumeirah Public Beach • Dubai Mall • Old Town Burj Dubai

La Maison D'Hotes

Escape from the Dubai hotel mantra of 'bigger and better' by checking into La Maison D'Hotes, a charming boutique-style venue on a leafy street in the residential suburb of Umm Suqeim. Made up of three converted villas, the hotel has a selection of rooms and suites, as well as a French restaurant, a coffee shop, a 22 seater conference room and two swimming pools.

The rooms and suites are each decorated differently from the next, with the common theme being Middle Eastern and Asian influence. From the deep purple opulence of the Kashmir Room to the monochromatic luxury of the Bagdad Executive Suite, each room has been planned in meticulous detail and has its own character. The Ceylan Kandy two-bedroom suite is a riot of fuschia and burnt orange, tamed by classic Arabian-style furniture and crisp white bed linen. Apart from two large bedrooms, this suite also features an inviting Jacuzzi bath. The Bagdad Executive Suite has a private dining area and views over one of the swimming pools – it makes a lovely venue for a romantic getaway.

Delectable French food, prepared by two resident French chefs, is available all day in the restaurant in the main building. This eatery serves a series of degustation menus, including, unusually for a French restaurant,

a vegetarian selection. The bright and sunny coffee shop, next door to the restaurant, is popular for pastries and tea in the afternoons. An important feature of the hotel is its open relationship with the arts. It is frequently used as an exhibition space for local artists and photographers, and large original pieces hang in the restaurant and coffee shop. Smaller works can be found in each of the rooms and suites, and all are available for sale. The beautiful gardens also feature numerous modern art sculptures. The onsite shop sells some beautiful hand-crafted items, as well as the bed linens used in the rooms.

In the reception area you'll find Elise, the knowledgeable and friendly tourism manager, who can make restaurant reservations, provide local area information, and book special activities not found in many other hotels in Dubai. She can organise hot air ballooning, falconry, catamaran cruises and many more unique activities. She can also book you in for a special Hummer desert safari with Beyond the Dunes (www.beyondthedunes.com) – a company focusing on individual attention and providing the ultimate desert experience in the dunes of Sharjah.

The hotel is centrally located and in cooler months you could walk to many nearby places such as Mercato Mall, the beach, and Town Centre. Jumeirah Beach Park is just a short taxi ride away.

Two important things to note about La Maison D'Hotes is that it does not serve alcohol or accept credit cards. However, for an intimate break with personalised service, it ticks all the right boxes.

Contact
Phone: +971 4 344 1838
Email: info@lamaisondhotesdubai.com
Web: www.lamaisondhotesdubai.com

Location
Villa 18, Street 83B, Jumeira. From Jumeira Beach Road, turn into 77B St. Take the second right onto 24D St, then a right at the T-junction. Turn left on to 20D St, and the hotel is in front of you opposite the T-junction.

Food & Drink
The Restaurant – French • Coffee Corner – cafe

Features
Two swimming pools • Gym • Five lounges • Gift shop • Babysitting

Nearby
Safa Park and Jumeirah Beach Park (www.dm.gov.ae) • Mall of the Emirates (www.malloftheemirates.com) • Wild Wadi Water Park (www.wildwadi.com) • Mercato Mall (www.mercatoshopping mall.com)

Dubai

One&Only
Royal Mirage

The most appealing aspect of The One&Only Royal Mirage is its isolation from its surroundings. The massive complex somehow manages to feel secluded and private, despite being located amid the ongoing construction and ever-increasing traffic of Al Sufouh and the Marina. Immediately upon entering the grounds, an air of tranquility sets in. The tree-shaded maze of roads connecting the three wings makes visitors forget they have only just left the dusty, washed-out and chaotic highways of Dubai.

The One&Only Royal Mirage is divided into three buildings, each offering its own charms, subtleties and amenities. The Palace, the largest of the three, succeeds in combining 246 sea-facing rooms and suites into what feels like a small, luxury beach resort. Next door sits the equally impressive Arabian Court. The third section of the resort is by far the most luxurious and personal. The Residence & Spa has only 50 rooms and suites, each of which leaves no detail ignored.

Upon entering the reception area, guests are welcomed by the most tasteful reproduction of traditional Arabic architecture that the city has to offer. Absent are the stucco-coated foam mouldings that are so commonly found in Dubai. In their place are real carved wood and formed plaster. Everything feels authentic, from the ornate, thick-iron lamps to the solid stone fountains.

Thankfully, the resort's professional and accommodating staff match their environment. The receptionists welcome newcomers with genuine hospitality and humility. In other words, they treat you as their most important guest. After an easy check in, you'll be led to your room, which will undoubtedly glow with the same quality workmanship as the grand entrance.

The spacious rooms are adorned with rich, fabrics, hand-made furniture and elegant accessories. The Arabic touches in the rooms are more subtle than the resort's public spaces, and help to create a complex, opulent style that manages to stay comfortable. To round out the package, the massive beds are the perfect match of firmness and comfort, and the well-lit bathrooms are spacious and modern. The only downside is that the resort offers so many activities and distractions that you may find it hard to choose between enjoying them all, or taking the time to relax in your personal luxury.

Once settled in your room, you'll want to tour the massive grounds to get an idea of everything you can do. First thing, you should head to the kilometre-long private beach which, unlike most other city resorts, doesn't give day passes to non-guests. There you'll find everything from catamaran sailing to parasailing. The absence of day users means there are always plenty of beach chairs and umbrellas, as well as plenty of space.

Next, head to one of the four temperature-controlled, palm tree-ringed pools. If swimming isn't on your list, take advantage of the Royal Mirage's proximity to the Emirates Golf Club, or just enjoy the walkways. Even at full capacity, the garden and beach areas are large enough to make each guest feel as though they have the resort to themselves. Nightly walks are a must, as the dimly lit pathways meander through massive trees and impeccably kept lawns and shrubbery. At one point or another, you should venture inside to relax in one of the resort's greatest assets: The Health and Beauty Institute, which houses both the Givenchy Spa and the Oriental Hammam, each offering unique, world-class therapies. Among its many available treatments, the Givenchy Spa offers 10 unique massage options, including the Canyon Love Stone Therapy, which uses warmed stones to

relieve stress. Even more memorable is the Oriental Hammam. Decorated almost entirely in marble, the hammam is a working replica of a traditional steam room. After changing into a traditional wrap, guests are guided through a maze of hallways before entering one of the two main steam rooms. In the centre of the room stands a massive heated marble slab, upon which guests are treated to a relaxing scrub with a variety of natural exfoliating compounds.

The Royal Mirage hosts some of the best restaurants and bars in the city. Morroccan-themed Tagine's interior is as close as you can get to authentic decor this side of the Suez. The food here is well-prepared and not prohibitively expensive. Alternatively, claim your table at Eauzone, where during the winter months you can enjoy a balmy alfresco dinner. All of the other restaurants are equally elegant and charming. The breakfast buffets are top notch, with expertly prepared, high-quality ingredients. Checking out of The Royal Mirage and driving out through the tree-shaded driveway and back into reality isn't pleasant. The resort is so well managed that every aspect of the place, from the impeccable interior design to the non-instrusive, personalised service, seems easy and unforced. The One&Only Royal Mirage is most definitely one of the best, most worthwhile escapes that the Gulf has to offer.

Dubai

Contact
Phone: +971 4 399 9999
Email: info@oneandonlyroyalmirage.ae
Web: www.oneandonlyresorts.com

Location
Al Sufouh Road (Beach Road), opposite Media City and near Palm Jumeirah.

Food & Drink
• The Rostisserie – European • Nina – Indian • Eauzone – Asian • Olives – Mediterranean • Tagine – Moroccan • Celebrities – international • Beach Bar & Grill – steakhouse

Features
Pools • Scented gardens • Beach • Spa • Salon • Fitness centre

Nearby
Emirates Golf Club (www.dubaigolf.com) • Dubai Media City • Madinat Jumeirah (www.madinatjumeirah.com) • Dubai International Marine Club (www.dimc-uae.com) • Palm Jumeirah (www.thepalm.ae)

The Palace –
The Old Town

One of the latest additions to the city's hospitality scene lies in the shadow of the Burj Dubai. Nestled at the base of the world's tallest building, The Palace hotel couldn't be more different from that modern monolith – looking like a tasteful castle for Arabic Barbie, it is actually built on the site of an old citadel. For some architects, symmetry is synonymous with luxury and with a grand archway and vast entrance (complete with dramatic water feature), this design strategy works. And the same principle spreads to other facets of the hotel's finer details: from beautifully designed staff uniforms to an outstanding spa, the hotel ticks all the upmarket boxes.

Aside from the feature at the entrance, the water theme continues inside, with guests greeted by rose petals floating in a huge fountain in the lobby, and an outdoor pool flanked by palm trees and recliners. And then there's the enormous faux lake that surrounds the hotel, which will eventually be used for transporting guests around the grounds by dhow.

The hotel boasts 242 guest rooms and suites, all with views of the Burj Dubai, the lake or Old Town. There are 131 deluxe rooms, 68 apartment suites, three royal suites and one imperial suite. The decor, regardless of the room size, is beautifully executed, with traditional Arabian designs mixed with Asian artefacts, resulting in a modern take on age-old luxury. The muted earth tones, ocean palettes and soft furnishings make for a relaxing stay and, despite being a relatively new hotel, the substantial and well-chosen pieces look like they have been in situ for years.

The quality continues to the bathrooms, where you'll find a two-person tub, with separate shower and toilet both sealed off with etched glass. Even the 'basic' deluxe rooms offer a high standard of finishing. The usual five-star extras are present: robes, slippers, an extensive collection of toiletries, hairdryer, satellite TV, minibar and room service. However, what makes sleeping at The Palace particularly special are the beds. So often overlooked – and clearly a crucial part of an overnight stay – the comfort factor of these mattresses is impressive.

Modern technology can be found throughout the hotel, and business travellers and Facebook addicts will be pleased to find free Wi-Fi and internet connections in all rooms. Alternatively, the Executive Lounge is open 24 hours a day with library, business centre, secretarial service, computer stations, Wi-Fi, newspapers, magazines and TVs.

For those looking to relax, the fitness centre and spa should impress. There are separate spas for men and women, steam and sauna areas, hammam and treatment rooms, shop and a relaxation lounge.

The hotel's restaurants, while relatively new on Dubai's dining scene, are quickly gathering the reputations they deserve. Breakfast is served in Ewaan, which is open for all day dining and offers Friday brunch, but for the evening, food fans are flocking to Asado and Thiptara. Asado is an Argentinian steak restaurant (to call it a 'steak joint' would be misleading) with a staggering wine list, live music, a fine selection of meat cuts and a cosy atmosphere rarely found in Dubai. Thiptara, meanwhile, takes advantage of its lakeside location with fire pits, tables by the water and an eye-popping view of the Burj. The views alone make it worth a trip, but the cocktail list encourages a longer stay. The authentic Thai food will delight, with delicious duck curries, spicy salads and royal fried rice with crab, but such dishes come at a price so this might be one place to save for a special occasion. For more casual dining, the pool bar serves snacks, icecreams, juices and alcoholic drinks from 10:00 to sunset, so you can lie back on your teak sun lounger with a cocktail in hand. It's a tough life.

The Palace has all the makings of a destination hotel. The fine dining, enviable spa and unique location mean it won't be an undiscovered gem for long. The opening of Souk Al Bahar also means that shopping fans can take a trip to Old Town to walk around this modern interpretation of a traditional market.

Luckily, it seems the hotel is prepared for this inevitable influx. The staff are quietly charming and clearly very well trained, there is no call for complaint about the rooms, and the kitchens are in full swing. From freshly made lemon-mint juice at breakfast to exquisite bife de chorizo for dinner, it's clear that a great deal of thought has gone into every detail. While prices might not be accessible to all, The Palace is certainly somewhere you can enjoy the luxury that you are paying for. In fact, the low-key sophistication will probably encourage you to order that extra bottle of red at Asado or book in for a Decléor facial at the spa. The hotel has a way of making you feel you deserve this outstanding treatment, so you'll probably be back again and again. The new take on old style with iconic views conspire to make a stay at The Palace a truly five-star experience.

Dubai

Contact
Phone: +971 4 428 7888
Email: reservations@thepalace-dubai.com
Web: www.thepalace-dubai.com

Location
Burj Dubai Blvd, Old Town, Downtown Burj Dubai, near Dubai Mall. Turn off Sheikh Zayed Road and at interchange 1 (Defence Roundabout), turn on to Doha Street.

Food & Drink
• Thiptara – Thai • Asado – Argentinian • Ewaan – Mediterranean & Middle Eastern

Features
Lake views • Arabian architecture • Large pool • Arabian tents • Boat cruises • Spa

Nearby
Souk Al Bahar • Old Town • Dubai Mall • Dubai World Trade Centre • Safa Park

Park Hyatt Dubai is at the opposite end of the five-star spectrum to its 'New Dubai' peers – geographically and stylistically. Where opulence and ostentation rule in Jumeira and Umm Suqeim, the charms are more endearing creekside. You approach the hotel through the manicured grounds of the Dubai Creek Golf and Yacht Club, eventually reaching a huge, whitewashed, Moorish dome – its Arabesque touches and tiling setting the tone of laidback luxury.

The Park Hyatt's architecture is unique among the city's hotels, and it goes a long way to

making your stay memorable. The low-rise blue and white domes have been cleverly dotted between pathways and water features, making for an intimate setting despite the hotel's 225 rooms (including 35 suites). The mood is tranquil, and the style brilliantly understated. There are two main focal points: the pool, with its carefully spaced loungers and general air of serenity, and the hotel's creekside dining options. The first is a palm-lined 25 metre affair – not that you'll be breaking into more than a gentle doggie paddle. Lie here for five minutes and you can't believe you're in Dubai, far less a stone's throw from the mania of Maktoum Bridge. At dusk, the pool is lit by

Park Hyatt Dubai

torchlight – a fitting sign-off to a blissfully peaceful day.

Creekside dining is the hotel's secret weapon. With little fanfare, you find one of the city's best Thai restaurants and arguably its best cocktail bar, both located seconds from your room. Thai Kitchen serves excellent tapas-style south-east Asian bites, with an excellent brunch on Friday, while The Terrace offers superb long drinks, with good tunes and a classic postcard view of the creek.

After all this pool lounging and cocktail drinking, you might think the quality of the rooms is irrelevant – but it isn't. The rooms are modern, stylish and full of all the facilities you want, like a huge big armchair, a big flatscreen TV, expensive soaps and lotions, and a stand-alone rain shower.

There is a range of room options, right up to the opulent Royal Suite, but the Park Room will satisfy even the most discerning weekend breaker. It's a large, open-plan affair, offering business-like chic. There's nothing business-like about the free-standing oval bath behind the bed, however, shielded by shutters that open or close, depending on your mood (and your room mate). Each room has a terrace; request one with views of the creek and harbour and your experience will be all the better for it.

A notch up the scale, the Park Executive suite comes with its own spa room and massage bench, but is aimed squarely at stressed out executives with generous expense budgets. Of the other dining options in the hotel, Café Arabesque offers more traditional flavours of the region at lunch and dinner, but serves a beautiful breakfast buffet, where you can overindulge on fresh fruit, good coffee and beautiful breads and pastries.

In comparison, the fine dining Traiteur is almost out of place. You descend a staircase into the main restaurant, where the hotel's neutral colours are abandoned for a slightly incongruous mix of nightclub hues. But the modern European food restores the status quo. You'll also have the choice of one of Dubai's longest wine lists.

If you want to just read the paper and recline with a brew, the Lounge is a peaceful, beautifully decorated retreat.

Although the Park Hyatt retains a loyal business and tourist clientele, it holds a special place for Dubai residents looking for a weekend escape or midweek treat.

One of the main reasons for this is the Amara Spa, which is rated highly amid the UAE's glut of pampering options. Pay for a treatment and you get access for the day to the pool – a real treat that more than justifies the outlay.

There are seven other private treatment rooms in the spa, each with an outside rain shower and mini garden designed to soothe. The massage and facial list is extensive, as is the range of potions and backing tracks you may choose to accompany your massage. The adjoining salon offers haircuts for men and women and the full range of beauty treatments. Staff make the experience one to savour. Should you feel the need to quicken the pulse afterwards, you could book a round of golf at the course next door, while the fitness centre is well stocked with equipment and helpful trainers. But it's usually empty. You don't visit the Park Hyatt to work up a head of steam, but to savour one of Dubai's diminishing number of genuine hideaways.

Dubai

Contact

Phone: +971 4 602 1234
Email: reservations.parkhyattdubai@hyatt.com
Web: www.hyatt.com

Directions

Inside Dubai Creek Golf & Yacht Club, Deira, opposite Deira City Centre.

Food & Drink

Traiteur – European • Café Arabesque – Middle Eastern • Thai Kitchen – Thai • Pistache – Patisserie • The Terrace – Vodka Bar

Features

Spa • Swimming pool • 18 hole golf course • Driving range • Gym • Private yacht charter

Nearby

Dubai Creek • Gold Souk • Spice Souk • Wafi Mall (www.wafi.com) • Deira City Centre (www.deiracitycentre.com) • Dubai Creek Golf & Yacht Club (www.dubaigolf.com)

Raffles Dubai

The eye-catching, pyramid-inspired architecture of Raffles Dubai is fast becoming a new city icon. The Egyptian theme continues into the interior of this grand hotel, from sphinxes carved into stone walls, pairs of pharaohs welcoming you through entrances, and carpets featuring the protective Eye of Horus. But the decor also makes a nod to both the Asian origins of the Raffles brand, as well as to the hotel's Middle Eastern location, so the result is an eclectic, beautiful and carefully planned fusion of Egyptian, Asian and Arabic influences.

Raffles is an all-suite hotel, and there are various levels of luxury spreading from the Signature Suite right up to the only-in-your-wildest-dreams opulence of the two Royal Suites (available at the wallet-busting price of Dhs.45,000 a night). At 70 square metres, the Signature Suite may not be vast, but it is certainly very comfortable and much has been made of the space available. The part-Arabic, part-Asian decor has a distinctively residential quality to it, so that you feel you are staying in a luxurious city apartment, rather than a hotel. Each suite has its own private balcony, complete with a pair of wicker sun loungers and of course a stunning city view. Back inside the room, the large, plush bed faces the windows and an inviting L-shaped couch faces the huge flat-screen TV, which swivels on its base so that you can also watch from the bed. Unique amenities such as an iPod docking station and a Lavazza coffee machine add to the luxury.

The bathroom is nothing short of superb, with soft lighting, neutral, earthy tones and spa amenities (the shower gel, shampoo and body lotion even come in a pyramid-shaped trio of bottles). The large corner bath invites lingering, and the separate rain shower is an invigorating addition. Shutter windows open up from the bathroom into the living area, creating a sense of space.

The hotel swimming pool features an intricate water fountain clock that not only creates a

tranquil ambience, but also tells the time. Wicker loungers and sheltered seating pods surround the pool, and thanks to a surface cooling system, you'll never singe the soles of your feet on the paving. It's a place for relaxing and keeping cool, although if you do want to do some exercise, there are two training pools (a bit like treadmills for swimmers) off to the side. The hotel also boasts a beautiful botanical garden, built to reflect the four elements of earth, wind, fire and water.

The Raffles Amrita Spa, on the fourth floor, is definitely one of the star attractions. Flooded with natural daylight, the spa common areas are an inviting and tranquil spot to spend an hour or two de-stressing. There are five treatment rooms and a couples' suite, where you can enjoy a range of top-notch treatments as well as the decadently extravagant signature gold facial.

Raffles' restaurant offerings are superb and already renowned as some of the best in the city. Noble House, the 17th floor Chinese fine-dining outlet, swept a recent restaurant awards, despite only having been open for a matter of months. But all accolades are well deserved; from the moment you are seated at your table and being treated to an elaborate tea-pouring ritual by the resident tea master, you know that this is no ordinary restaurant. Asiana, on the same floor, offers delectable far eastern cuisine for lunch and dinner. Upstairs from Asiana is the New Asia Bar, which is an ideal location for a pre-dinner cocktail and, as it turns into a nightclub at around midnight, a great place to end the evening too. Various theme nights bring in the crowds; Thursdays are international nights, Friday is house, Sunday is a popular 80s night and Wednesday brings the urban sounds of R&B and hip-hop. Upstairs yet again, in the pinnacle of the pyramid, you'll find the city's big spenders, movers and shakers in the China Moon Bar, which screams exclusivity from the distinctive stairs (lit up to look like champagne bubbles) to the Dhs.5,000 per table minimum spend (on weekends).

Fire & Ice is the Raffles signature restaurant, and offers the unique gastronomical concept of preparing food using liquid nitrogen. The brick walls, open kitchen and large wine cellar, offering 600 different labels, make this a restaurant you will enjoy for many different reasons. If the thought of the ice menu is a little extreme, you can enjoy the fire menu, which features a delectable range of grilled dishes. Rounding out the food and beverage options in the hotel are the Crossroads Cocktail Bar, where you can enjoy signature cocktail the Dubai Sling (based on the more famous Singapore Sling), and Azure, which features all-day dining.

As city breaks go, you will find it difficult to beat the unique qualities of Raffles Dubai, which has stormed on to the hotel scene to give other five-star hotels a serious run for their money in terms of top spot. The luxury of its suites, the tranquility of its spa, and the quality of its restaurants make this an ultimate location for a weekend away.

Contact
Phone: +971-4 324 8888
Email: dubai@raffles.com
Web: www.raffles.com

Location
Sheikh Rashid Road, Dubai. Raffles is located next to Wafi City, on Sheikh Rashid Road between Zaabeel Park and the Grand Hyatt.

Food & Drink
Raffles Salon – afternoon tea • Crossroads – cocktails • Azure – international • Fire & Ice – contemporary • Asiana – Far Eastern • Noble house – Chinese • New Asia – bar & club • China Moon – champagne bar

Features
Spa • Botanical gardens • Boutique • Swimming pools • Babysitting service

Nearby
Wafi Mall (www.wafi.com) • Dubai Museum (www.dubaitourism.ae) • Dubai Creek • BurJuman (www.burjuman.com)

The Westin Dubai Mina Seyahi

The new star name on the block, before Atlantis opened its doors, The Westin Mina Seyahi is a striking, neoclassical European-style residence on Beach Road just before the entrance to Dubai Marina. Opened in May 2008, The Westin is twinned with its neighbour, the longstanding Dubai favourite Le Meridien Mina Seyahi, to form one large beach resort where guests of either establishment can take advantage of both sets of facilities. The entrance to the grounds is particularly grand, with the ornate renaissance-style architecture and fountain adding a touch of class before you've set foot inside. Through the doors, the lobby area is vast, in both floor area

and height. Step beyond the check-in reception through to a large, relaxed communal area, with formal sofas and designer armchairs scattered over a marble-tiled floor. Guests can enjoy coffee or drinks here, get stuck into some reading material from the library shelves round the perimeter, and listen to live music played from the grand piano in the evening. The lobby's centrepiece is the 30 foot designer chandelier that hangs from the domed ceiling of the atrium, and the Roman floor mosaic that sits beneath it. The mosaic took a team of Italian craftsmen six months to put in place, and if you want to get a full view of it, head up to the seventh floor and peer over – it takes on a clever 3D perspective when viewed from above.

The lobby and atrium may be vast, but the rooms are spacious yet homely. Tastefully decorated in creams and browns, they are stylishly finished, with some excellent modern touches. A 42 inch LCD television hooks up to a DVD player, for which you can borrow movies from the reception. A chrome remote control panel, operating everything from lights to air conditioning and electrical appliances, sits next to the bed. And, possibly uniquely but definitely appropriately for a hotel room, it's the bed that's the centrepiece. The signature Westin Heavenly Bed is used in all of the hotel chain's premises worldwide, and the

design was a result of extensive research that involved a host of sleepers who gave their opinion after lying down on the job. The result is that it works like a dream – you won't want to get up in the morning (they're so popular that The Westin actually sells the bed to smitten guests). Something that will help you wake up from your Heavenly slumber though is the in-room coffee-making facility – this is no sachet of instant and a plastic kettle; here, in keeping with the Italian flavour of the hotel, you get your very own state-of-the-art espresso machine to kickstart yourself. The minibar also goes one step further, extending to offering a mini-cosmetics and a mini-accessories shop, with various useful and luxury items in the cupboard available for purchase. Not all the rooms are sea-facing (approximately 20% look towards the road and Dubai Media City), so request a beachfront one when booking if you're after that relaxing sea panorama. Also worth asking for is one with a balcony, which provides a lovely spot for having breakfast. Adjacent rooms can also connect to form family rooms.

The hotel is particularly family oriented at weekends. Down at sea level, there are three swimming pools to choose from – a kids' play pool, a lap pool, and the impressive 150m long winding pool, which snakes along the entire front of the hotel. There's also the Penguin Club to keep little ones busy with games and entertainment while parents take it easy. Kicking back on the beach is a relaxing experience; the beachfront feels like a secluded spot, sheltered by the Palm Jumeirah to the north and the marina wall to the south. As with all the facilities, Westin guests also have access to Le Meridien's Waterports Centre, from which you can get wet in a variety of sporty ways. Sailing, waterskiing, wakeboarding and boat charters are all offered. For leisure time of a more sedate nature, the Heavenly Spa offers treatments for both men and women.

Eating and drinking is an area where The Westin excels. Coffees, high teas, snacks, and the signature 'Jing tea' are all available from

The Atrium in the lobby. Here you'll also find Sin, which serves up enough cocoa varieties of food and drink to make any chocoholic laugh and cry all at the same time.

The Blue Orange is the hotel's 24 hour eatery, serving international food, buffet style, with the fare freshly prepared from live cooking stations. More specialist cuisine is offered at The Spice Emporium, which dishes up firey Asian dishes, from Indian to east Asian, while hearty meat lovers can opt for a steak in Hunter's Room & Grill.

If you're visiting The Westin in the cooler months, the outdoor pizza terrace at Bussola is a fantastic option, while the indoor area below serves up more classical fare.

For evening entertainment, there are a couple of lively bars – the buzzing Senyar, which also serves tapas, and the classy Oeno, a split-level wine bar that has an impressive cellar and a delightful cheese shop (you can take tasting courses in both). Both bars have live entertainment in the evening too, and you've also got all the food and drink outlets at Le Meridien to choose from as well – including Dubai's most popular beach bar, Barasti.

Contact
Phone: +971 4 399 4141
Email: serviceexpress.dubai@westin.com
Web: www.westin.com

Location
Al Sufouh Road (Beach Road) at the entrance to Dubai Marina, next to Le Meridien Mina Seyahi and opposite Media City.

Food & Drink
• Blue Orange – international • Bussola – Italian • Spice Emporium – Asian • Hunter's Room & Grill – steakhouse • Senyar – bar • Oeno – wine bar

Features
Three pools • Heavenly Spa • Watersports centre • Beach volleyball • Gym • Tennis courts • Conference facilities • Ballroom • Kids' club

Nearby
Dubai Marina • Mall of the Emirates (www.malloftheemirates.com) • Emirates Golf Club (www.dubaigolf.com) • The Montgomerie (www.themontgomerie.com) • The Palm Jumeirah (www.thepalm.ae)

Dubai

XVA Art Hotel

The XVA is one of Dubai's most interesting art galleries – not least because of its unique position in the heart of the restored area of Bastakiya, where the city's rarely seen history and heritage are on display at every turn. The museum itself is located in a converted traditional windtower; buildings that were designed to trap every whisper of the wind and funnel it down to the rooms below in the days before air conditioning. Apart from a fascinating collection of art, the museum is home to what is undoubtedly one of Dubai's hidden gems – a little hotel on the upper level. With just eight rooms, you'll feel like you're part of an elite group of hipsters who have rejected the glitz and glamour of the beachfront resorts in favour of a quiet weekend in 'real' Dubai. You won't find modern touches like in-room LCD television screens, DVD players, work stations and remote-control curtains, but if that is likely to disappoint you, XVA is probably not your cup of tea. Instead, the hotel appeals to a discerning audience, one that appreciates fine art, local culture and a tranquil atmosphere. Rooms are cosy but adequate, and all have en suite bathrooms. Unlike the uniformity you'll find in most hotels, here each room has been lovingly and individually decorated, and features the works of local artists. If you choose to stay in the hotel's master suite, you will have more room, as well as your own personal terrace, from where you can survey the hustle and bustle of the Bur Dubai district and gaze across the rooftops towards Deira. Free Wi-Fi is available throughout the hotel. As already mentioned, there are no TVs in the rooms, but there is a communal TV lounge off the central courtyard, equipped with a TV, a video player (how retro), comfy seating and relaxing lighting.

Inside your room you'll find a fridge with a small selection of snacks for when hunger strikes, but it's unlikely you'll need it after a delicious dinner prepared by the in-house chef. In cooler months you can enjoy your meals in the courtyard; in summer, however, you'll want to seek out a table in the air-conditioned lounge area.

Many of the soft furnishings throughout the hotel have been hand-crafted by the XVA's very own tailor, using a selection of fabrics found at the nearby textile souk. The tailor is on hand to create personal items of clothing for hotel guests, should you wish to take a unique souvenir home with you. A range of his designs can also be purchased from the shop, which is located at the entrance to the gallery. You'll also find some very creative little gifts and knick-knacks in there.

The XVA has its own abra on the creek, with plenty of room for a group of people. It is possible to arrange dinner on board by prior arrangement. The abra captain will sail you up and down the creek for as long as you like while you enjoy the views (although since the abra has no loo onboard, your ability to ignore the call of nature may dictate how long you stay on the water).

The eight rooms at the XVA Gallery may not match other hotels for luxury, modernity or five-star service, but if you're looking for a charming base from which to explore Dubai's most interesting historical area, and maybe enjoy some souk shopping, you're always welcome.

Bastakiah Nights
There are some meals where the mood is as important as the food – Bastakiah Nights, right near the XVA Gallery, combines the two effortlessly. Choose from fixed menus or individual a la carte items, and enjoy the blend of local cuisine with authentic local culture. 04 353 7772

Contact
Phone: +971 4 353 5383
Email: xva@xvagallery.com
Web: www.xvagallery.com

Location
Bastakiya, Bur Dubai, next to the creek and near to Dubai Museum.

Food & Drink
XVA Cafe – vegetarian

Features
100 year old Dubai house • Art-furnished boutique hotel • Wireless internet access • Traditional courtyards • Wind towers • Art gallery on premises

Nearby
Dubai Museum • Abra station • BurJuman (www.burjuman.com) • Deira fish market • Gold souk • Carrefour • Creek Park • Al Meena Bazaar • Art galleries

Abu Dhabi

Dubai might get most of the international recognition, but it's Abu Dhabi that is both the UAE's biggest emirate and capital city – and is a must-see destination for anyone living in the region.

Much like the relationship between Sydney and Canberra, or New York City and Washington DC, Dubai is widely seen as the glamorous commercial boomtown of the UAE while steady Abu Dhabi is the federal centre. Life in the capital is certainly more calming and less hectic than madcap Dubai, but if as a Dubai resident you fancy getting away for a break in a city where being the flashiest or the biggest isn't everything, and where building is largely (at least comparatively) complete, then a stay in the capital is just the ticket.

In between the calm green gardens, high-rise apartment blocks, elegant fountains, stunning Corniche and the luxury villas is a city brimming with vibrancy and plenty of places to explore. The island city of Abu Dhabi is growing rapidly, and its evolution from quiet village to thriving metropolis has been remarkable. It's not just the size and shape of buildings that will impress in Abu Dhabi either – there's a serious emphasis on cultural and entertainment experiences too. From exhibits of artists such as Picasso and concerts by the likes of Elton John at the Emirates Palace, to forthcoming attractions such as the Formula One Grand Prix course on Yas Island and the UAE's very own proposed Guggenheim museum, there's much of interest to get involved in.

The Corniche itself is designed for play, with beautiful parks, walkways, cycle paths and picnic areas all bordering the turquoise waters of the Arabian Gulf. Further inland,

Clockwise from top left: Liwa, Marina Mall, National Bank of Abu Dhabi

Abu Dhabi

the skyscrapers make way for beautiful villas, low-rise apartment blocks and quieter, tree-lined streets, where local life plays out among public gardens and hidden palaces.

Travelling around the island will provide plenty of photo opportunities. The city is known for its many fountains and its public art; Cannon Square dominates the surrounding buildings with its magnificent water fountain and enormous concrete replicas of traditional Arabic artefacts, and there are several souks selling all kinds of wares.

To the east of the capital, but still within the Abu Dhabi emirate, is Al Ain, a picturesque oasis town on the edge of the desert and on the border with Oman, while to the south-west lies the Rub Al Khali (Empty Quarter), the largest sand desert in the world. It's a beguiling but harsh landscape, populated only with pockets of habitability, including the spectacular Liwa Oasis.

Other Areas

Al Ain

Al Ain is the second city in the Abu Dhabi emirate, and of great historic significance in the UAE. Its location on ancient trading routes between Oman and the Arabian Gulf meant that the oasis was of strategic importance, and the source of longstanding disputes for the UAE, Oman and Saudi Arabia. The city actually straddles the border with the Sultanate of Oman; the UAE side is known as Al Ain and the Oman side as Buraimi. In more recent times, it gained special status as the birthplace of the first ruler of the United Arab Emirates, the late, revered Sheikh Zayed. Commonly known as 'The Garden City', Al Ain features oases and lovely patches of greenery, as does Buraimi. The shady oasis is a pleasant stretch of vegetation among the harsh surroundings, and the palm plantations have plenty of examples of the ancient 'falaj' irrigation system.

Already naturally fertile, Sheikh Zayed instigated a programme to 'green' the city. The seven natural oases are now set amid tree-lined streets and beautiful urban parks,

all of which make the city a very pleasant place to drive around.

Its unique archaeological heritage and historic identity means that Al Ain is home to a variety of interesting sights and attractions. Hili Archaeological Garden is the source of many ancient finds, most of which are now displayed in Al Ain Museum, where displays of traditional Bedouin life and photographs show how much the area has changed. Hili Fun City offers entertainment for the whole family, while Al Ain Wildlife Park & Resort is a modern and enjoyable animal park with lots to see for all ages.

Liwa

The Liwa oasis sits at the entrance to the Rub Al Khali. For 650,000 square kilometres the surrounding landscape offers a breathtaking panorama in the world's largest continuous area of sand. Most of it is uninhabitable, with Bedouin tribes occupying only the outer fringes of the desert. The Liwa area, situated on the perimeter of the desert, is a fertile crescent that stretches over 150 kilometres, and is dotted with many small villages.

The emptiness and size of this area offers a unique location that is largely unscathed by mass tourism, providing peaceful exploration for those keen on a sandy adventure.

The main gateway to the desert is through the town of Mezaira'a. It holds little more than a few grocery stores and a petrol station, and most visitors are either on their way to the Empty Quarter or are seeking a peaceful break at the white converted sheikh's palace sitting at the top of a sand dune – Liwa Hotel (p.148).

Accommodation Options

If you want a weekend visit to Abu Dhabi but fancy something a little different to the hotels featured in this book, there are plenty of other accommodation options in the capital.

If you really like to indulge, then look no further than Emirates Palace (02 690 9000, www.emiratespalace.com), Abu Dhabi's answer to Dubai's Burj Al Arab. For the price of a week's holiday at most other establishments, you can book one of the

To the south-west of Abu Dhabi lies the beguiling, harsh landscape of the Rub Al Khali, the largest sand desert in the world.

Abu Dhabi

Sir Bani Yas Island

This idyllic island, home to an abundance of wildlife, is now accessible to guests of the Desert Islands Resort & Spa. Promoting the perfect mix of nature and luxury, this new resort offers a beautiful collection of rooms and suites, various bars and restaurants and a swanky spa. Guests can explore the island on foot, by bike, or in an air-conditioned 4WD, while the waters surrounding the island are excellent for diving. +971 2 801 5400, www.anantara.com

spectacularly opulent hotel's 394 suites for a night and live like, or quite possibly next to, royalty.

In fact, a recent promotion at Emirates Palace is its Million Dollar package, which will cost you exactly $1 million. If you've got that kind of cash, you can look forward to first-class flights from any international destination (with Etihad), a seven-night stay in the Palace Suite, a chauffeur-driven luxury car at your disposal for the entire week, daytrips in a private jet to Iran, Jordan and Bahrain, plus a selection of luxurious spa treatments, activities, and gifts. Back in the real world, most international big name chains have a presence in the city, such as Rotana (02 644 3000, www.rotana.com), Crowne Plaza (02 621 0000,

www.crowneplaza.com), Le Meridien (02 644 6666, www.lemeridienabudhabi.ae) and Sheraton (02 677 3333, www.sheraton.com). There are local three and four-star options too, including the Al Ain Palace Hotel (02 679 4777, www.alainpalacehotel.com), known locally as 'Ally Pally', Al Diar group of hotels (www.aldiarhotels.com), Al Sharia Hotel (02 563 8557) and the Saba Hotel (02 644 8333). For those who like a stylish city break, The Village (02 495 2000, www.onetoonehotels. com) is a boutique hotel perfectly positioned for pounding the pavement and has a number of pools to cool off afterwards. If you're travelling from afar and arriving by air, the Abu Dhabi Airport Hotel (02 575 7377) is a convenient spot to rest up.

In Al Ain, options include the Hilton Al Ain (03 768 6666) and the three-star Ain Al Fayda Hotel (03 783 8333). Another Al Ain option is the fully furnished Green Mubazzarah Chalets (03 783 9555), set at the base of Jebel Hafeet in an open public park with plenty of green spaces for a picnic, or afternoon lounging in the sun. The park has a toboggan run, miniature railway and boating lake, as well as natural hot springs.

Above: Carpet Shop, Below: Cultural Foundation

Camping

Campsites are impossible to find in Abu Dhabi city, but the emirate of Abu Dhabi boasts the country's most spectacular camping spot of all: Liwa. It will blow you away with its massive expanses of amazing desert, and the biggest dunes this side of the Sahara. Adventurous off-road driving and incredible scenery make the long trip well worth it.

While there are hotels in Liwa, camping is the most popular way to spend the night, and can be an unforgettable experience. Go to bed enjoying the magical, silvery appearance of unspoiled dunes under the moonlight, and wake up to views of endless waves of sand rolling away into the distance. You can camp just about anywhere, so take any of the roads or tracks into the desert off the main road through the oasis. Find somewhere near to where you'd like to start the next day's driving, but make sure that you are far enough away from roads, habitation and activity to pitch in a peaceful spot. Try to get settled in your campsite long before the sun goes down, both for safety reasons and so that you can enjoy the sunset.

One particularly good camping area is on the road to Moreeb Hill, passing the Liwa Resthouse. This minor paved road heads into the desert for 11.5km, leading you into some of the best dunes, and crossing many sabkha flats – any one of which allows you to get off road and into some sheltered areas, far from disturbances, easily and in quite a short time. If you want to camp near Al Ain, you'll find some good desert and mountain spots on routes to north of the city that are suitable for pitching up. There are some nice dunes off the Mahdah to Madam road, as well as just out of the city limits off the Airport Road See the *UAE Off Road Explorer* for all you need to know about heading off the beaten track.

Shopping

If shopping is your preferred activity on a weekend away, you won't be disappointed in Abu Dhabi. The number of malls rival Dubai for choice, while the souks and markets give an interesting, cheaper alternative. The attractive, imaginatively designed modern shopping centres are a major draw to the city, particularly during summer when the air conditioning offers a welcome relief from the stifling temperatures.

Highlights include the recently expanded Marina Mall (02 681 8300, www.marinamall. ae), situated on the Breakwater, which as well as a huge range of fashion and other retail outlets also features a cinema, bowling alley, ice rink and snow park.

Of equal importance on the local scene is Abu Dhabi Mall (02 645 4858, www. abudhabi-mall.com), which, with more than 200 retail outlets, is one of the country's largest shopping centres. It's a family-friendly place, with facilities for babies and kids and a sizeable foodcourt to help keep those shopping energy levels up.

A new arrival is the glistening Al Wahda Mall off Airport Road (02 446 6622, www.alwahda-mall.com), which contains some pleasant European restaurants, as well as a spacious sunroof design.

If you like your shopping experiences a little less rarefied, there are several souks in town where you can hone your bargaining skills, or simply stand back and watch the action; at the Fish, Fruit and Vegetable Souk at Port Zayed you can get up close and personal to a great range of fresh (and odorous) produce. Get there early for the best fish action – catches start to be unloaded from as early as 04:30. For goods that have a lengthier sell-by date, head to the Gold Souk in Madinat Zayed for a huge choice of jewellery and watches. There's an interesting souk in Al Ain too, although the wares on offer here are more modern domestic than old Arabian, and also a huge shopping centre in the Garden City – Al Ain Mall (03 766 0333), complete with all the usual mall-based entertainments.

Going Out

As befits a capital city, pretty much any type of food you want is available in Abu Dhabi – from hotel restaurants to local cheap and cheerful cafes, there's a diverse range. The swankiest places to eat are undoubtedly to be

Rappelling down Jebel Hafeet

Abu Dhabi

Father Information
The name Abu Dhabi translates to 'Father of the Gazelle', and was named so by the Baniyas tribe in the late 1700s due to the abundant wildlife found on the island.

found in the top-end hotels (also the place to go if you want a glass or two of wine with your meal, due to licensing restrictions).

Most large hotels have at least two or three restaurants. However, you should not miss the opportunity to eat at one of the many local roadside cafes and independent restaurants, where you can often find the most authentic regional cuisine from India, Sri Lanka and the Middle East.

The only real culinary hardship you'll encounter in a city with so many choices is deciding where to eat first. Below are some of Explorer's recommended outlets:

Al Fanar – Magnificent panoramic views of the city and the Corniche await at this revolving restaurant, as does top-quality international cuisine. Le Royal Meridien, 02 674 2020

Al Mawal – Welcoming staff bring baskets of bread and olives to your table while you select a range of dishes from the exhaustive Lebanese menu. Hilton International Abu Dhabi, 02 672 7337

Cristal – This tranquil champagne and cigar bar is perfect for a posh night of luxurious decor, bottles of bubbly and live jazz. Millennium Hotel, 02 626 2700

Kwality – Authentic Indian food, from north Indian tandoori to Goan dishes, at a great price. Delicious appetisers like naans, spicy poppadoms and tangy chutney make your mouth water. Al Salam Street, 02 672 7337

Mezzaluna – A heavenly Italian eatery in the regal Emirates Palace. Fresh pasta, seafood creations and succulent meat dishes are all delicious, and the prices are reasonable. Emirates Palace, 02 690 7070

Rosebuds – Serving an international buffet for breakfast, lunch and dinner, and offering one of the city's most popular family Friday brunches, Rosebuds is always a good choice. Beach Rotana, 02 644 3000

Sayad – Superb seafood, luxury touches and a wine list that features the top eight varieties from every wine-producing region in the world combine to make this a sublime experience. Emirates Palace, 02 690 7033

Zaitoun – An award-winning restaurant with wonderful service. The menu is a good mix of traditional and modern with an Arabic twist. Great specials and personal recommendations from the staff make this a standout venue. Danat Resort Jebel Dhanna, 02 801 2222

Downtown Abu Dhabi

Abu Dhabi Corniche

The grand Corniche is the heart of the city and a great place to pause and gaze out to sea. It's beautifully landscaped and is a popular spot for runners, walkers, roller bladers and cyclists. The Corniche is currently being upgraded and will eventually feature new restaurants, amusement centres, parks and shopping malls. Taking one of the boat cruises that run along the coast offers a good alternative perspective.

Grand Mosque

The newly finished Sheikh Zayed Grand Mosque, one of the world's largest, most beautiful Islamic places of worship, stands at the entrance to the city, and is arguably the country's most impressive piece of architecture. The $350 million project features stunning traditional design, has a Makrana marble facade and provides space for 40,000 worshippers.

Al Ain Oasis

The impressive oasis in Al Ain is home to many palm plantations, most of which are still working farms. You are free to wander through the cool and shady area, where all you'll hear is birdsong and the rustle of the palm fronds. Some farms have signs welcoming visitors inside, and there are plenty of examples of 'falaj', the traditional irrigation system. Just next door is the atmospheric Livestock Souk, full of local colour.

Dune Bashing

If your car can take the heat, follow the locals at Liwa as they ride the ridges and climb the slopes of some of the biggest dunes in the UAE. If you haven't got the appropriate wheels, you can hire a dune buggy. The routes around Sabkha are a good challenge, but you can choose a path as arduous as you like.

Must-Do Experiences

Whether you're looking for city attractions or desert adventures, Abu Dhabi has a range of features to help you plan your ideal weekend.

Abu Dhabi

Al Raha Beach

The best maintained public beach in Abu Dhabi, Al Raha has some excellent facilities. One section is for women only, and the other is open to all. For those on a budget, staying in a city centre hotel, or looking to get away from the more confined hotel-based beach settings, this is definitely the place to go.

Camel Market

Al Ain's camel market is the last of its kind in the UAE, and provides an excellent opportunity to view the 'ships of the desert' up close, and to see and hear the traders discussing the price and merits of their animals. Although it is only open in the mornings, it is always busy and offers some excellent photo opportunities, but be careful where you point your lens and always seek permission first.

Heritage Village

For a look into the history and culture of the Abu Dhabi region, check out the Heritage Village. It offers a glimpse into a way of living that is far removed from the city life that exists today. Test the effectiveness of a wind-tower, the earliest form of air-conditioning, or get up close to a camel or Arabian horse.

Al Ain Rotana

to bedtime. The en suite bathroom is bigger than some small apartments with luxury toiletries and the obligatory fluffy bathrobe. Each room has the usual amenities such as internet connection and satellite TV, plus an extensive room service menu and well-stocked minibar in case you don't feel like leaving the comfort of your room.

If traipsing through the hotel to your room is too much effort, try one of the self-contained villas that overlook the pool. Spread over two floors, the villas are furnished to a high standard, and come with a personal car parking space. Ideal for longer stays, or bigger groups, you can cook up your own feast in the modern kitchen and then dine while enjoying the views from the terrace.

Outside of the rooms, the large pool and Jacuzzi are a great place for a day of relaxation, while for those keen on working up a sweat, the sauna, fitness centre, and choice of two squash and tennis courts will help rid the stresses of a working week. Strictly speaking, the hotel does not have a spa, but Bodylines, the health and fitness centre, offers a range of massages in addition to aerobics classes. Kids are well catered for with their own shaded pool and a play area.

After a hard day by the pool, the diverse selection of eating and drinking venues will

Nestled close to the Oman border, Al Ain is far removed from hectic city life, making it a great option for a break with a change of pace. Fittingly, while the Al Ain Rotana may be a five-star hotel, it has none of the pretensions of many of its big city contemporaries, opting instead for understated style and good service. There are no gold statues or gimmicks when you walk into the lobby, just an impressive emphasis on the friendliness of the staff. Having recently undergone renovation, the hotel now boasts 200 rooms and suites. All are well designed, presented with crisp white linen and pillows that sink perfectly when it comes

leave you spoilt for choice. Trader Vic's is a large restaurant and cocktail bar, offering a varied menu featuring dishes that range from delicious noodles to juicy steak, flambéed at your table – not one to order if you don't like being the centre of attention. If you are more into cocktails than coq au vin there is a large bar area, and with an extensive drinks menu you're likely to be tempted into trying a couple, but be warned: they are potent. Min Zaman, an authentic Lebanese restaurant, is a more refined affair that is quiet until just before midnight, when the music cranks up and an impressive belly dancer wriggles her way around the room. The decor may be plain with a slightly formal feel (before the entertainment starts), but the food is full of flavour, and the array of colourful dishes set out before you make for a visual feast. The staff are happy to advise what's what, or give personal recommendations and suggested combinations; the best option is to order a few dishes to share. Because this is a popular spot for local residents who usually dine late, you may find you have the restaurant to yourself before 22:00.

If it's too difficult to make a culinary decision, why not have a bit of everything at Gardinia. All-day dining is available if hunger strikes early, and the buffet has something to suit most palates. Breakfast here brings plenty of choice too, and is the perfect opportunity to pile your plate high and refuel after one too many the night before in Trader Vic's.

The Rotana is an ideal base for exploring the visitor attractions of Al Ain, such as the zoo, or even a drive to the top of Jebel Hafeet. While the interior may not be as flashy as some, it is certainly luxurious enough to leave the sightseeing for another trip. The small but personal touches make the hotel stand out, whether that is returning from dinner to find your bed turned down and fluffy slippers at the side, or the staff remembering your name.

Contact
Phone: +971 3 754 5111
Email: alain.hotel@rotana.com
Web: www.rotana.com

Location
The Rotana is situated on Sheikh Zayed Road in Al Ain between the Glazlan and Moatared Roundabouts, just off the E22 road that connects Al Ain with Abu Dhabi. If you are coming into Al Ain from Dubai on the E66, take a right at the Clock Tower Roundabout.

Food & Drink
Trader Vic's – Polynesian food & cocktail bar • Min Zaman – Lebanese • Gardinia – Mediterranean • Atrium Café • Aquarius – poolside drinks and snacks

Features
Duplex villas • Children's pool • Leisure and fitness club • Squash courts

Nearby
Al Ain Golf Club • Al Ain Mall (www.alainmall.org) • Al Ain National Museum (www.aam.gov.ae) • Al Ain Oasis • Al Ain Wildlife Park & Resort • Gold Souk • Green Mubazzarah Park • Hili Archaeological Garden • Hili Fun City • Jahili Fort & Park • Jebel Hafeet

Al Raha Beach Hotel

Al Raha Beach Hotel is located on the coast of the mainland, sheltered by the islands of Abu Dhabi, and is one of the first inhabitants of what will, in a few years, be the in-demand Al Raha Beach area.

At time of writing, apart from the hotel and neighbouring Al Raha Mall, there isn't much else in the vicinity – but that's one of the plus points. Al Raha Beach Hotel has all the resort trimmings that you need for a weekend break, and its relative isolation makes it all the more desirable as a location where you can really get away from it all.

One of the first things that will strike you about the hotel (once you've got over the grandeur of the lobby, complete with marble tiling and gold leaf ceiling) is the size of the rooms. The standard rooms are generously sized, with plenty of floor space, so you can spare yourself that small-room shimmy around the furniture every time you need to go to the bathroom. Huge beds, a work desk, an alcove with a minibar and tea and coffee-making facilities, and a large, bright bathroom make this the kind of hotel where you can spend a bit of time in your room, in total comfort. If you're in the mood for extravagance you can check into an executive, diplomatic or royal suite, where big bucks equals big benefits.

The leisure facilities at Al Raha are quite spectacular, and it could be argued that this is the primary reason to consider this hotel as your next weekend getaway. The main swimming pool, with an infinity horizon, is large and inviting, bordered by comfy sun loungers and attentive waiters. The nearby children's pool goes above and beyond what most kids would expect – it is part swimming pool and part aqua playground. Never deeper than about half a metre, the shallow centre is home to a vast climbing frame, complete with slides – you'll have a hard time getting your brood to leave the water. Fortunately, the sun loungers are never far away, so you can indulge in some lazy sunbathing while the kids tire themselves out within your line of sight. The hotel gym is similarly large and well equipped, with modern equipment, an aerobics studio, squash courts and a team of personal trainers. The third floor of the hotel houses the hotel spa, with three treatment rooms offering a range of massages, facials and scrubs. The treatment rooms are located around the large, tranquil indoor swimming pool and Jacuzzi, lit from above by attractive skylights. All these leisure facilities add value to your weekend break, but there is a downside. The hotel offers health club memberships to non-guests, and given the facilities, it is hugely popular. This means that, on a Friday, the swimming pool can feel a little overcrowded, which may not suit those who like a bit of calm while swimming.

There's an adequate collection of food and beverage establishments within the hotel grounds. For light meals around the pool, you can eat at La Piscine or walk along the boardwalk to Al Manzil. The latter is actually located near the pool for the luxury villas (also part of the hotel), and although only villa residents may use the pool, hotel guests are welcome to eat here. Back at the main pool, La Piscine also does regular barbecues and is a popular shisha cafe after 19:00.

The Sevilla restaurant, just off the lobby, is the hotel's all-day dining outlet. It serves an impressive and varied buffet for breakfast, lunch and dinner, and a la carte options are also available. Sevilla does a popular Asian-themed buffet on a Wednesday night, and a Mediterranean offering on Mondays. The Black Pearl Piano Bar is open till late and serves a wide range of beers, wines and cocktails; there is live music most nights. Finally, the Enigma nightclub, with its huge dancefloor surrounded by bars, offers an eclectic mix of music, including Arabic pop on Wednesdays and a Bollywood night on Saturdays.

There's no doubt that the Al Raha Beach area is yet to be fully developed, and the out-of-city location may not appeal to all. But with five-star leisure facilities and great rooms, it's definitely worth a visit for a weekend getaway.

Abu Dhabi

Contact
Phone: +971 2 508 0555
Email: info@danatresortalraha.ae
Web: www.danathotelgroup.com

Location
Located approximately halfway along the E10 road that connects the E11 Dubai and E22 Al Ain roads. Al Raha Beach is on the right as you approach from Dubai.

Food & Drink
Sevilla Restaurant – international • Al Manzil Clubhouse • La Piscine – snacks and shisha • The Black Pearl Piano Bar • Enigma – nightclub

Features
Sea views • Swimming pool • Health club • Spa • Squash courts

Nearby
Abu Dhabi Golf Club (www.adgolfclub.com) • Al Ghazal Golf Club (www.alghazalgolf.ae) • Al Raha Beach • Al Raha Mall • Mangroves • Maqtaa Fort • Sheikh Zayed Grand Mosque • Yas Island

A two-hour drive across desert plains from Abu Dhabi, the five-star Danat resort is a welcome sight after the long journey.

The hotel is modest in size, which gives it an intimate feel; staff are friendly and the service has a personal touch. The resort manages to strike the perfect balance between being quiet and relaxing, with a pervading air of calm, and being a family-friendly destination where kids are allowed to be kids.

Modern, comfortable rooms with sweeping sea views are the order of the day. The usual amenities like robes and slippers, TV and satellite channels, plenty of wardrobe space and large, fully equipped bathrooms help you

Abu Dhabi

Danat Resort Jebel Dhanna

settle in and leave all stresses at the door. The beautiful white sandy beach that skirts the front of the resort is postcard perfect, and spending long periods lounging there while watching the crystal clear water lap gently on to the shore is certainly no hardship. The sea is shallow for quite a distance from the shore, so you can wander out and be alone with your thoughts, and the fish.

Comfy cushioned loungers await your return to shore; lie back, relax, and wait for the staff to come round with cold towels and Evian spritz to lower your chillout temperature even further. For a change of scenery, lay claim to one of the huge hammocks on the lawn, or book yourself a massage down by the beach. Those with an aversion to sand in their swimwear can hang out by the pool instead. Onsite activities include garden chess, arts and crafts, banana boats, kayaks, tennis, squash, waterskiing and windsurfing. A children's pool and play area keeps little ones busy, and there is also a gym and a spa for adults seeking a bit of me-time. Sailing, fishing and snorkelling trips can be arranged by the hotel.

As for food, this resort is home to Zaitoun, an award-winning restaurant that deserves all the praise it gets. The menu – full of modern Italian dishes, with an Arabic twist – is consistently excellent. Ask your waiter for any specials or recommendations and then try them – the personal touch found throughout the hotel extends to this restaurant and you won't leave disappointed.

Tides is the all-day dining outlet, where you can enjoy an international buffet for breakfast, lunch and dinner. Al Bahar serves fresh seafood, and can bring you a poolside meal as you work on your tan. You can also dine alfresco at Al Bahar, although only in the cooler months. The glass-fronted lobby cafe overlooks the hotel grounds, and is a pleasant spot to enjoy a nice cup of tea in the afternoon or a drink before dinner.

The resort doesn't go wild once the sun goes down, although it is a popular social venue for the employees of the nearby oil and gas plants. L'Attitude is a fairly popular pub with a dartboard, pool table and, most importantly, a generous happy hour. Live music and DJs pump up the atmosphere in the later hours. There aren't too many nearby attractions here, although there is a nationally important one: the recently reopened Sir Bani Yas Island, a haven for wildlife. Trees, lakes and olive groves provide a welcoming habitat for oryx, gazelles, giraffes and ostriches, in addition to 170 species of birds and butterflies. It is only accessible by boat, and there are three crossings a day (the hotel can arrange the boat trip for you).

Further afield, Delma Island features a fascinating insight into the culture and history of the region and its people. There are also several 'desert islands' – small spits of sand in the ocean, some of which will be developed with eco-resorts; again, there are regular boats to these from close to the hotel.

Jebel Dhanna lies within Al Gharbia region of Abu Dhabi emirate, so expect further attractions to roll out over the next few years as huge financial resources have been allocated to develop this area into an important ecotourism destination.

If you're not put off by the long drive, a weekend at Jebel Dhanna is certainly worth the trip for the quiet sense of isolation, the friendliness of the staff, who seem to appreciate just how far you've come, and of course for a meal in Zaitoun, which is almost worth the journey on its own.

Contact
Phone: +971 2 801 2222
Email: reservations@danatresortjd.ae
Web: www.danathotelgroup.com

Location
Jebel Dhanna is in Al Gharbia region, 240km west of Abu Dhabi along the E11. Once past Ruwais, you're almost there. Follow the signs and keep a look out for the signpost marking the turn-off to the Danat Resort.

Food & Drink
Tides – all-day dining bistro • Al Bahar – seafood and grill • Zaitoun – Arabic • L'Attitude – bar

Features
Wave pool • Swimming pool • Health club • Sauna • Tennis courts • Golf • Beach • Watersports

Nearby
Delma Island • Desert Islands (www.desertislands.com) • Sir Bani Yas Island

Hilton
Abu Dhabi

The huge lobby is home to a range of shops and amenities, as well as a business centre catering to the Hilton's working guests. There is also a hair salon, a florist, car hire desks and a beauty salon, plus several jewellery stores and a souvenir shop. Check-in is a friendly affair, facilitated by professional and multilingual staff, and an iced tea dispenser provides a refreshing start to your weekend. Rooms have all the usual amenities needed for a comfortable stay, including bathrobes and slippers, a great room service menu and a large TV with a selection of satellite channels. Ample in size, each room has a large bed, seating area and en suite bathroom, but the real showpiece is the view of the sea and the Corniche from the window.

An alluring feature of the Hilton is the private beach, pool and health club area which is situated across the road, and accessed using a pedestrian underpass. Here guests can use the gym, which is large and fitted out with a range of modern equipment, or opt to chill out by the beautiful open-air pool and bar. A selection of invigorating and relaxing treatments is available in the spa. You can enjoy various watersports, including sailing, windsurfing and snorkelling, on the beach, and there are floodlit tennis courts at the back of the hotel. Speak to any staff member about making full use of the sports facilities.

Abu Dhabi is arguably a little less glitzy than the logic-defying architecture of Dubai, or not quite as stunning as the mountainous backdrop of Muscat. But then you get to the Corniche, and you suddenly get why Abu Dhabi residents say they wouldn't live anywhere else. Wide walkways border the perfectly blue water, and a collection of fascinating islands (some dedicated to nature, some dedicated to tourism) can be seen just offshore. It is along this beautiful strip that the Hilton is situated, making it an excellent choice for weekend breakers looking for ocean views, leisurely walks and a fascinating window on the character of the city.

The Hilton houses some of the finest restaurants in Abu Dhabi, and is an important venue on the social scene for many local residents. Mawal is one of the most highly respected Lebanese restaurants in the region, and here you can enjoy traditional Arabic fare as well as live entertainment courtesy of a singer and belly dancer. Royal Orchid, open for lunch and dinner, is an elegant outlet serving cuisine from Thailand, Mongolia and China. The ultimate ambience, however, is to be found in Vasco's. It is situated across the street from the hotel, with tables arranged on a waterfront terrace overlooking the Gulf. Soft, pretty lighting and water fountains make it a wonderful romantic spot or a great place to take out-of-towners. Spot-on service and a vast international menu, featuring succulent steaks and seafood, seal the deal. Linger in the atmosphere a little longer while you wait for the chef to prepare your chocolate soufflé – sinful but worth it.

Hemingway's is the stuff of Abu Dhabi legends – popular with locals thanks to quiz nights, ladies' nights and live music. The Jazz Bar next door consistently features an excellent live band, as well as a great fusion menu for when those midnight munchies set in. Other outlets in the hotel include La Terrazza (Mediterranean) for all-day dining, Coconut Bay, a beachside restaurant serving light meals (open for lunch only), and BiCE, which is well known for its modern Italian menu and beautiful views.

Should you wish to leave the hotel to explore the surrounding area, or maybe take in a bit of shopping at nearby Marina Mall, there is a speedy taxi service available just outside the front entrance.

Contact
Phone: +971 2 681 1900
Email: auhhitw@eim.ae
Web: www.hilton.com

Location
The hotel is on the Corniche at the northwest corner of Abu Dhabi island. It is close to Emirates Palace and the road that connects to Marina Mall.

Food & Drink
La Terrazza – Mediterranean • The Jazz Bar & Dining – Fusion • Coconut Bay – Lunch • Vienna Plaza – cafe • BiCE – Italian • Hemmingway's – Latin American • Mawal – Lebanese • Royal Orchid – Asian • Vasco's – international

Features
Beach • Bicycling • Fishing • Fitness room • Playground • Kids' club • Sailing • Sightseeing tours • Snorkelling • Walking track • Windsurfing

Nearby
Abu Dhabi Mall (www.abudhabi-mall.com) • Abu Dhabi Golf Club (www.adgolfclub. com) • Al Ghazal Golf Club (www. alghazalgolf.ae) • Emirates Palace • Fish Market • Hemisphere Gallery (www.hemisphere.ae) • Heritage Village • Lulu Island • Marina Mall • Port Mina Zayed • Sheikh Zayed Grand Mosque

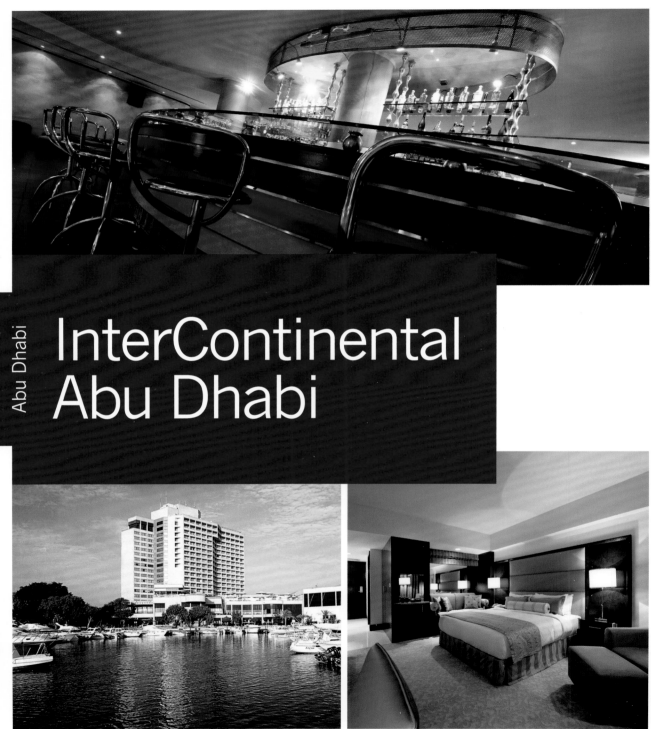

InterContinental
Abu Dhabi

Abu Dhabi

The subtle grandeur of the InterContinental Abu Dhabi is its characteristic feature: slender silver classical Greek columns gracing the reception, its marble floors leading effortlessly through to the centrepiece of the ground floor, the Piano Lounge, complete with pianist and chandeliers. A recent refurbishment has resulted in an air of modern elegance; it's the kind of place where you could imagine diplomats enjoying an evening cocktail or an earl grey tea in the afternoon.

Rooms are comfortable and of a reasonable size. Amenities such as interactive flat-screen TVs with satellite channels, a well-stocked minibar and 24 hour room service aim to make you feel right at home. Bathrooms have both wet and dry zones – an intriguing idea aimed at maximising your chillout period.

The large private beach has its own marina, and here you can enjoy a range of watersports, including jetskiing, waterskiing, or a thrilling ride on a giant inflatable. The health zone offers therapeutic massages, a well-equipped gym and tennis courts; a tennis pro is on hand to give lessons if needed.

The outdoor swimming pool is a gorgeous area and probably where you'll spend most of your weekend. A lovely bar serves refreshing drinks and light snacks throughout the day, and there is a good view of the marina down below. Families are welcome here; childcare and babysitting services can be arranged, and interconnecting rooms are available for groups or larger families. There is a grassed recreational area near the Fishmarket restaurant, and plenty of space for football on the beach of course.

The InterContinental is home to a good variety of food and beverage outlets. Selections is the all-day dining outlet, offering an excellent buffet for breakfast, lunch and dinner. Boccaccio is the place for delicious Italian fare, from risottos to pizzas, and has a terrace where you can enjoy alfresco dining in the cooler months; and Chamas, the new Brazilian restaurant, offers authentic food and lively entertainment in the evenings. One of the best-loved restaurants here is the Fishmarket, down by the marina. Select your choice of fresh seafood, from succulent lobster to catch of the day. A helpful waiter will then whisk it off to the kitchen where it will be prepared specially for you.

Party people can head to the onsite nightclub, a.m.p.m., where a resident DJ plays to a packed dancefloor. Despite being one of the city's hotspots, light sleepers needn't worry about the noise disturbing them – the club is tucked away and soundproof enough that you won't hear a thing.

Abu Dhabi

Contact
Phone: +971 2 666 6888
Email: abudhabi@interconti.com
Web: www.intercontinental.com

Location
The hotel is on Bainunah Street at the north-west corner of Abu Dhabi island. It is close to Emirates Palace.

Food & Drink
Fishmarket – seafood • Boccaccio – Italian • Selections – international • Chamas Brazilian Churrascaria – Brazilian • Piano Lounge – drinks & snacks • a.m.p.m. – nightclub

Features
Private beach • Sauna • Jacuzzi • Gym • Outdoor swimming pool • Tennis court • Squash court • Children's activities • Live entertainment • Newsstand • Beauty salon • Gift shop

Nearby
Abu Dhabi Mall (www.abudhabi-mall.com) • Abu Dhabi Golf Club (www.adgolfclub.com) • Al Ghazal Golf Club (www.alghazalgolf.ae) • Emirates Palace • Fish Market • Hemisphere Gallery (www.hemisphere.ae) • Heritage Village • Lulu Island • Marina Mall • Port Mina Zayed • Sheikh Zayed Grand Mosque

InterContinental Al Ain Resort

This resort appeals to all kinds of fun seekers: couples can enjoy romantic sundowners while taking in the dramatic scenery; party-goers can dance the night away in Luce, an Italian restaurant that transforms into a nightclub at midnight; and families can benefit from interconnecting rooms and a babysitting service. It is this mix-and-match approach to customer service that gives the hotel a unique, refreshing personality. The InterContinental Al Ain Resort seems to have no illusions of grandeur and instead is simply a very friendly, warm hotel where fun takes priority over opulence.

The rooms are spacious enough and each has a balcony with a view of either the pool and gardens, or of Jebel Hafeet. In-room facilities are as you would expect – minibar, internet, satellite TV, and a pillow menu should you be adverse to those provided.

There are two pools, one for a spot of volleyball or in-pool bar propping, and the other for the serious swimmers making a splash from starting blocks. Kids can wear themselves out in the dedicated play area and babies can paddle in the small but functional kids' pool. Just behind the paddling pool is a play area, which is close enough to keep an eye but far enough to save the ears. The Jacuzzi is a good spot for indulging in one of the poolside bar's cocktails (virgin or not).

For those with surplus energy (as if the volleyball and 33 metre lap pools weren't enough) there are two squash courts, four tennis courts, a gym (which can get a bit crowded with external members) and, if you can get a scrum together, a rugby pitch.

If you prefer rest and relaxation to reps and rucks, there is a small spa offering a wide range of massage treatments.

After a day of fun and frolics there is an excellent selection of dining and drinking options to keep you amused into the early hours. Tanjore is a traditional Indian restaurant which could have been lifted straight out of Rajasthan. The waiters, proudly dressed in intricately adorned costume, are both enthusiastic and helpful. They will dazzle you with a list of delights presented in aromatic pots that you'll never see the bottom of. Take your time to enjoy the intimate booths, the exposed brick decor and rustic Indian furnishings.

If you can move at the end of the meal, the recently refurbished Horse and Jockey next door transports you from the Indian subcontinent to the somewhat less exotic shores of middle England. The interior may hide no surprises but the newly extended terrace is a popular spot where you can enjoy a barbecue every Thursday evening. Live sports, a chillout night, party night and quiz night also appear on the weekly menu, which keeps punters pouring in.

The Wok, a Far Eastern offering, has a relaxed ambience with lots of bamboo, ceiling fans and red lanterns. There is a small bar should you fancy an aperitif, and poolside dining is an option, although a little less sophisticated. Sushi features heavily on the menu, while the exposed kitchen is busy concocting noodle and rice dishes and crowd pleasers such as 'surf & turf'. A rather up-close-and-personal band strums an array of generation spanning ballads, and the casual dining atmosphere encourages the drinks to flow.

Contemporary Italian restaurant Luce is the hotel's hotspot, memorable for everything from the orange interior to the late-night clientele. The food pleases too, and pitches above the standard fare on offer in most Italian restaurants, scoring especially well with its seafood options. The wine list is equally digestible with enough to please even the fussiest of palates. However, it is the post-dinner drinking and dancing that is the real draw. Local Al Ainers flood in by around 23:00 to enjoy the surprisingly skilled DJ who seamlessly slips from R&B to popular dance and from hands-in-the-air anthems to Arabic hip-shakers.

If dancing is not your scene then an after-dinner duel in Shooters snooker bar may be more appealing. Just be aware that while girls are allowed, men prevail around the felt, with snooker faces that may wander, so dressing appropriately for long shots is advisable.

Finally, Arabesque is the location for breakfast, as well as lunch and dinner if buffet is your idea of culinary heaven. Chocolate fountains and endless shiny pots hiding feasts from all four corners of the globe will excite over-zealous appetites.

The InterContinental Al Ain Resort certainly has enough to keep you busy for a weekend break, and is well positioned to visit the heritage sites nearby. What it may lack in obsessive attention to detail and rich extravagance it most definitely makes up for in personality. A multiple personality of course.

Contact
Phone: +971 3 768 6686
Email: alain@icalain.ae
Web: www.intercontinental.com

Location
The hotel is on the corner of Khaled Ibn Sultan Street and Al Salam Street, to the east of Al Ain Oasis and close to Buraimi – look out for purple signposts.

Food & Drink
The Wok – Oriental • Arabesque – Arabic • Tanjore – Indian • Luce Ristorante – Italian • Horse and Jockey – bar

Features
Three swimming pools • Health & fitness centre • Spa • Daycare & children's activities • Aqua aerobics • Karate lessons • Rugby • Football • Tennis • Squash

Nearby
Al Ain Golf Club • Al Ain Mall (www.alainmall.org) • Al Ain National Museum (www.aam.gov.ae) • Al Ain Oasis • Al Ain Wildlife Park & Resort • Gold Souk • Green Mubazzarah Park • Hili Archaeological Garden • Hili Fun City • Jahili Fort & Park • Jebel Hafeet

Le Royal Meridien Abu Dhabi

The distinctive 31 storey tower of Le Royal Meridien, topped by a UFO-like pod containing a revolving restaurant, has been something of a landmark on the Abu Dhabi skyline for a number of years. And, after a couple of name changes (and a complete refurb in 2004, when a smaller, second tower was added), the hotel maintains its position as one of the capital's most prestigious five-star destinations. Check-in in the spacious lobby is a graceful affair, helped along by cold towels, a welcome drink, contemporary surroundings and excellent service.

Le Royal Meridien has 276 rooms and suites, split between the two towers. The original 31 storey building – the Deluxe Tower – is home to the 'classic rooms'. While they're the cheapest option, these rooms are still a good size and feature generous king size beds (or twin singles), an armchair, coffee table and desk. Classic rooms have either a city or sea view. The smaller Royal Tower offers a choice of superior and Royal Club rooms, and junior, executive and Royal Club suites. In keeping with those in the Deluxe Tower, these rooms and suites are spacious and uncluttered, and feature modern decor with dark wood furniture. Suites have a lounge area with contemporary furnishings, a TV and DVD player, and not one but two minibars. Royal Club suites have a dining table and chairs. The newer rooms and suites in the Royal Tower feature bathrooms with standalone 'claw-foot' baths and rain showers, as well as bathroom products courtesy of Hermes. Accommodation in the Royal Tower is mostly sea-facing, and, as with the Deluxe Tower, the higher your room, the better your view of the sea.

For added exclusivity, you can pay extra when booking and opt for the Royal Club experience

Royal Club guests get rooms on their very own floor (complete with personal butler) and gain access to a lounge on the ground floor serving complimentary continental breakfast and evening drinks.

There is a small gym on the fourth floor of the Deluxe Tower, with an equally compact indoor pool alongside. But the most impressive leisure facilities are saved for the outdoor pool, and, oddly, the neighbouring hotel.

Given its city centre location, the ground level swimming pool area is surprisingly spacious and pleasantly green, with plenty of foliage and palm trees. The inviting pool is big enough for serious swimmers, but is really better suited to floating around, cooling off and chilling out. A separate kids' pool is shaded by a large canopy. With the gleaming hotel towering above, and sheltered from the surrounding roads and buildings, the pool area is an attractive oasis where you could easily spend the majority of your stay.

In addition, guests get free access to the amenities at the neighbouring Al Ain Palace Hotel, which include a bigger gym, Jacuzzi and plunge pool, and two squash courts.

So, the accommodation is good, as are the leisure facilities, but the big draw at this hotel is undoubtedly the variety and quality of food and drink outlets.

The pick of the bunch is Al Fanar – a revolving restaurant offering birds'-eye views over the city and superb international cuisine. It's not cheap, but it's worth it. Italian restaurant Amalfi is light and airy with clean, modern decor and an outdoor terrace overlooking the pool area. The menu features some familiar favourites alongside less common Mediterranean dishes.

The all day dining option (and the breakfast venue) is L'Opera Brasserie, which offers a selection of dishes from around the world. Oceans Seafood Kitchen and Lounge is part cocktail bar, part seafood restaurant, with a Polynesian feel and a popular terrace.

Soba is a chic oriental restaurant serving sushi, sashimi, tempura and noodles, and a selection of light and healthy food options, while Sax offers fine food, flashy cocktails and live jazz.

Guests looking for some faux Dublin fun and charm could do worse than PJ O'Reilly's, the lively Irish boozer that dishes up pints, pub grub, televised sports and a quiz night. Next door, in a standalone villa beside the pool area, is the unique Zari Zardozi, which will transport you from Abu Dhabi to exotic India through its trad-meets-mod decor. This three-in-one experience consists of the Zari restaurant, the Z'dozi Lounge and Zardozi Hukka (www.zarizardozi.com).

There's also a poolside bar and a choice of two lounges off the lobby for light lunches and pre-dinner drinks. And if you have any energy left, Illusions nightclub is the place for late-night dancing with a party atmosphere. Should you feel the need to stray beyond the confines of the hotel, Le Royal Meridien operates the Shuja yacht, which sets sail from the marina (guests get a free transfer) for sunset cruises along the Corniche.

Abu Dhabi

Contact
Phone: +971 2 674 2020
Email: info.lrmad@lemeridien.com
Web: www.lemeridien.com

Location
Le Royal Meridien is locatred at the north end of Abu Dhabi island, on Sheikh Khalifa Street (Street Number 3).

Food & Drinks
Al Fanar – revolving restaurant • Amalfi – Italian • L'Opera Brasserie – French • Oceans – seafood • Soba – Japanese • Shuja Yacht – dinner cruise • Zari Zardozi – Indian • Sax – jazz bar • The Piano Lounge – cocktails • P. J. O'Reilly's – Irish pub • Illusions – nightclub

Features
Watersports • Fitness centre • Indoor & outdoor pool • Spa • Jacuzzi • Squash • Golf courses • Tennis courts • Waterskiing • Jetskiing • Boating

Nearby
Abu Dhabi Mall (www.abudhabi-mall.com) • Al Ghazal Golf Club (www.alghazalgolf.ae) • Emirates Palace • Fish Market • Heritage Village • Marina Mall • Port Mina Zayed • Sheikh Zayed Grand Mosque

Liwa Hotel

The Empty Quarter, or the Rub Al Khali, is the largest sand desert in the world, and is bordered by Oman, Saudi Arabia, Yemen and the UAE. For those who want to explore the fringes of this fascinating place, The Liwa Hotel is the ideal getaway.

Liwa is actually a large oasis, more than 100km long, and even the lengthy drive to the hotel provides a tantalising introduction to the desert scenery. The hotel was originally conceived as a sheikh's palace, but prior to occupation was converted into a hotel. While its four-star comfort may not quite match royal standards, it certainly makes for an enjoyable weekend break with a difference.

The unique selling point of this hotel is its spectacular location. If you think you've seen the desert, think again; nothing quite compares to the vast, pristine dunes of Liwa, and the Liwa Hotel offers beautiful, peaceful views of the desertscape. Serenity runs throughout the hotel too, from the friendly welcome at check-in to the hushed background noises in the evenings.

The 58 standard rooms all have their own large terrace, complete with table and chairs so you can relax and enjoy the scenery. Just make sure to request a room on the second floor, otherwise you may find you have a lovely view of the carpark.

Five suites are also available, and larger families and groups can stay in one of the three villas, which have three bedrooms, two bathrooms, private swimming pools and large living and dining areas. The decor is fairly basic, but it fits in with the calm, minimalist surroundings, only interrupted every now and then by the occasional revving of a 4WD or quad bike on its way back from a jaunt on the nearby dunes.

Outside of the rooms, you'll find a large swimming pool and surprisingly lush grounds, perfect for relaxing. There is also a sauna, Jacuzzi and steam room, tennis and volleyball courts, a separate kids' pool and play area. But the real star of the show is the great outdoors – the surrounding desert, where you can climb up a dune to enjoy the views at sunset.

If it's desert adventure you're after, you can head off to the big dunes, some of which are hundreds of metres high. While the hotel used to work with local tour companies to offer desert excursions, unfortunately you currently have to make your own arrangements. You can either contact a local tour operator, such as Off Road Adventures (www.arabiantours.com), or explore in your own vehicle. Don't undertake the second option lightly though – you need to be fully prepared, always travelling in a convoy, preferably with GPS and armed with a copy of *UAE Off-Road* by Explorer Publishing.

If you do nothing else, at the very least aim to have an evening barbecue on the dunes during your stay – it's a Liwa must-do and you can find a perfect dune just a short drive from the hotel. The nearby Moreeb Hill is worth a visit, if only to gaze in wonder at the 4WDs attempting to climb the steep peak before their inevitable descent back down to ground level. While there will be many others exploring the area, the desert is so vast that it won't be hard to find a quiet spot.

At the hotel you can enjoy a buffet breakfast or dinner at the Al Mezoon restaurant, which is situated at the far end of the lobby. The terrace overlooks the hotel gardens, and serves international and local cuisine. Expect simple yet tasty dishes such as fish curry,

vegetable biryani, lasagne, samosas and steamed vegetables. The breakfast manu offers a range of pastries, scrambled egg, pancakes, lebneh and Arabic bread. If you'd like a spot on the terrace, be sure to book early as the restaurant does fill up. For a little privacy, you can order from the room service menu and enjoy dinner on your balcony.

The nightlife at the hotel is modest, with just one bar, Al Misyal. The bar is seemingly frequented by few hotel guests, and is fairly quiet. However, it houses a few arcade machines, a dartboard, a pool table and a good range of cocktails and drinks.

The hotel and indeed the town of Liwa may not cater for those looking for a raucous night on the town. Instead, it suits families, groups of desert thrill seekers, and those looking for a genuine escape from city life in the remoteness of the Empty Quarter.

Abu Dhabi

Contact
Phone: +971 2 882 2000
Email: liwahtl@emirates.net.ae
Web: www.danathotelgroup.com

Location
Liwa Hotel is located in Al Gharbia region, 230km from Abu Dhabi city, in the Rub Al Khali desert (also known as the Empty Quarter). The hotel lies just south-west of the town of Mezaira'a.

Food & Drinks
Mezoon Restaurant – international

Features
Fitness centre • Sauna • Jacuzzi • Four floodlit tennis courts • Climate controlled swimming pool • Children's pool and playground • Volleyball court

Nearby
Moreeb dune • Desert • Oasis • Fish farm • Forts

What the Mercure Grand Jebel Hafeet lacks in Emirati extravagance it makes up for in character and old-school charm. It is a UAE hidden gem, one of the few places that has remained untouched by the country's new-found drive for all-round opulence.

This 'under-the-radar' tag doesn't equate to uninteresting either; quite the contrary, since the Mercure has its fair share of attention-grabbing qualities.

The journey up to the hotel forms a spectacular beginning to your weekend away. The approach weaves up the majestic Jebel Hafeet, and you can stop to make the most

Mercure Grand Jebel Hafeet

Abu Dhabi

of the panoramic views over Al Ain and the surrounding desert.

The hotel lobby is a verdant display of local wildlife, with a vine waterfall forming the backdrop. The lived-in, almost mismatched, decor is far from distasteful, and should provoke a smile if you've grown tired of cookie-cutter hotel lobbies. The rooms are modest in size, each with a very small balcony. However, if it's vistas you're after you can head to the hotel's viewing platform for more space and a lofty perspective of the landscape.

Apart from the surrounding aesthetics, which are worth taking the time to admire, there is a range of activities to keep you busy. Tennis courts, a small gym, a steam room, sauna and beauty treatments, as well as a pitch and putt green and a small climbing wall, give the hotel a kitsch, holiday camp feel.

Kids (and kidults) will love the water slides, while the swim-up bar keeps spirits high. There is also a decent baby pool, and families make up a substantial quota of the hotel guest list. However, couples and non-family groups are more than welcome, and can find retreat in the warm and friendly Lawrence's Bar for a cocktail and some of Al Ain's favourite entertainers. Alternatively, the tranquil mountain location is the perfect setting for a puff of shisha at Al Khayma.

Dining choices are a bit limited, but enthusiasm and good service feature prominently. Le Belvedere is the hotel's main restaurant, serving breakfast, lunch and dinner. Decor may not be the speciality here, but the food satisfies the appetite with an interesting mix of French-Mediterranean and Moroccan fare.

The prime location for dining for most guests, however, is Eden Rock, otherwise known as the terrace behind the pool.

As you enjoy the unobstructed view from your table on the edge of the mountain, you can fill up at the buffet – a different theme every night makes repeat visits possible.

The setting is truly wonderful, with a gentle mountain breeze and twinkling fairy lights adding to the special ambience.

With the attractions of Al Ain and the surrounding great outdoors there is enough on offer at the Mercure Grand to keep you occupied for a weekend break. For the longer-staying guest, the hotel runs a number of tours, from desert safaris to guided shopping sprees. However, the main attraction here, and it is one that won't break the piggy bank, is the secluded setting of the hotel, which really adds meaning to the phrase 'getting away from it all'.

Contact
Phone: +971 3 783 8888
Email: resa@mercure-alain.ae
Web: www.mercure.com

Location
From Al Ain, follow the signs for Jebel Hafeet, which is to the south of the city. The hotel is located on the mountain itself.

Food & Drink
Eden Rock – international • Le Belvedere – Mediterranean • Oriental Café – Asian • Lawrence's Bar – wine bar

Features
Three swimming pools • Tennis court • Wi-Fi access • Fitness centre • Kids' playground • Mini-golf

Nearby
Al Ain Golf Club • Al Ain Mall (www.alainmall.org) • Al Ain National Museum (www.aam.gov.ae) • Al Ain Oasis • Al Ain Wildlife Park & Resort • Gold Souk • Green Mubazzarah Park • Hili Archaeological Garden • Hili Fun City • Jahili Fort & Park • Jebel Hafeet

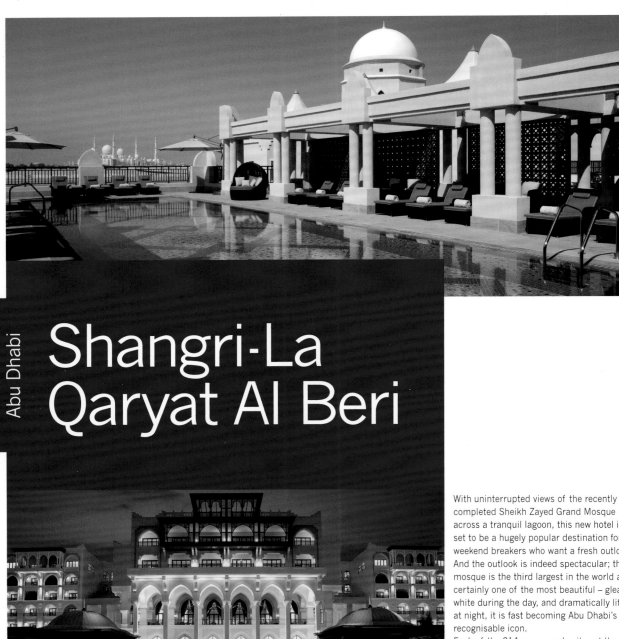

Shangri-La Qaryat Al Beri

With uninterrupted views of the recently completed Sheikh Zayed Grand Mosque across a tranquil lagoon, this new hotel is set to be a hugely popular destination for weekend breakers who want a fresh outlook. And the outlook is indeed spectacular; the mosque is the third largest in the world and certainly one of the most beautiful – gleaming white during the day, and dramatically lit up at night, it is fast becoming Abu Dhabi's most recognisable icon.

Each of the 214 rooms and suites at the Shangri-La has a generous balcony or terrace, from which you can enjoy the magnificent view of the mosque and the rest of Abu Dhabi city stretching out behind it. If you can tear yourself away for long enough, you'll discover that the interiors of the rooms are almost as magnificent – all have been decorated to high standards, and the bathroom and the large cupboard area are built into alcoves within the room, further enhancing the traditional Arabian decor. Luxurious touches, like a large bath and separate walk-in shower, an LCD television complete with satellite TV and a DVD player, a fruit basket and an elegant mini bar, make you feel more like you are staying in a suite than in a 'standard' room.

Outside the room, the hotel has an impressive collection of leisure facilities. The renowned Shangri-La spa brand, CHI at Shangri-La, is present here, and features an extensive spa menu that can obliterate stress in an instant. Experience the traditional Arabian Hammam treatment here, where they can recreate the ancient ritual for up to four people at a time. The spa also offers a selection of signature therapies, half-day packages, and CHI journeys, which are complete treatments for the body and mind. Aside from the spa, the Shangri-La also has a dedicated well-being zone, which houses two gyms, a swimming pool and a yoga room.

There are an additional four swimming pools in the 8.5 hectare grounds, all with plush sun loungers, ample shade and a food and beverage service. There is a separate children's pool. Alternatively, you can choose to sun yourself on the beach, which stretches for a kilometre along the front of the hotel. Since the water lapping on to the sand is actually part of the lagoon that separates the island of Abu Dhabi from the mainland, the waters are calm and safe; nevertheless, there is a lifeguard on duty just in case.

Rounding off the long list of relaxing experiences that can be had here at the Shangri-La is the opportunity to watch the sun set from the balcony of the Al Hanah Bar. With a cocktail in hand and the sky changing colours as the sun goes down, you'll realise why this is the perfect location for a weekend break.

After sundowners, you have the difficult choice of where to enjoy dinner. The Shangri-La has

four excellent restaurants that are popular with hotel guests and external diners alike. Experience French fine dining made with imported ingredients at Bord Eau, which can also be noted for its superb wine list. Alternatively, take a culinary journey eastwards with modern Vietnamese cuisine at Hoi An or contemporary, authentic Chinese food at the much-lauded Shang Palace. All-day dining hits new highs in Sofra bld, where the buffet is both imaginative and extravagant (chocolate fountain for breakfast, anyone?). Finally, the Lobby Lounge is open from early till late, serving a fine range of light meals and drinks. The hotel sits on an 8.5 hectare complex that offers further attractions. The Souk is a shopping area based on a old-style Arabian market, where traditional abras (small motorised boats) await to transport you from shop to shop along a waterway.

So with shopping, fine dining, a world-class spa, a well-being complex, numerous swimming pools, spectacular views, impeccable service and, possibly most important of all, luxurious, comfortable bedrooms, Shangri-La Qaryat Al Beri truly ticks all the boxes for the ultimate weekend break. Highly recommended.

Abu Dhabi

Contact
Phone: +971 2 509 8888
Email: slad@shangri-la.com
Website: www.shangri-la.com

Location
From National Exhibition Centre using 30th street ahead straight after mussafah bridge follow the sign going to Shangri-La Qaryat Al Beri.

Food & Drink
Bord Eua – French • Hoi An – Vietnamese • Shang Palace – Chinese • Sofra Bld – local & international

Features
Modern Arabic style • Pools & private Pools • Spa • Yoga room • two gymnasiums

Nearby
International Airport • Golf course • Convention centre • City centre • Abras • Arabian market • Sheikh Khalifa Park • Al Maqtaa Fort

Northern Emirates

The northern emirates encapsulate the natural beauty of Arabia, with rugged mountains, rolling dunes, an attractive coastline and quiet towns offering a traditional regional experience.

Running up the coast from Dubai are the northern emirates, comprising Sharjah, Ajman, Umm Al Quwain and Ras Al Khaimah. Sharjah is a little smaller than its neighbour Dubai, but has almost the same level of activity, and a completely different character. The other emirates are all much less developed, and have a more relaxed pace of life. In them you'll find diverse scenery, adrenaline-pumping sports and activities, historic forts, off-road routes, relaxing spas and museums packed with Arabian culture.

Sharjah

Sharjah was once one of the wealthiest towns in the region, with fishing, pearling and trading providing affluence for its inhabitants. Although it has now been eclipsed by Dubai, Sharjah has far more culture and heritage, and an impressive array of attractions. While many people staying in Sharjah also visit Dubai, there's not many who do the journey the other way, but they really are missing out. The city centres are only 20 kilometres away from each other, but seem a world apart in terms of feel and things to see and do. Noted for its museums and heritage, it was named the cultural capital of the Arab world in 1998 by Unesco because of its flair for culture and art, together with its desire to preserve local heritage. It is possibly the most conservative of all the emirates, with stricter laws than the others. No hotels or restaurants serve

Clockwise from top left: Ras Al Khaimah, Souk Al Arsah, Sharjah Heritage area, Al Qasba

alcohol, and visitors should dress a little more discreetly in public places.

The city is based around the creek, Khalid Lagoon, in the middle of which is Al Jazeera Park. Around the water's edge, Buheirah Corniche is a nice place for a stroll when the weather is cool. Joining Khalid Lagoon to Al Khan Lagoon, Al Qasba is home to a variety of cultural events, exhibitions, theatre and music – all held on the canalside walkways or at dedicated venues. There are also many waterside restaurants and cafes serving up Arabic, Asian and Mediterranean cuisine. At the mouth of Al Khan Lagoon, Sharjah Aquarium (06 528 5288, www.sharjahaquarium.ae) is the city's newest attraction. It opened its doors in 2008 and is already attracting crowds of visitors.

On the north side of the creek, in the city centre, two areas have been developed with masses to see and do: Sharjah Heritage Area and the Arts Area. The Heritage Area (www.sharjahtourism.ae) is a great place for people with an interest in local history, and is home to a number of old buildings including Al Hisn Fort, Sharjah Islamic Museum, Sharjah Heritage Museum (Bait Al Naboodah), the Majlis of Ibrahim Mohammed Al Midfa and the Old Souk (Souk Al Arsah).

The Arts Area is another place visitors should take in, featuring a selection of galleries and museums, including Sharjah Art Museum (www.sharjahtourism.ae). Housing over 300 paintings and maps belonging to the ruler of Sharjah, the oil paintings and watercolours on display here capture life from around the Arabian world.

For shopping, modern malls such as Sharjah City Centre, Sahara Centre and Mega Mall are the most popular destinations, but the Blue Souk (officially named Central Souk) shouldn't be missed while you're there. It is an impressive sight, with two long, blue buildings running parallel to each other and connected by footbridges. Constructed according to Islamic design, it houses over 600 shops selling jewellery and gifts. The fruit and vegetable markets near the creek are also worth perusing, as is Souk Al Arsah in the Heritage Area.

Ajman

The smallest of the emirates, Ajman is situated around 10 kilometres from Sharjah, and the two cities merge with each other along the coast. There is a nice stretch of beach and a pleasant corniche – a great place to enjoy a stroll – and an increasing number of facilities to tempt the visitor. Ajman Kempinski Hotel & Resort is a grand offering for those who want a luxurious stay, while there are some other cheaper options along the beach. Ajman Museum (06 742 3824, www.am.gov.ae) houses a variety of interesting displays in a restored fort that is worth visiting as much for the building itself as for the exhibits. Ajman is known for being one of the largest dhow building centres in the region, and while it is mainly modern boats that emerge from the yards these days, you may catch sight of traditionally built wooden boat sailing out to of the harbour to sea. The souk is a reminder of a slower pace of life, while Ajman City Centre is a modern mall with plenty of shops and a cinema.

Umm Al Quwain

Next up the coast from Ajman, Umm Al Quwain is the second-smallest emirate, where life has changed very little for generations. Many people still earn their living from fishing and farming, although the emirate has not escaped the attention of the developers, and there are a couple of major projects already underway. The city is located on a peninsula sticking out on the west side of the lagoon, which has masses of mangroves, islands and bird and marine life. It is a popular place for boat trips and watersports, as it is sheltered and free of dangerous currents.

However, this whole area is set to undergo massive change with the planned Umm Al Quwain Marina, a Dhs.12 billion project to create a waterfront town of more than 9,000 homes around the lagoon and on the islands. Construction started in 2005 and is planned to be completed in 2012, but it remains to be seen what the effects of this will be on the area's natural wildlife. .

The emirate has several old watchtowers and forts, while in the city there are a number

Cover Up
Sharjah is a conservative place: don't kiss in public or wear revealing clothing in public places and remember that consuming, and even transporting alcohol, in the emirate is prohibited.

Fossil Rock
Officially called Jebel Maleihah, this is a large outcrop in the Sharjah desert close to Al Dhaid. It gets its name from the profusion of marine fossils on its slopes. Popular with off-roaders, it can be reached with a fairly easy drive through the desert. This is a great route for beginners and experts – easy enough to cut your teeth on, but also with some areas that will challenge expert desert drivers. The orange-red colour comes from the iron oxide in the sand.

Central Souk

of budget beach hotels, a ladies spa, the Umm Al Quwain Marine Reseach Center & Aquarium (www.uaq24.com/aquarium) and Umm Al Quwain Marine Club, the new home of Dubai Water Sports Association (050 492 7445, www.dwsa.net), where you can go wakeboarding or waterskiing.

East of the city and the lagoon, the area next to the Ras Al Khaimah road is home to several options for activities, catering for all tastes. UAQ Aeroclub (06 768 1447, www.uaqaeroclub.com) is the original aviation sports club in the Middle East, and offers flying, microlighting, skydiving and air tours – the perfect way to view the beautiful lagoons and deserted beaches. If it's high-speed thrills you are after, Emirates Motorplex (06 768 1166, www.motorplex.ae) hosts all types of motorsport events. UAQ Shooting Club (06 768 1903) has a shooting range and an outdoor paintballing course. With 25 rides in landscaped grounds, Dreamland Aqua Park (06 768 1888, www.dreamlanduae.com) is one of the largest water parks in the world, with rides ranging from wild to relaxing. you can also stay in fixed tents.

Ras Al Khaimah

Ras Al Khaimah is the most northerly of the seven emirates, and has arguably the best scenery in the UAE. The majestic Hajar Mountains rising just behind the city provide the backdrop and the sparkling Arabian Gulf offers natural beaches. Inland you will find the start of the desert, and also an incredibly fertile and green area near the airport.

The city is divided by a creek, with the old town of Ras Al Khaimah on one side and the newer Al Nakheel area on the other. The old town is worth visiting for the souk and the National Museum of Ras Al Khaimah, which is in a fort. On the other side of the creek, shopping and leisure opportunities include Manar Mall, which has a cinema and a family entertainment centre, Tower Links Golf Course (07 227 9939, www.towerlinks.com) among the mangroves around the creek, and Ras Al Khaimah Shooting Club (see p.160). There are also many smaller hotels and independant restaurants.

Outside the city, the ancient sites of Sheba Palace and Shimal are worth seeing. To the south are the natural hot springs at Khatt, along with a number of places to stay around the springs, an ostrich farm and a camel race track at Digdagga. The track is located in the middle of an amazingly green area where leafy lanes wind past fertile farms, and there is even a forest of hardy ghaf trees.

Following the direction set by Dubai and Abu Dhabi, Ras Al Khaimah has started to move forward with plans for developments to appeal

Photo Opportunities
- The striking exterior of Sharjah's Central Souk, or in its tiny shops.
- In among the various cultural attractions along Al Qasba canal.
- The ornate Magferah mosque.
- The mysterious Fossil Rock at sunset.
- Ajman Museum (housed in a classic Arabian fort).
- Umm Al Quwain from the air.
- The camel racing at Digdagga.

The peaceful pace of life in the Northern Emirates offers a real glimpse into traditional Arabian culture. Sharjah in particular is home to a wide range of cultural attractions, such as the famous Central Souk, the Sharjah Heritage Area, and Al Qasba, which stages theatrical productions, music recitals and art exhibitions throughout the year.

to both new residents and tourists, including
using its tremendous natural potential to
position itself as the destination for outdoor
activities in the UAE. Projects such as Al
Hamra Village, Marjan Island, Dana Island,
Polo Amusement Park, Mina Al Arab and Jebel
Al Jais Mountain Resort will add five-star
hotels, dining and entertainment options,
exciting new attractions and leisure facilities,
including an outdoor ski slope.

Ras Al Khaimah is also a good place to start
discovering the rugged Hajar Mountains
from. Although previously the start of the
Wadi Bih route to Dibba, this is now closed
at the UAE border post to all non-Emirati or
Omani traffic. It is still possible to drive the
route starting from Dibba though, and you
can access all the way west into Wadi Bih,

including the hikes, climbing and camping
spots. From the west side, you can drive in
towards Wadi Bih, then turn off onto the
new road being constructed up to Jebel Al
Jais Mountain Resort. Although it won't be
completed until 2010, the finished part of the
road already takes you up a picturesque wadi
to amazing views over the mountains.
There are also chances to get into the
mountains up the coast north of Ras Al
Khaimah, such as Wadi Ghalilah and the areas
around Rams and Shams, and also south
of RAK in Wadi Nakhab and Jebel Yibir – the
tallest mountain in the country, where a new
track now takes you nearly all the way to the
top for spectacular panoramic views over the
surrounding mountain tops.

Clockwise from top left: Camels in Ras Al Khaimah, Al Hisn
Fort, Ras Al Khaimah

Northern Emirates

Al Qasba

The beautiful Al Qasba in Sharjah is a kilometre-long canal with eateries, shops and stalls along its banks. The emphasis is on culture, with a calendar that includes Arabian poetry and film, art exhibitions, music and theatre. The Tent of Wonders is a permanent 'big top' featuring shows from around the world. But perhaps the biggest draw is the Eye of the Emirates – a 60 metre high observation wheel that offers amazing views over Sharjah and across to Dubai. www.qaq.ae.

Sharjah Heritage Area

This area is home to a collection of beautifully restored historic buildings including Al Hisn Fort (Sharjah Fort), Sharjah Islamic Museum, Sharjah Heritage Museum (Bait Al Naboodah), the Majlis of Ibrahim Mohammed Al Midfa and the Old Souk (Souk Al Arsah). Among the traditional architecture, you can see life described, depicted and displayed as it was from over 150 years ago up to more recent times.

Must-Do
Experiences

Heritage, culture, wildlife, amazing scenery and activities all combine for weekends of fun for all.

Northern Emirates

Dreamland Aqua Park

One of the largest water parks in the world, with a variety of rides from the 'Black Hole' to a wave pool and high-salinity pool for floating. There's also a go-kart track. You can stay overnight in a tent provided for you, or in a cabana hut. For prices and opening times visit www.dreamlanduae.com or call 06 768 1888.

Sharjah Desert Park

A world-class attraction located just outside Sharjah, this park is home to the Natural History Museum, the Arabian Wildlife Centre, the Children's Farm and the recently opened Sharjah Botanical Museum. All combine education and enjoyment in the most dynamic of atmospheres, with excellent care given to the animals, and a fascinating day can be spent exploring them all. The park is about 25km from Sharjah on the Al Dhaid Road (E88). Call 06 5311999 or see www.sharjahtourism.ae.

Mountains & Wadis

A trip to the northern emirates would not be complete without witnessing the grand scenery of the spectacular Hajar Mountains. An old favourite – the legendary Wadi Bih route – is still open for business from Dibba, and remains one of the most dramatic drives in the UAE. In contrast, the new track up Jebel Yibir, the highest mountain in the UAE, opens up a brand new area for off-roaders, with stunning panoramic views over the surrounding mountains and a myriad of hiking trails strewn across the hillsides.

Ajman Kempinski

It may be in the 'forgotten' emirate of Ajman, but the Ajman Kempinski is a weekend break gem. As the only five-star hotel in the tiny emirate, competition is not exactly fierce, but it is up there with the best beach resorts in the country.

Peacefully located at the end of the sparsely populated hotel beach strip, the Kempinski looks out to sea from right next to Ajman's small harbour, where dhows and fishing boats sail out into the gulf.

The hotel is a modern, attractive building, inside and out, and the range of facilities and entertainment will satisfy even the most active of guests. Dining options include

four restaurants, a cafe, a sports bar, a beachside snack bar, and a private dining experience available right on the beach. The comprehensive leisure facilities include a gym and health club, two separate spas, a dive centre, a bowling alley and kids' club.

A wide range of rooms and suites are available. All are sea facing, with differing size, costs and levels of facilities. The basic rooms, although compact, are very comfortable and finished in sophisticated colours. A recent lobby upgrade has spruced things up a bit, and a new bar has been added. Off the reception there is a small shopping arcade providing all the usual tourist essentials such as beachwear and souvenirs.

The grounds of the hotel are not expansive, but the well-kept gardens are attractive and filled with a mix of trees and plants, extending along the building around both sides. To one side, in between tall mature palm trees, is a putting green and tennis courts.

Sports and leisure facilities also include a gym and a dive centre that offers the full range of courses and, for PADI certified divers, tours out to explore the wrecks and reefs in the Arabian Gulf.

Spa lovers can enjoy some heavenly indulgence at the hotel's two wellness centres: the Softouch Ayurveda Spa has many types of relaxing Indian massages, while the Laguna

Spa offers a range of exotic treatments, including private sessions in the Balinese hut next to the beach.

The pool lies in a sheltered stretch between the hotel and the curving wing of cabana accommodation, and invites long, leisurely afternoons spent alternating between comfy sun loungers and the cool water. Temperature control keeps the pool from feeling like a tepid bath, even in the height of summer. It is a good size, with a swim-up bar, and next to it there is a dedicated children's pool complete with mini deckchairs.

The nearby Kempi Kids' Club offers supervised children's facilities and organised activities. Both the indoor playrooms and the outdoor playground are well equipped, modern and bright, and the staff work hard to make sure your little ones are having fun.

Take a short stroll on the path through the trees and you'll reach one of the resort's big selling points: the beach. This half-kilometre stretch of clean white sand, with expansive views out over the beautiful turquoise-blue ocean, is nothing short of paradise. There's not a man-made island or dredger in sight, providing an uncluttered view that is almost impossible to find in Dubai or Abu Dhabi nowadays.

As one of very few entertainment and leisure spots in the emirate, the hotel is Ajman's party central, and plays host to an interesting collection of local residents every night. The cafe on the first floor (appropriately named Café on First), with an outdoor terrace, is a popular hangout for coffee and business through the day, or for enjoying shisha in the evenings. It is also a common venue with the local community for functions such as weddings and receptions in the ballroom or the gardens. It's not uncommon to see rifle-twirling dancers out on the lawns in the evening either. At the other end of the hotel, the World Cup Sports Bar – part sports bar, part British pub – and the Cosmic Bowling ten-pin alley provide fun for a lively crowd of hotel guests and Ajman residents.

The hotel's buffet restaurant, Café Kranzler, is a cut above standard hotel offerings, with excellent breakfasts including particularly tasty home-baked breads and croissants. As well as dining inside, there is a lovely shaded terrace that looks out through the grounds towards the sea. Lunch is served from 12:30 until 15:30, and, in the evenings, every night has a different theme – but with several speciality restaurants also in the hotel, most guests head elsewhere for dinner.

The main restaurants are quite highly priced, but offer top-class food. Hai Tao serves authentic Cantonese and Szechwan food cooked by the resident Chinese chefs, Sabella's offers Italian cuisine, and Bukhara serves up classy and award-winning Indian food.

It can take as little as 20 minutes to get to the Ajman Kempinski from Dubai – a far shorter length of time than to other common destinations, so you can benefit from your break without getting tired from the drive there and back. Despite this, the journey to Ajman is just long enough to feel like you're heading somewhere different – and the route through Sharjah on Friday is a pleasure. You should, however, time your drive carefully on any other day of the week – if you attempt to get there during rush hour you'll experience the traffic jams that Sharjah is infamous for.

Northern Emirates

Contact

Phone: +971 6 714 5555
Email: ajman.kempinski@kemp-aj.com
Web: www.ajmankempinski.com

Location

From Emirates Road, follow signs for Ajman. In the city, take Sheikh Khalifa Bin Zayed Street all the way to the sea, then turn right onto Sheikh Humaid Bin Rashid Al Nuaimi Street and the hotel is at the end on the left.

Food & Drink

Café Kranzler – international • Bukhara – Indian • Hai Tao – Chinese • Sabella's – Italian • World Cup Sports Bar – American bar

Features

Gym • Health club • Bowling • Jetskiing • Parasailing • Surfing • Tennis courts • Diving • Temperature controlled Swimming pool • Kids' pool • Private beach • Putting green • Kid's club

Nearby

Ajman City Centre Mall • Ajman Souk • Boat yard • Sharjah • Umm Al Quwain

Al Hamra Fort Hotel & Beach Resort

Although it might seem somewhat dated compared to the bling-bling, five-star resorts of Dubai, the Al Hamra Fort Hotel and Beach Resort is a great place to escape the hustle and bustle of city life. Built in the style of a traditional Arabic fort, complete with traditional windtowers, the hotel is set among well-maintained gardens along a long strip of sandy beach, providing a real weekend break atmosphere just an hour's drive out of Dubai. Most of the hotel's accommodation is made up of villa rooms, which are widely spread throughout the lush gardens, and arranged in small groups, creating a haven of privacy and seclusion in this large resort. Each of the villa rooms has a large private balcony or terrace with garden or beach views. Rooms are spacious and comfortable, and have all the usual amenities – satellite television, a well-stocked mini bar, a safe – although compared to the exceptional lavishness of Dubai, they can feel a little on the basic side. Whether you see this as a good thing or a bad thing depends on your opinion of over-the-top opulence. Most rooms have interconnecting doors for families.

In keeping with the holiday village atmosphere, Al Hamra has numerous dining options. There are six main restaurants spread throughout the grounds, offering a mix of traditional Arabic and international food. Each restaurant has a different ambience, depending on the theme and the cuisine. The main hotel restaurant provides different themed buffets each night, and the outside terrace has nice views over the garden and pools towards the beach. For sundowners or to enjoy your meal on the beach, try Le Chalet, or for solid Italian fare in fun, faux-trattoria surroundings try Don Camillo (but ask for a table towards the back to avoid views of the lobby). There is also a 'nightclub' on site, with the DJ playing the usual dancefloor fillers so you can pull out your best robot and running man moves until the early hours.

Al Hamra's best quality is undoubtedly its vast collection of leisure activities, which make it the perfect weekend break for families or

groups of friends looking for a break from the city, but with a bit of excitement thrown in. The beach club offers an extensive range of watersports, including kayaking, windsurfing, sailing, waterskiing, wakeboarding and jetskiing. Alternatively, gather a team together for beach games such as volleyball or boules. A certified dive centre onsite offers lessons and organised dives; the northern location of the hotel makes dive sites on the Musandam peninsula and east coast easily accessible. The hotel also has tennis courts and two golf courses: an 18 hole championship course and a nine-hole academy course for beginners. Both courses are floodlit, so you can avoid the heat of the day in warmer months.

This hotel is very near to Al Hamra Cellar, MMI's tax-free bottle store, so you can combine your stay here with a booze run (www.mmidubai.com).

In a nutshell, you won't find too many venues that beat Al Hamra Fort Hotel and Beach Resort for a family getaway – kids will love it, and so will frazzled mums and dads who don't want to spend their weekends worrying that their offspring will get bored, or disturb other guests.

Contact
Phone: +971 07 244 6666
Email: hamfort@emirates.net.ae
Website: www.alhamrafort.com

Location
Situated on the E11 coast road, south of Ras Al Khaimah, next to the new Al Hamra Village.

Food & Drink
Le Chalet – fastfood and bar • Al Shamal – international • Don Camillo – Italian • Al Jazeera – Lebanese • Club Malibu – nightclub • Sirocco – lounge Bar • Seafood Market Restaurant – seafood • Pool Bar – fastfood and bar

Features
Fitness centre • Massage room • Outdoor Jacuzzi • Temperature-controlled swimming pool • Kids' paddle pool • Two tennis courts • Mini golf • Male and female saunas • Watersports

Nearby
Al Hamra Golf Club and Resorts (www.alhamragolf.com) • RAK National Museum (www.rakmuseum.gov.ae) • Khatt Hot Springs • RAK Shooting Club (07 236 3622) • Tower Links Golf Club (www.towerlinks.com) • Digdagga camel racetrack • Mountains • Desert • Dreamland Aqua Park (www.dreamlanduae.com) • Umm Al Quwain

Dreamland Aqua Park

Dreamland might not be the first choice for a weekend break, but if nothing else it's not many places you can sleep over in a water park. Whether you have the excuse of taking the kids or not, a 36 hour stint aqua-side makes good on the 'fun for all the family' cliche, as well as everyone's favourite sell line, 'great value for money'.

Accommodation comes in the form of chalets, with built-in air-conditioning, an inflated mattress, and sleeping bags. Chalets vary in size, with the three to five sleepers having the added feature of a terrace. You can comfortably survive with the bedding provided, although you may opt for bringing your own 'blankey' if the thought of sleeping in a strange sleeping bag feels a bit odd. Don't expect the European version of a holiday chalet – these are more garden shed than *gite*, but then again you are just dossing overnight in a water park. Happy campers can pitch their tents if chalets seem a little too 'soft'. Overnighters can check in from 15:00 onwards, get settled in and hit the slides (probably around 15:05). Dreamland has the luxury of having more space than its Dubai rival, Wild Wadi, and has green areas ideal for a game of Frisbee, an extremely relaxed lazy river, plenty of sun-drenched spots for tanning (although there are many shady spots too), and, perhaps most importantly, a swim-up bar. There are enough rides to keep all ages happy, including looping tubes, the black hole, a family raft, and the super-scary kamikaze rides. The most humorous ride (or most disgusting, depending on your viewpoint), is the whirlpool ride that simulates being flushed down a toilet. There is a gentle wave pool, and for younger kids, the central pool has plenty of mini slides and showers.

Dreamland has a lot of character, and will take you back to the water parks you visited on family holidays as a child, when it wasn't all about being the world's biggest, shiniest or scariest. The volcano pool, complete with plastic hippos, the usually unpopulated arcade, and a small animal farm seem somewhat random, but they are all part of this much-loved UAE institution. There is a reserved area within the water park itself for overnight guests.

Your overnight stay is all-inclusive, with dinner coming in the form of an impressive barbecue kit, including plenty of meat, salads and breads for do-it-yourself alfresco dining. A buffet breakfast is served before the park opens, and lunch is served at the food stall, Snack Attack. The bar remains open until midnight (although at certain times of the year it closes at 18:00, so it's best to check before you arrive), and at around 22:00 there is a belly-dancing show – although you might want to lurk at the back if you plan on leaving with your dignity intact.

Toilets and showers are located a short walk from your chalet, but don't expect scented hand towels and complimentary toiletries. This is just a step or two up from camping; if you're a seasoned camper then you'll think it is far from 'roughing it'; if you'd like to camp but are nervous that it will be too hardcore for you, then a stay here is a gentle introduction. But don't forget why you've come here – because you get to SLEEP in a water park!

Contact
Phone: +971 6 768 18 88
Email: info@dreamlanduae.com
Web: www.dreamlanduae.com

Location
In Umm Al Quwain follow the Shk Zayed Bin Sultan Al Nahyan Rd (E55) for 2.9km. Leave Shk Zayed Bin Sultan Al Nahyan Rd (E55) and turn right into Al Ittehad Sq (E11). Stay on for 4,5 km. Leave Al Ittehad Sq (E11) and head straightforward onto Al Ittehad Rd (E11). Stay on for 14 km.

Food & Drink
Atlantis Restaurant – All day dinning
• Taj Mahal Restaurant – Indian and Asian
• Snack Attack – snacks • Saj Zaman & Shisha Majlis – snacks & shisha

Features
Aqua Play • Bumper Boats • Wave Pool • Dream Stream • Twister • Family Raft Ride • Kamikaze • Twisting Dragons • Slide 5 • Mighty Go Round • Hippos Island • Pool Bar • Dead Sea • Buheira Grande • Go Kart Circuit • Mini Pet Land • Tennis

Nearby
Barracuda Beach Resort • Emirates Motors Flex • UAQ Aeroclub

Hilton Ras Al Khaimah

On first impressions, the Hilton Ras Al Khaimah may not appear a prime spot for an escape from the city. A plain, functional-looking building situated on the edge of the city centre in a commercial area, externally this hotel bears all the hallmarks of being business accommodation; that feeling extends to the polite but efficient check-in too.

It's only when you move beyond the reception area, into the lounge, restaurants and bars, that you realise the hotel actually has a laid-back vibe and is full of holidaymakers. Families and groups from Germany, France and the UK come here for relaxing package holidays – and that's because, although the hotel is not located in the most glamorous part of the UAE, the affilliated Hilton Beach Club and Hilton Resort & Spa (p.170) are only a short shuttle bus ride away, transporting guests from edge of town to beautiful beach in a matter of minutes.

The decor inside the hotel is somewhat dated, with brown and green soft furnishings being the theme, although the rooms are spacious, and there are sophisticated touches such as Crabtree & Evelyn products in the bathrooms – this is a Hilton after all. Standard rooms feature a king-size bed, a television with the usual satellite channels, as well as a sofa, coffee table and writing desk. You'll also have access to high-speed internet if you need to bring your laptop.

One tip though: if you're there on a Thursday or Friday night, request a room at the back of the hotel if you're a light sleeper, as beats from the neighbouring nightclub, while not overly intrusive, may keep you awake – unless you're there for a party, in which case you won't have far to stumble back after a night on the dancefloor.

If you've got cash to splash for a more luxurious weekend, executive rooms and junior suites are also available.

A variety of food and drink is served in the onsite restaurants and bars. The Al Khor international buffet and barbecue is the most popular, as the all-inclusive packages and half and full-board rates cover this restaurant. Choose from a variety of foods, ranging from Arabic to Mediterranean, as well as special theme nights. In the outdoor section of Al Khor you can eat from the live cooking menu. This is the place to come for breakfast too.

As the name suggests, the Hoof 'n' Fin restaurant dishes up steak and seafood. The atmosphere in this eatery is more upmarket, perfect for an intimate dinner for two.

If you've been on one of the hotel's fishing trips (and been relatively successful) you can have your catch cooked for you here – seafood doesn't get much fresher than that.

Next door is Cuban lounge Havana Bar, featuring Central American food, plus Cuban music, cigars and cocktails. If you're up for some late night Latino dancing, Havana Bar stays open until 02:00. The Arab style Lobby Lounge is open until midnight for coffee and nibbles, while creekside fare is available by the pool in the form of beers and snacks from Aqua.

For the energetic, there's a good-sized gym to work up a sweat in, and a fantastic outdoor LA-style swimming pool on site, all sharp lines and white and blue contrast. From the pool deck and restaurant terrace there's a good view over the creek (if you

don't mind the processing plant on the other side – but that can add a kind of gritty urban chic, in a certain light). There are also a few boutique shops and a tour operator desk in the hotel lobby.

The real attraction of a break at this Hilton though is not the hotel – it's the beach club. A regular shuttle bus whisks guests the couple of miles to the sea throughout the day. The club, next to the new Hilton Resort & Spa, has split-level pools, a swim-up bar, a kids' club, beach activities including volleyball, a beach bar and an outdoor massage table (or you can get a more pricey treatment at the neighbouring spa). The Beach Club is adjacent to the new resort (p.170), and as this facility nears completion, expect the beach club facility to be upgraded.

Activities such as snorkelling, scuba diving and fishing can all be arranged from the beach club (for an extra cost), and your boat can take you right back to the hotel along the creek. And if you have a good day with the fishing rod, be sure to take your catch to Hoof 'n' Fin to enjoy the most satisfying fish supper you'll ever have.

Contact
Phone: +971 7 288 8888
Email: ras-al-khaimah@hilton.com
Web: www.hilton.com

Location
Once in Ras Al Khaimah, turn right at Clock Tower Roundabout, go straight at the next roundabout, and past the golf club. At the first signal turn left, then left again at the junction after Manar Mall. Take the first right, and the hotel is on the left. It is signposted from within RAK.

Food & Drink
Al Khor – international/Arabic • Hoof 'n' Fin – seafood & steaks • Havana Bar – Latin

Features
Private beach • Watersports • Swimming pool • Fitness room • Fishing • Jogging track • Table tennis • Pool • Diving • Sightseeing tours • Tennis court • Walking track • Golf course • Playground • Snorkelling • Waterskiing • Windsurfing

Nearby
RAK National Museum (www.rakmuseum.gov.ae) • RAK Shooting Club (07 236 3622) • Khatt Hot Springs • Tower Links Golf Club (www.towerlinks.com) • Digdagga ghaf forest • Mountains • Desert

Hilton Ras Al Khaimah Resort & Spa

Tucked away on an exclusive bay to the north of the creek, out of sight of the city, the Hilton Ras Al Khaimah Resort & Spa is the perfect place for a beach break.

With the magnificent Hajar Mountains dominating the skyline in one direction, and the blue gulf waters in the other, a stay at this new addition to the UAE hotel roster offers a superbly relaxing experience, only a 90 minute drive from the city lights of Dubai (and five minutes from RAK city).

The resort has been developed in two stages. A line of beachside villas that stretch most of the length of the bay opened fully in 2008, while the main hotel complex building, with 325 rooms, is scheduled to open in early 2009. When the resort building is complete, there will be an increased range of restaurants, bars and entertainment facilities to choose from, but for now, however, you really can't go wrong with a peaceful villa stay.

The villas are largely split into four suites – two upstairs and two downstairs – and are spacious and beautifully decorated. What's more, their key selling point is that the majority of them sit right on the beach – meaning you can breakfast on your terrace or balcony literally a pebble's throw from the lapping waves.

The villas are surrounded by luscious landscaped gardens, hosting a verdant variety of palms and plants, plus the odd rustic water feature. Each room has a separate entrance, and feels completely private. Junior suites, which occupy the ground floors, have a lounge area as well as a king size bed. You can walk straight onto the beach from the patio, and there's even a small, low-set shuttered window which means you can view the sea from the optimum relaxation position – lying in bed. Arabian decor gives a subtle but sultry exotic flavour, with hanging lamps, arched bed heads and dark wood furniture all working well together. Large flat-screen TVs provide the entertainment in both the lounge and the bedroom, and MP3 players can be hooked up to the radio if you prefer your own music. Bathrooms come with his-and-hers sinks, a separate bath and shower, and supplies of Crabtree & Evelyn for that extra splash of luxury. Standard rooms are equally nice, but don't have the lounge room. Be aware that a handful of the villas are located poolside rather than right on the beach, so be sure to specify when booking if you want the latter option.

The main leisure draw is, without question, the beach. You can choose to spend the whole day lying on loungers in front of your room, cooling down with the occasional dip in the sea. If you want to be more active, you can sign up for some watersports – most forms of water-based propulsion are available, as is fishing. A printed update – *Guest Press* – keeps you informed of what activities are on offer. There are a number of pools too (with more to come when the main resort building is open) if you prefer bathing of the freshwater variety, including a kids' pool. A playground and children's club are also on hand to keep the little ones happy.

You won't have to wander far for some refreshments either – the Dhows Beach Bar is nicely positioned on the north end of the bay, serving up a variety of eating options and drinks throughout the day from a shaded terrace.

More dining can be found in the Waterfront Restaurant at the far end of the beach. As well as Asian cuisine in the indoor dining area, there is a terrace featuring live cooking stations and shisha tents, while upstairs the rooftop Lighthouse Bar is a truly memorable place for a sundowner or a night under the stars, nestled in a cushioned booth, relaxing drink in hand.

Between the villas and the new resort building lies the Hilton Spa. It features a number of treatment rooms as well as hammams for men and women, plus steam rooms, saunas and Jacuzzis. It's all hugely calming, with soft lighting, water features and candles creating a soothing atmosphere. The separate gym upstairs boasts ultra modern equipment – the running machines have their own TV screens to keep you distracted while you slog

The dynamics of the resort will undoubtedly change once everything is fully open, with more facilities and choice available, but for now the Hilton Resort & Spa certainly has everything you need for a relaxing beach stay.

Contact
Phone: +971 7 228 8888
Email: ras-al-khaimah@hilton.com
Website: www.hiltonworldresorts.com

Location
Once in Ras Al Khaimah, turn right at Clock Tower Roundabout, go straight at the next roundabout and past the golf club. At the first signal turn left, and then turn left at the second signal on to Al Jazah Road. Turn right at the first roundabout and left at the next. Follow the road towards the sea, and the resort is on your left. It is signposted from the city centre.

Food & Drink
Passage to Asia – Asian • The Dome – pool & beachside bar • Lighthouse – bar • Al Bahar – seafood & grill • Waterbreaker – international

Features
Spa • Two hammams • Sauna • Salon • Fitness centre • Five swimming pools • Two children's swimming pools • Watersports centre

Nearby
RAK National Museum (www.rakmuseum.gov.ae) • RAK Shooting Club (07 236 3622) • Khatt Hot Springs • Tower Links Golf Club (www.towerlinks.com) • Digdagga ghaf forest • Mountains • Desert

The UAE certainly has its share of luxurious spas where you can relax and revitalise for a few hours or even a full day, but until now tranquil spa weekend getaways involved checking into a top-end hotel and using the in-house facilities.

Enter Imar Spa, one of the first spas to offer overnight stays, meaning you can really get away from it all for longer periods.

The spa is a little off the beaten track, situated along the coast of Umm Al Quwain. It has a small private beach, a tranquil terrace where you can sun yourself in peace, and an alfresco dining area. There is also an indoor heated pool and an aquatic sea therapy pool (salt water). The atmosphere is relaxed, spacious and luxurious, and Imar Spa is a welcome retreat for a girly getaway. And because it is a female-only spa, you can comfortably wander around in your slippers and cotton robes without having to worry about encountering any men. Accommodation consists of just five rooms: three single and two twin. The small occupancy means it never gets too crowded, yet although it is a tranquil, hushed setting, you won't feel as though you can't have a chat with your fellow guests.

The entire spa is pristine and airy, and you can relax fully from the moment you check in. The rooms are modern and neat, and each is fitted with a wide-screen TV and a complimentary mini bar; but before you whoop for joy at the prospect of free bubbly, remember that this is strictly an alcohol-free zone – you're here to embrace your holistic side, after all. In the bathroom, creamy neutrals encase a powerful shower unit and wash basin complete with Kérastase hair products and heaps of fluffy towels.

There is only one option for eating at the spa:

Imar Spa

the Bon Bon Café offers a healthy selection of light meals, as well as some more yummy (but less virtuous) dishes. Everything is given a calorie rating, so you can track exactly what you are putting into your body. The food is good – vegetarians are well looked after, while for meat eaters the steak sandwich with fries is particularly satisfying, especially when chased with a slice of decadent chocolate cake. More dedicated detoxers may want to stick to the salads, soups and fruit, as well as the super-fresh smoothies and juices. All items on the menu are available as room service.

From 21:00 onwards, a security guard patrols the grounds and the main doors are locked for the night – a nice touch that makes you feel completely safe and secure. But you needn't worry about feeling penned in: you can open up your room doors and wander out to your private patio for a breath of fresh sea air before turning in for a good night of beauty sleep. The treatments are the main drawcard here, and, with over 60 on offer, there's plenty to choose from. You should try to reserve your treatments as early as possible before arrival, as the spa gets fairly booked up with day visitors (a day spa pass is available for Dhs.50 plus the cost of any treatments). Treatment rooms are pristine, and the staff are highly proficient. Choose from natural ayurveda treatments, Karin Herzog chocolate-based facials and body scrubs, crystal microdermabrasion, or the French finesse of Décleor and Carita to take care of the face, mind and body. 'Spa days' (costing from Dhs350), bridal programmes and a cosmetic surgery clinic covering everything from Botox to tummy tucks mean the potential for transformation is staggering.

Experience the ultimate Arabic treatment by booking a hammam (starting from Dhs.175), which will leave you feeling clean, refreshed and relaxed, although it's not recommended for the shy. Shift a few pounds with a course of Hypoxi training, intense slimming treatments and super detox programmes.

For those with a more conventional approach to fitness, there is a fully equipped gym (with the option of a personal trainer), as well as

a fitness room offering classes such as aqua aerobics, step, body balance and tae-bo. Classes run from 10:15 to 19:30 daily.Finish off your day of bliss by pampering your crowning glory at the on-site hair salon – a professional L'Oréal colourist works wonders, while untamed manes are styled, shaped and blow-dried to suit the gleaming new you.

For a spa getaway, a night or two at Imar can work out to be surprisingly reasonable. Packages start at Dhs.950, ranging from one to seven night stays, including health food, personal trainer and use of all facilities.

Contact
Phone: +971 6 766 4440
Email: imarspa@eim.ae
Web: www.imarspa.com

Location
From Dubai or Sharjah, follow the directions to Umm Al Quwain on the E11. Just north of Hamriya Free Zone, turn left at Al Ittihad Roundabout, and then at Clock Tower Roundabout turn right. Turn left at the T-junction, go straight over Fish Roundabout, and the spa is on the left.

Food & Drink
Bon Bon Café & Juice Bar – international

Features
Indoor swimming pool • Aquatic Sea therapy pool • Jacuzzi • Hammam • Spa • Gym • Aerobics studio • Hair & beauty studio • Beach • Ayurveda treatments • Detox clinic • Cosmetic surgery clinic

Nearby
UAQ Aeroclub • UAQ Shooting Club • Dreamland Aqua Park • Emirates Motorplex • UAQ Marine Research Centre & Aquarium • Ajman

Khatt Springs Hotel & Spa

If you are craving a simple 'hush hush' getaway and some soothing spa treatments to complement your break, Khatt Springs Hotel & Spa offers serenity away from the city without complications or over-fussy decor to distract you. Who needs convoluted chandeliers and ruffled red carpets when you can have mountain views and uninterrupted tranquility?

The hotel is situated on a hilltop, just 20 minutes away from Ras Al Khaimah city. Accommodation is made up of 150 rooms (standard, superior and deluxe), with double or twin sharing options. Rooms are simple and neat, containing a TV, mini-bar and other convenient amenities. The bathrooms, decorated in calming neutral tones, feature a powerful massage shower.

But the real draw at the hotel is the spa, a beautiful basement escape with separate facilities for men and women. Subdued candle light flickers over earthy tones to create a haven of peace and quiet where you can enjoy a range of relaxing treatments. As a guest of the hotel, you have free access to the sauna, steam room, ice grotto (to close the pores after a good steam), hydro pool and relaxation room.

More than a hundred treatments make up the spa menu, which draws on the best therapies from around the world. The spa offers a range of packages, which vary in price from Dhs.650 to Dhs.1,200. The signature treatment is the Precious Stone Therapy, traditionally practised in China, which involves using suitable gemstones and oils selected according to your birth date and mood to stimulate reflexology zones on the spine. Ayurvedic therapies, Swedish and Thai massage, shiatsu, reflexology and sports massage are also available. For a treatment with a difference, try the Cleopatra Bath, where you can rejuvenate your skin by soaking in a tub of camel's milk.

Apart from the spa, the Harmony Ayurveda Centre is located just outside the main hotel building. It focuses on Indian therapies, with male and female ayurvedic doctors available for consultation and treatment. Meditation and yoga training are also offered here, as are special child-care programmes. Next door to the hotel, you can take a dip in the public Khatt Hot Springs – piping hot water which, it is claimed, has curative powers for various remedies. However, the quality of the experience here is not as high as the spa in the hotel.

If you are looking for a fun-filled break, an array of watersports such as kayaking, waterskiing, jetskiing, windsurfing, sailing, diving and fishing are available at Al Hamra Fort Beach Resort, the resort's sister hotel, just a short drive away.

The hotel restaurant offers a buffet of international cuisine, including, rather surprisingly for a spa hotel, a range of delicious desserts. Alcohol is available too. A complimentary shuttle service will transport you to the mall for a few hours of leisurely shopping, or for a day on the beach, which you can enjoy all the more knowing that, when you return to your hotel later, a bevy of friendly staff and talented practitioners are on hand to help you relax.

Contact
Phone: +971 7 244 8777
Email: gmoffice@khatthotel.com
Web: www.khatthotel.com

Location
Follow signs for Ras Al Khaimah International Airport, and at the Airport Roundabout, turn left. Head straight at the next roundabout, towards Khatt, then turn right at the third roundabout. You will see the hotel up on the hill straight ahead of you.

Food & Drink
La Palmeraie – international • Bar Springs – cocktail bar

Features
Natural hot springs • Outdoor pool • Two indoor hydropools • Ice grotto • Sauna • Gym • Spa • Mountain & desert tours

Nearby
Saqr Park • Camel race track • Tower Links Golf Course (www.towerlinks.com) • Manar Mall • RAK NAtional Museum • Mountains • Desert • Ghaf forest

Radisson SAS Resort, Sharjah

The grand, Aztec temple-like exterior of this hotel is an impressive sight. This is a majestic hotel inside and out; in the reception area are the sights, sounds and smells of a rainforest. There's a waterfall, Indian mynah birds nesting in lush vegetation, and a babbling pool inhabited by Japanese koi fish.

The standard guest rooms are large and comfortable, all with flat-screen televisions and satellite channels, huge beds and great bathrooms. As with so many hotels however, the abundance of facilities make it almost impossible to simply lounge around in your room, no matter how plush. And the Radisson is no exception: a full range of leisure and sports activities exist to make your weekend break a busy one.

The Bay Club is a full-service health club offering two gyms (one for ladies only), saunas, a plunge pool, tennis courts and a kids' zone.

Sunseekers can position themselves on a comfy lounger around one of the two swimming pools, or on the private beach. If taking it easy is not your thing, the hotel offers watersports and a range of organised activities most afternoons, including windsurfing lessons in the lagoon. Massages and treatments are also available at The Bay Club, from the ultra-relaxing aromatherapy massages to the more vigorous Swedish ones. The resort even has its own bowling alley, set next to an American-style fastfood outlet (there are also pool tables).

As it is set in the dry emirate of Sharjah, there's no drinking allowed at this hotel. However, there are several excellent restaurants on site. Café at the Falls is the hotel's signature all-day-dining restaurant, where you can sit under a gazebo in the subtly lit dining area, within earshot of the waterfall and birdcalls. Buffets with a seemingly endless choice of international cuisine are available for breakfast, lunch and dinner. Evening selections feature locally caught seafood and a live-cooking station, as well as the standard meat, chicken and vegetable dishes.

The Chillout Café (open 24/7) offers huge, comfy chairs where you can sink down and enjoy a few hours with a good book or interesting company. Shahzadeh Persian & Moroccan Restaurant serves the best of these two rich cuisines, and China Garden dishes up delicious, modern Cantonese specialities. A poolside snack bar offers sandwiches and snacks, and there is also a 'bar' near the private beach, serving much-needed refreshments like milkshakes and juices (but not alcohol).

Essentially this is a family-friendly resort with peaceful surroundings. A shuttle service is available to Sharjah's many cultural highlights, and also to neighbouring city Dubai.

Contact
Phone: +971 6 565 7777
Email: info.sharjah@radissonsas.com
Web: www.sharjah.radissonsas.com

Location
From Al Wahda Street, turn off at King Faisal Square and head west towards the corniche along King Faisal Street. Go straight through the complicated Al Soor Square and follow Corniche Street around next to the water. The hotel is on the left by the second large roundabout.

Food & Drink
Shazadeh – Persian & Moroccan • China Garden – Chinese • Café at the Falls – international • Latitudes – cafe/snacks

Features
Private beach • Fitness club • Spa • Gym • Tennis courts • Swimming pools • Watersports • Leisure boats

Nearby
Sharjah Aquarium • Sharjah Heritage Area • Al Jazeera Park • Al Qasba • Central Souk • Al Hisn Fort • Sharjah Arts Area • Sharjah Desert Park

East Coast

The UAE's east coast is a popular destination for west coast city dwellers looking to unwind. With its golden beaches bordered by the Gulf of Oman on one side and the rugged Hajar Mountains on the other, it should definitely be on your list of places to visit.

The east coast is a placid escape, popular with residents from throughout the UAE. Fujairah is less than two hours from Dubai, and can be reached in three hours from Abu Dhabi. The drive skirts the Hajar Mountains, a stark, craggy range that stretches on into central Oman. The east coast desert and mountains inland provide plenty of opportunities for sampling the great outdoors, from camping to some great off-road driving. The mountains are just a small part of the appeal, and most visitors head east for the relatively peaceful beaches to relax, snorkel or dive. The diving is considered some of the best in the country, mainly because of increased visibility. Snoopy Island is a favourite spot for snorkelling.

The area is home to a few interesting diversions, many of which are free to explore. The site of the oldest mosque in the UAE, Bidiyah, is roughly half way down the east coast, north of Khor Fakkan. Fujairah Fort has undergone a renovation programme, and is due to open as a museum. The main part of the fort is believed to be more than 500 years old, with other sections being built about 150 years later. Fujairah Museum itself, opposite the ruler's palace, offers an insight into the emirate's history. Further south, Khor Kalba's mangroves are great for exploring by canoe, while Dibba to the north offers deserted beaches and a glimpse of a more relaxed pace of life.

Clockwise from top left: Idyllic beaches, Imposing mountains, Calm waters

East Coast

Fujairah

Overlooking the atmospheric old town is the recently restored Fujairah Fort. The surrounding hillsides are dotted with ancient forts and watchtowers, which add an air of mystery and charm. Most of these appear to be undergoing restoration work, too. Fujairah is also a busy trading centre, with its modern container port and a thriving free zone attracting companies from around the world. Off the coast, the seas and coral reefs make a great spot for fishing, diving and watersports. It is also a good place for birdwatching during the spring and autumn migrations since it is on the route from Africa to Central Asia. The emirate has started to encourage more tourism by opening new hotels and providing more recreational facilities. Since Fujairah is close to the mountains and many areas of natural beauty, it makes an excellent base to explore the countryside and discover wadis, forts, waterfalls and even natural hot springs. On Friday afternoons during winter, crowds gather between the Hilton Hotel and the Khor Kalba area to watch 'bull butting'. This is not bullfighting as many people know it, rather a traditional sport between two bulls headbutting one another until one admits defeat and walks away. The animals rarely get hurt, with the main injuries being bruised egos for the bulls' owners.

Dibba

Located at the northern-most point of the east coast, on the border with Musandam (part of Oman), Dibba is made up of three fishing villages, each coming under a different jurisdiction: Sharjah, Fujairah, and Oman. The three Dibbas share an attractive bay, fishing communities, and excellent diving locations – from here you can arrange dhow trips to take you to unspoiled dive locations in the Musandam. The Hajar Mountains provide a wonderful backdrop, rising in some places to over 1,800 metres. There are some good public beaches too, where your only company will be the crabs and seagulls, and where seashell collectors may find a few treasures. It's possible to camp on the beach here.

Kalba

Just to the south of Fujairah you'll find Kalba, which is part of the emirate of Sharjah and renowned for its mangrove forest and golden beaches. It's a pretty fishing village that still manages to retain much of its historical charm. A road through the mountains linking Kalba to Hatta has recently been completed, creating an interesting alternative if you are returning to Dubai.

Khor Kalba

South of the village of Kalba is Khor Kalba, set in a beautiful tidal estuary (khor is the Arabic word for creek). This is the most northerly mangrove forest in the world, the oldest in Arabia and home to a variety of plant, marine and birdlife not found anywhere else in the UAE.
The mangroves flourish in this area thanks to a mix of saltwater from the sea and freshwater from the mountains, but worryingly they are receding due to the excessive use of water from inland wells. For birdwatchers, the area is especially good during the spring and autumn migrations when species such as the reef heron can be spotted. It is also home to a rare subspecies of the white collared kingfisher, which breeds here and nowhere else in the world. There are believed to be only 55 pairs of these birds still in existence. A canoe tour is an ideal opportunity to reach the heart of the reserve and you can regularly see over a dozen kingfishers on a trip. Desert Rangers (04 340 2408) has canoes for hire.

Accommodation Options

The east coast is beginning to catch the tourism bug, with a number of new hotels popping up in recent years. In addition to the hotels listed in the following pages, just south of Dibba there's a couple of budget options in the shape of the Holiday Beach Hotel (09 244 5540) and the Royal Beach Al Faqeet Hotel (09 244 9444, www.royalbeach. ae). Further south is the popular Sandy Beach Hotel & Resort (09 244 5555, www.sandybm. com) which overlooks the snorkelling spot of

Khor Kalba is home to a rare subspecies of kingfisher. Despite there being only around 55 pairs in existence, you stand a good chance of seeing one during a canoe trip through the mangroves.

Snoopy Island. With individual chalets and bungalows, this is a good option for groups who wish to get away together. The wide range of watersports, including a dive centre, means this is very popular with water babies. The hotel also has a pool, restaurant and bar. In Khor Fakkan, the Oceanic Hotel (09 238 5111, www.oceanichotel.com) has a range of F&B and leisure facilities, although the accommodation isn't as smart as the newer hotels further up the coast.

Camping

While the recommended hotels in this section are perfect for a weekend break, the diversity of the east coast makes it a great place to camp, especially for a long weekend. Dibba beach is a good spot – drive as far north as you can towards the rocks and pitch on the sand; in the morning you can flop into the sea to wake yourself up. Just outside Dibba there's a plateau above the village of Sana which is perfect for camping. A seven-kilometre climb from the Masafi to Dibba road, this spot offers a cool breeze and great views. Further inland, Wadi Madhah and Wadi Shis have some of the most fascinating scenery on the east coast, and camping spots are close to traditional falaj irrigation channels and pools to swim in (take care not to leave any rubbish or waste in falaj channels or streams, as this water is used by rural families). Drive to the end of Wadi Madhah to find a remote site where you're guaranteed peace and quiet. The *UAE Off-Road Explorer* has further details of the routes.

Going Out

The east coast is not really known for all-night partying, with only the hotels having licensed premises, but there's good food and good times to be had if you look. The hotels may be quieter than those in the cities, but bars often have music, and some often have live bands. In 2008, a new karaoke bar opened in the Sandy Beach Hotel, adding even more character to this quaint venue.
If you can find a bar or restaurant with a terrace, sipping alfresco sundowners while gazing at the mountains or the sea really can't be beat. The east coast doesn't have many options for independent restaurants serving international fine dining, but the towns of Dibba, Fujairah and Khalba all have an array of basic restaurants and cafeterias offering bargain Middle Eastern and Indian specialities.

Coastal mountains

Khor Kalba

This beautiful tidal estuary is home to the most northerly mangrove forest in the world and a variety of plant, marine and birdlife not found anywhere else in the UAE. Visit during spring and autumn to see birds migrate from Siberia to Central Asia, or to see the rare white-collared kingfisher, which despite their numbers are a relatively common sight. Khor Kalba is best seen from the water, and canoes are available to rent from Desert Rangers (04 340 2408).

Friday Market

Just outside Masafi (where the water comes from) is the famous Friday Market. Although open during the week, there is a special buzz on a Friday, with people travelling to buy, sell, and browse. Everything is available, from carpets and plants, to local produce, some of which you may not recognise. The wide selection of knick-knacks can often include some bizarre items (such as an inflatable Santa Claus).

Bullfighting

This ancient Portuguese sport consists of two huge bulls going head to head for several rounds, until after a few nudges and a bit of hoof bashing, a winner is determined. It's not as cruel or barbaric as other forms of bullfighting, but animal lovers may still want to avoid it. A new wire fence protects spectators from any angry runaways. The bullfights take place every Friday around 16:30 (except during the summer) near the Fujairah – Kalba bridge area, near the Hilton Hotel.

Must-Do Experiences

Choose from market knick-knacks and glimpses of the past, or fish, bulls and birds on the UAE's varied east coast.

Bithnah

The village of Bithnah, outside Fujairah, is ideal for history buffs due to its fort and archaeological sights. The fort itself is very impressive, but make sure you visit the main archaeological sight known as the Long Chambered Tomb. It was excavated in 1988 and is thought to date back to 3,000BC. Fujairah Museum has a detailed display of the tomb.

Fujairah Museum

Fujairah Museum (09 222 9085), opposite the ruler's palace, offers an insight into the emirate's history. This may be a little less colourful than neighbouring emirates, but is interesting nonetheless. You can see permanent exhibitions on traditional ways of life, including the recent Bedouin past. There are also weapons from the bronze and iron ages, finely painted pottery, carved soapstone vessels and silver coins. The museum is closed on Saturdays.

Explore Snoopy Island

Snoopy Island is one of the best places to see the marine life of the UAE. The island is a good 10 minute swim from the beach, but at low tide you can walk almost the whole way, and the reef starts closer to the shore making it ideal for novice snorkellers. It can get busy here, but there is plenty to explore. While you can take your own equipment, Sandy Beach Hotel (09 244 5555, www.sandybm.com) allows non-guests to use their beach and hire snorkelling equipment for a fee. Their onsite dive centre also runs diving trips and courses.

Fujairah Rotana Resort & Spa

The Fujairah Rotana was completed in 2007, just in time for Hurricane Gonu to undo all the hard work. It has had a good spit and polish since, and sits next to the imposing Le Meridien Al Aqah (p.190), where the Hajar Mountains crumble into the Gulf of Oman. On arrival, guests are seated and given a fruit cocktail while a member of staff runs through the check-in formalities. The entrance foyer feels like a business hotel, with plenty of marble, bright lights and airport lounge seating. However, the guests tapping away on laptops (there is Wi-Fi throughout) are more likely to be European tourists on a package trip. Step beyond the foyer and you get a truer feel for the place. Its two low-rise wings spread out in a V of motel-style rooms around a large pool and gardens. It has a distinct family feel, and resembles resorts in southern Europe. Ping-pong and foosball tables sit in a shady concrete bandstand, and while parents eat at the buffet restaurant Mozaique in the evening, children scamper around the gardens, where shrubs and ferns provide ample opportunities for hiding.

There is also a kids' club, Flippers, to keep the little ones occupied during the day. In a move that is either wonderfully in touch with

the wants of modern 4 to 14 year olds, or drastically overestimating the agoraphobia of today's youth, most of these activities take place indoors. There is a games room, with a graffiti wall to inspire aspirant artists and vandals, a cinema area with a library of DVDs, and a multimedia room, with game consoles and a workstation where teens can get online. Grown ups have some relaxing options too. The Zen spa offers the usual treatments for destressing and detoxing, and a spa food menu is available, so health conscious guests don't undo all the good work by gorging on hummus. There is also a tent on the beach where you can get a half hour Thai or Swedish massage on your back, shoulders and neck. But, there are more active options too. The hotel's pool is big enough for a few lengths if you fancy a swimming workout, and there are tennis and squash courts and a decent gym for those intent on getting sweatier.

One nice touch is the inclusion, for free, of waterskiing, windsurfing, glass bottom boat trips, kayaks, pedalos and snorkelling gear. You can also pay for PADI diving, desert safaris, quad biking and camel rides.

And of course, as with any destination on the east coast, the main appeal lies beyond the confines of a resort. The hotel entrance faces the Hajar Mountains, whose vertiginous rock formations look both inhospitable and inspiring. If you can find a perch with a good view at sunrise or sunset, the rocks briefly glow the colour of blood oranges.

To ensure the best view, you need to get into the mountains themselves. A stroll from the hotel will only get you so far, so many choose to take a drive. For the more active, the Rotana offers mountain biking trips with tour firm Dream Adventures. The company will take out slow pedalling families or free wheeling adrenalin junkies, and can tailor routes and the length of trips accordingly.

And after the exercise, there are a couple of options for replenishment. Mozaique is the hotel's main restaurant, and serves buffets at breakfast and dinner. The food is decent, with a selection of Arabic and western staples. The wine list is reasonably priced.

Waves, down by the beach, offers a better view and menus rather than a buffet. There is also a pleasant pool bar, as well as Tabu, which serves up cocktails and shots.

The UAE's east coast is a popular spot for quick breaks, particularly among those in northern Oman, Dubai and the eastern emirates, and as a result it is well served for hotels. This Rotana fills a mid-range void between the opulence of Le Meridien Al Aqah (p.190) and the cheap and cheerful functionality of the Sandy Beach Hotel (09 244 5555, www.sandybm.com). There's enough to keep families amused, and the rooms are plusher than the motel layout might suggest from the outside. Balconies are big enough to encourage loafing over sunset views, and staff are eager to please.

Contact
Phone: +971 9 244 9888
Email: fujairah.resort@rotana.com
Web: www.rotana.com

Location
Located on the coast road, 18km south of Dibba and 16km north of Khor Fakkan.

Food & Drink
Waves – international • Mozaique – international • Tabu – cocktails • Sharkeys – snacks

Features
Private beach • Temperature controlled swimming pool • Watersports Snorkelling trips • Deep sea fishing • Volleyball • Mountain biking • Musandam trips • Desert safaris • Gym • Spa • Squash & tennis courts • Kids' activities

Nearby
Bidiyah Mosque • Dibba Castle • Boat trips • Snoopy Island • Mountains • Wadis • Fujairah Fort

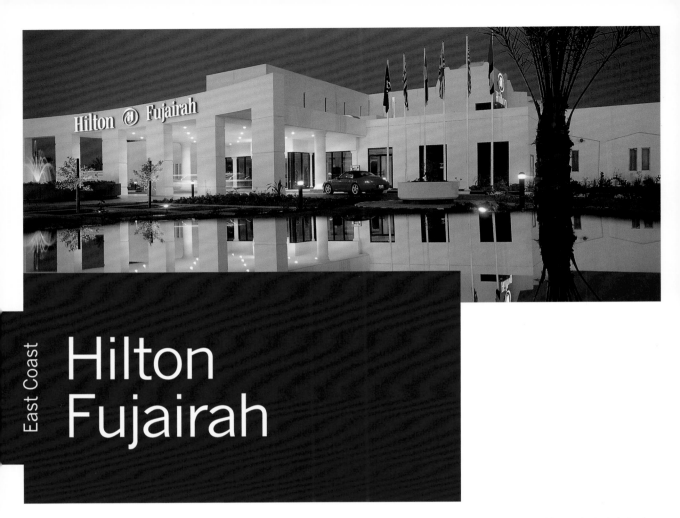

Hilton Fujairah

At first glance, the shoddy construction and empty streets of Fujairah city don't seem like the perfect setting for a relaxing weekend away. Step inside the easy-to-find Hilton Fujairah, however, and the friendly staff will change your mind. From the first taste of the welcome dates you'll be offered, the relaxation begins.

Unlike some of the stuffier hotels in the UAE, this Hilton strives to impress its guests with superior service, rather than overwhelming architecture and flash. At nearly 30 years old, the seaside resort is in surprisingly good shape. You won't find any million-dollar contemporary chandeliers or mile-high aquariums; instead, you'll find spotless lobbies, clean corridors and private balconies with great views of the Indian Ocean.

As one of the less expensive hotel resorts in the region, it's a perfect place to take children. You won't need to worry about your brood bothering any snooty millionaires around the pool, or knocking over a priceless sculpture. Instead, you can let them run round the massive gardens or splash up a storm in the kids' pool while you carry on with the important job of relaxing.

That said, childless couples needn't be concerned that their romantic weekend away will turn into a kiddie-infested hell either. Try to book a sea-facing room on the second floor and you'll end up with a private balcony that's perfect for holding hands while watching the sea. Despite their age, the rooms couldn't be cleaner and all of the furniture is relatively new.

Although lounging around the temperature-controlled pool is pleasant (and, indeed, compulsory for maximum relaxation), the hotel also suits active vacationers. The two well-kept, floodlit tennis courts are usually available without reservation, and there is a pitch and putt golf green, basketball court, petanque court and Frisbee golf course. Best of all is the watersports centre, which lets guests take sea kayaks into the Indian Ocean, charter a fishing boat, or just borrow some snorkelling gear and flop around in the waves. Guests can also get their workout fix in the recently renovated gym, which houses a full range of quality free weights and ample cardio machines.

After you've worked up your appetite, head to one of the restaurants. The aptly named Neptunia Restaurant has one of the best buffets on the east coast, with a rotating menu that ranges from barbecue Thursdays to seafood Mondays. If you'd rather order your meal, the Mediterranean a la carte menu has enough variety to cater to any taste.

Peckish sunbathers not wanting to don their trousers tend to have their lunch at the Beach Café, which overlooks the tanker-studded sea. The grill-oriented menu serves standard pool food – the grilled seafood is a must.

With the Hajar Mountains separating you from Dubai and Abu Dhabi, the Hilton Fujairah's main goal is to increase the feeling of isolated bliss by providing a relaxing setting. It accomplishes its goal by providing the type of service that you'd expect from a bed and breakfast. Somehow it seems that each member of the staff has perfected the 'genuinely friendly but never intrusive' service that so many other resorts fail to provide. Towels are handed out and picked up with a smile and rooms are always cleaned by the time you get back from a swim, no matter what time you walk out the door. Best of all, you never feel as though you're being watched. Not everything is perfect though. The

surrounding town of Fujairah doesn't provide many distractions, so choose this hotel only if you plan on lounging around the grounds for most of your stay.

Contact
Phone: +971 9 222 2411
Email: reservations.fujairah@hilton.com
Web: www.hilton.com

Location
Located on Al Ghourfa Street in Fujairah, next to the Coffee Pot Roundabout.

Food & Drink
Neptunia – mediterranean • Sailor's – seafood • Octavia – international • Fez – cocktail bar

Features
Swimming pool • Basketball • Bicycle rental • Fishing • Fitness room • Jetskiing • Playground • Pool table • Sightseeing tours • Snorkelling • Waterskiing • Windsurfing • Golf • Health club

Nearby
Fujairah Fort • Fujairah Museum • Al Hayl Fort • Bithnah Fort • Bidiyah Mosque • Boat Trips • Snoopy Island • Khor Kalba • Mountains • Wadis

Hotel JAL Fujairah Resort & Spa

The hotel, which has more than 200 rooms, has managed to muscle itself a prime view, with Dibba Rock in the foreground, the impressive Hajar Mountains looming to the left and, straight ahead, a pleasant private beach punctuated with luxurious loungers.

All rooms face the Gulf of Oman, with sizeable balconies and ergonomic chairs to help you appreciate the scene. You have the choice of a standard room, a two or three-bedroom option or one of four sakura grand suites. Unless you've got kids in tow or deep pockets, the standard is more than adequate. The surprisingly big space echoes the hotel's pitch: stylish minimalism with a nod to the far east. A flat-screen TV, a semi-open-plan bathroom and a plentiful bed are enough to forgive the slightly corporate whiff of the corridors. There's nice shampoo, too.

The Japanese-owned JAL Hotel group is big in its own country, and although this is their only property in the Middle East, following openings in the US and Europe, they clearly know what they're doing. From the lobby to the library, the hotel's clean lines and wholesome tones are reminiscent of a mood-enhancing spa; the neat design a nod to the simplicity of countryman brands such as Muji.

Bright pink, angular and vaguely reminiscent of 1980s Benidorm, Hotel JAL Fujairah is an incongruous addition to the east coast of the UAE. Its hodgepodge pastel exterior might be acquired taste, but what lies within will meet with universal approval.

This stretch of the UAE's coastline at Dibba is unrecognisable from a few years ago, when only the Sandy Beach Hotel and Holiday Beach Motel kept Dubai daytrippers entertained. Now there is serious competition, and little sand left – thanks mostly to the surprisingly vast JAL, which butts up against the rocks before the UAE becomes Oman.

Facilities are hugely impressive and deceptive given the hotel's size and price.

Diving and snorkelling trips to Dibba Rock and the perennially popular Snoopy Island can be organised through the adjacent Palms Dive Centre, or alternatively you can just slip into a kimono at Spa Zen and enjoy the range of treatments. There is also a hairdressers and beauty salon.

A small library provides calm, a small selection of local magazines, and access to the internet, while a decent-sized gym has enough equipment for a good sweat.

In keeping with its tardis-like feel, JAL offers guests a choice of six cafes and restaurants. Breeze, and its seaview, is where you go for the buffet breakfast – where yoghurt is served in a martini glass – and Mediterranean cuisine the rest of the day. Icho is the only teppanyaki restaurant this side of Dubai. Traditional and fairly workmanlike Lebanese fare can be found at Al Nokhada. You'll find Asian staples at Marco Polo, beachside bites at Grand Bleu and cocktails and shisha at Moon Beach. The lack of a killer bar or terrace is a shame, but not a stumbling block.

JAL's upscale vibe will attract young couples, but the beach and myriad diversions make this a great family spot too. Kids have a limited outside entertainment space, complete with worn-in foosball table (and table tennis on request), but inside they are spoilt for choice. There is the kodomo kid club, which is free of charge for guests and open from 09:00 to 18:00, and a video games room, with PlayStations, DVD players and air hockey, that will keep them goggle-eyed until 21:00.

But the main attraction is the private beach and semi-infinity pool, where you can slump, swim, or simply gaze as boats bob back and forth from Dibba Rock. The beach loungers are more like beds: vast, comfortable and conducive to instant napping. Pull the hood up and pretend there aren't 200 balconies behind you.

Despite the number of rooms, guests and the resort bustle, there's a relative peace to JAL that's reminiscent of Musandam up the coast or Muscat a lot further south. In fact, you could be in either if it wasn't for the fellow beachgoers in tight trunks loudly strutting their stuff.

This is a five-star hotel in all but price and deserves your attention – hideous paintjob or not.

East Coast

Contact
Phone: +971 9 204 3111
Email: reservations@jalfujairahresort.ae
Web: www.jalfujairahresort.ae

Location
Next to the Holiday Beach Motel, 6km east of Dibba's dolphin roundabout.

Food & Drink
Breeze – mediterranean • Icho – japanese • Al Nokhada – arabic • Marco Polo – asian • Grand Bleu – seafood & steakhouse

Features
Fitness centre • Swimming pool • Beach • Diving & fishing trips • Spa • Library • Children's facilities

Nearby
Bidiyah Mosque • Dibba Castle • Boat Trips • Snoopy Island • Mountains • Wadis • Fujairah Fort

Le Meridien
Al Aqah

Situated on a private stretch of beach on the shores of the Indian Ocean, the modern 22 floor building isn't exactly designed to blend in with the local landscape, towering impressively against the jagged Hajar Mountains. The interior is modern, light and airy, and despite its size, the hotel is calm and peaceful. All rooms are ocean facing with full-size windows, and offer stunning, unobstructed views over the attractive pool and gardens, along the coast and out to sea. To the back of the hotel, the stark brown mountains stretch into the distance.

The grounds are beautifully landscaped with pools, lush plants, plenty of shady trees, winding paths, and one of the largest swimming pools in the UAE. The shallow end slopes gently, and is a perfect place for kids, lounging or taking part in the water aerobics. There is a swim-up, shaded pool bar with seating, and an 'infinity wall' with views over the deeper pool and gardens. The second section goes a lot deeper, and is long enough for a proper swim. It is the location for activities such as water volleyball and beginners' dive courses. The beach is well equipped, and the clear waters perfect for swimming. Hurricane Gonu changed the topography a little, with some rocks now uncovered by the loss of sand, but for interesting marine life and some of the best snorkelling in the UAE, you can head down the

If one hotel in the UAE embodies all that a weekend break resort should be, Le Meridien Al Aqah could well be it. Since opening in 2002, this hotel has become an incredibly popular destination for weekends away with people from the west coast (half of all weekend guests are residents of the UAE, and you'll often have to book well in advance – even in the summer). It has won several awards in its first few years, such as the 'Middle East's Leading Beach Resort' at the World Travel Awards, two years running. Although competition in the area has increased recently, Le Meridien's popularity shows no sign of fading.

coast a few hundred metres to Snoopy Island. As a true resort should, Al Aqah offers an extensive range of sports and leisure facilities, and there are special programmes of events and activities every day. Outdoors there is tennis, mini golf, volleyball, watersports, and a branch of Al Boom Diving that offers diving and snorkelling trips to various sites along the east coast or up into Musandam.

Inside, there is squash, table tennis, billiards, a video arcade, a mini cinema, a selection of shops and a high quality spa. In serene surroundings, the Balinese staff can refresh and pamper you with a variety of massages and Ayurvedic treatments, all as either individual sessions, or as part of half or full day packages. If you're staying for just a weekend there's no chance of getting bored (you're likely to be planning your next trip before you even leave), but for visitors staying longer the hotel also offers sightseeing tours around the east coast as well as boat trips and fishing trips.

It is a particularly good choice for families, with a significant number of weekend break guests coming with kids. The excellent Penguin Club offers supervised indoor and outdoor facilities, and there are child-minding and babysitting services. Events and activities are organised regularly, such as stage shows for children and families, kids' discos and campfires.

Compared to many other hotels, the rooms are huge. Almost all are identically sized (48 sq m) with the same design and facilities, and the extra space really makes a difference – you feel comfortable. Beds are fitted with crisp linen sheets; bathrooms have baths and walk-in showers, and are fully outfitted with all kinds of accessories. Some have private balconies. There are also some executive suites, which are double the size, with a lounge, dining area and a kitchenette, and all have balconies.

There are three restaurants and one cafe in the hotel, as well as an additional restaurant in the gardens, snack bars on the beach and at the pool, and a top floor bar. Views is the largest and most popular venue, especially for breakfast and lunch. Massive windows look out onto the gardens, and in the evenings a live band serenades diners from the sweeping staircase. It offers a good quality buffet and a live cooking station, with the theme changing on a daily basis, alongside some international staples. You can also order a la carte.

Taste serves excellent Thai food, as delicious and authentic as you'll find anywhere else in the country, with dining on the balcony when the weather permits. The other in-house restaurant is Swaad, which offers good Indian food, while Baywatch is an alfresco restaurant in the gardens, which has a real holiday feel. On a terrace under the shelter of a wooden roof surrounded by luxuriant greenery, it specialises in pizzas in the daytime and seafood at night. For entertainment, Astro's Bar on the top floor is a great place for views and sundowners or pre-dinner drinks, getting livelier later with the help of a live band. Big sports games are regularly shown on TV. Although it's less than two hours from the west coast, Al Aqah feels like a very different place, and with all that the hotel offers, a weekend won't seem long enough. This is a place you'll want to come back to again and again, so check the website for the special deals offered at certain times of the year.

Contact
Phone: +971 9 244 9000
Email: reservations@lemeridien-alaqah.com
Web: www.lemeridien-alaqah.com

Location
Located just off the coast road, 18km south of Dibba and 16km north of Khor Fakkan.

Food & Drink
Taste – thai • Swaad – indian • Baywatch – seafood • Baywatch Beach & Pool Bar – refreshments

Features
Outdoor pools • Billiards • Tennis lessons • Squash court • Fitness centre • Spa • Scuba diving • Kids' club • Snorkelling trips • Watersports • Deep sea fishing • 4WD Expeditions

Nearby
Bidiyah Mosque • Dibba Castle • Boat trips • Snoopy Island • Mountains • Wadis • Fujairah Fort

Residents' Guides
All you need to know about living, working and enjoying

 Abu Dhabi
 Amsterdam
 Bahrain
 Barcelona
 Beijing
 Berlin
 Dubai
 Dublin
 Hong Kong

 Kuala Lumpur
 Kuwait
 London
 Los Angeles
 New Zealand
 Oman
 New York
 Paris
 Qatar

 Shanghai
 Singapore
 Sydney
 Tokyo

Mini Guides
The perfect pocket-sized Visitors' Guides

 Abu Dhabi
 Amsterdam
 Bahrain
 Barcelona
 Beijing
 Dubai
 Dublin

Hong Kong
London
Los Angeles
New York
New Zealand
Oman
Paris

Shanghai
Singapore
Sydney

Calendars
The time, the place, and the date

 Abu Dhabi 2009
 Bahrain 2009

 Dubai 2009
 Oman 2009
 Qatar 2009

Activity and Lifestyle Guides
Drive, trek, dive and swim... Life will never be boring again

 UAE underwater
 Oman trekking
 Oman off-road
 UAE off-road
 DUBAI YACHTING & BOATING
 POSH NOSH CHEAP EATS & STAR BARS
 Weekend Breaks Oman & UAE

Maps

Wherever you are, never get lost again

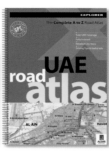

Photography Books

Beautiful cities caught through the lens

Retail Sales

Our books are available in most good bookshops around the world, and are also available online at Amazon.co.uk and Amazon.com. If you would like to enquire about any of our international distributors, please contact;
retail@explorerpublishing.com

Bulk Sales & Customisation

All our products are available for bulk sales with customisation options. For discount rates and further information, please contact;
corporatesales@explorerpublishing.com

Licensing & Digital Sales

All our content, maps and photography are available for print or digital use. For licensing enquiries please contact;
licensing@explorerpublishing.com

Check out

www.explorerpublishing.com/products

The No.1 off-road guide to the UAE

The ultimate accessory for any 4WD, *UAE Off-Road Explorer* helps drivers to discover this region's 'outback'. Just remember your 4WD was made for more than just the school run.

UAE Off-Road Explorer

What your 4WD was made for

Includes
Dhs.250
voucher for
Off-Road Zone

Proudly supported by

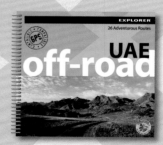

www.liveworkexplore.com

live it, love it
...log on

www.liveworkexplore.com

- Communities
- Updates
- Competitions
- Discounts
- Explorer expeditions
- Shop online

Index

Weekend Breaks Oman & UAE Team
Lead Editor: Jane Roberts
Contributing Authors: Pamela Afram, Tim Binks, Annabel Clough, Katie Drynan, Claire England, Tracy Fitzgerald, Kate Fox, Richard Greig, Tom Jordan, Sean Kearns, Jenny Lyon, Jake Marsico, David Quinn, Helen Spearman
Designers: Ieyad Charaf, Pete Maloney, Jayde Fernandes
Photographers: Victor Romero, Pete Maloney, Mohsen Al-Dajani, Sharjah Commerce & Tourism Development Authority
Cartographers: Sunitha Lakhiani

Publishing
Publisher Alistair MacKenzie
Associate Publisher Claire England
Assistant to Associate Publisher Kathryn Calderon

Editorial
Group Editor Jane Roberts
Lead Editors Tim Binks, Tom Jordan
Online Editor Helen Spearman
Deputy Editors Jake Marsico, Pamela Afram, Siobhan Campbell
Senior Editorial Assistant Mimi Stankova
Editorial Assistants Grace Carnay, Ingrid Cupido

Design
Creative Director Pete Maloney
Art Director Ieyad Charaf
Account Manager Christopher Goldstraw
Junior Designer Jessie Perera
Layout Manager Jayde Fernandes
Designers Rafi VP, Shawn Zuzarte
Cartography Manager Zainudheen Madathil
Cartographers Juby Jose, Noushad Madathil, Sunita Lakhiani
Traffic Manager Maricar Ong
Traffic Coordinator Amapola Castillo

Photography
Photography Manager Pamela Grist
Photographer Victor Romero
Image Editor Henry Hilos

Sales & Marketing
Media Sales Area Managers Laura Zuffa, Paul Santer, Pouneh Hafizi, Stephen Jones
International Media Sales Manager Peter Saxby
Corporate Sales Area Manager Ben Merrett

Corporate Sales Executive Hannah Brisby
Sales & Marketing Coordinator Lennie Mangalino
Marketing Manager Kate Fox
Marketing Executive Annabel Clough
Marketing Assistant Shedan Ebona
Digital Content Manager Derrick Pereira
Web Coder Anas Abdul Latheef
International Retail Sales Manager Ivan Rodrigues
Business Relations Manager Shyrell Tamayo
Retail Sales Coordinators Sobia Gulzad, Michelle Mascarenhas
Retail Sales Supervisor Mathew Samuel
Retail Sales Merchandisers Johny Mathew, Shan Kumar
Distribution Executives Ahmed Mainodin, Firos Khan
Warehouse Assistants Ashfaq Ahmad Thachankunnan, Mohamed Riyas Chakkiyath, Najumudeen K.I.
Drivers Shabsir Madathil

Finance & Administration
Finance Manager Michael Samuel
Junior Accountant Cherry Enriquez
Public Relations Officer Rafi Jamal

IT
Senior IT Administrator R. Ajay
Senior Software Engineer Bahrudeen Abdul Kareem

Contact Us

Reader Response
If you have any comments and suggestions, fill out our online reader response form and you could win prizes.
Log on to **www.explorerpublishing.com**

General Enquiries
We'd love to hear your thoughts and answer any questions you have about this book or any other Explorer product.
Contact us at **info@explorerpublishing.com**

Careers
If you fancy yourself as an Explorer, send your CV (stating the position you're interested in) to **jobs@explorerpublishing.com**

Designlab & Contract Publishing
For enquiries about Explorer's Contract Publishing arm and design services contact **designlab@explorerpublishing.com**

PR & Marketing
For PR and marketing enquries contact **marketing@explorerpublishing.com**
pr@explorerpublishing.com

Corporate Sales
For bulk sales and customisation options, for this book or any Explorer product, contact **sales@explorerpublishing.com**

Advertising & Sponsorship
For advertising and sponsorship, contact **media@explorerpublishing.com**

Explorer Publishing & Distribution
PO Box 34275, Dubai, United Arab Emirates
www.explorerpublishing.com
Phone: +971 (0)4 340 8805
Fax: +971 (0)4 340 8806